Commercial Cultures

Economies, Practices, Spaces

Edited by
Peter Jackson, Michelle Lowe, Daniel Miller and Frank Mort

BERG

Oxford • New York

First published in 2000 by
Berg
Editorial offices:
150 Cowley Road, Oxford, OX4 1JJ, UK
838 Broadway, Third Floor, New York, NY 10003-4812, USA

© Peter Jackson, Michelle Lowe, Daniel Miller, Frank Mort 2000

Berg is an imprint of Oxford International Publishers Ltd.

Library of Congress Cataloging-in-Publication Data
A catalogue record for this book is available from the Library of Congress.

British Library Cataloguing-in-Publication Data
A catalogue record for this book is available from the British Library.

ISBN 1 85973 377 8 (Cloth)
1 85973 382 4 (Paper)

Typeset by JS Typesetting, Wellingborough, Northamptonshire
Printed in the United Kingdom by Biddles Ltd, Guildford and King's Lynn

Contents

List of Contributors

Kate Brooks, Postgraduate Researcher, Department of Geography, University of Sheffield

Alison Clarke, Tutor in the History of Design, School of Humanities, Royal College of Art, London

Louise Crewe, Reader in Geography, University of Nottingham

Nicky Gregson, Reader in Geography, University of Sheffield

Peter Jackson, Professor of Human Geography, University of Sheffield

Marianne Lien, Associate Professor in the Department of Social Anthropology, University of Oslo

Michelle Lowe, Senior Lecturer in Geography, University of Southampton

Daniel Miller, Professor of Anthropology, University College London

Christopher Moore, Reader in Marketing, Department of Consumer Studies, Glasgow Caledonian University

Frank Mort, Professor of Cultural History and Director of the Raphael Samuel Centre for Metropolitan Cultural History, University of East London

Sean Nixon, Lecturer in Sociology, University of Essex

Don Slater, Senior Lecturer in Sociology, Goldsmiths' College, University of London

Paul Stallard, Research Associate, Department of Geography, University of Hull

Nick Stevenson, Lecturer in Sociology, Department of Sociological Studies, University of Sheffield

Janice Winship, Lecturer in Media Studies in the School of Cultural and Community Studies, University of Sussex

Neil Wrigley, Professor of Geography, University of Southampton

Introduction: Transcending Dualisms

Peter Jackson, Michelle Lowe, Daniel Miller and Frank Mort

The juxtaposition of 'culture' and 'commerce' in our title might at first seem like a doomed attempt to bring together two irreconcilable ways of seeing the world. At least in its colloquial form the term 'culture' is associated with meaning and creativity, with works of the imagination and aesthetic practices. 'Commerce', on the other hand, has traditionally been regarded as founded on a 'bottom-line' of profitability, and commercial agents may take delight in representing themselves and participating in a vulgar and materialistic, amoral world where human agency is subordinated to the logic of capital. As Bourdieu (1984) showed in his analysis of modern taste, economic and cultural capital often define each other by opposition.

The commitment made by this book in its inception, its composition and its execution is to find a way to transend that dualism and to explore the way that various aspects of cultural production – in fashion, publishing and retailing among other sectors – are inherently concerned with the commodification of various kinds of cultural difference – of gender and generation, ethnicity and sexuality, youth and the body. Conversely, we aim to show how the apparently rational calculus of the market is inescapably embedded in a range of cultural processes. We are not seeking to 'reduce' the cultural to the economic (or vice versa), or to show that either side of the equation is more significant than the other. Rather, we assume that the world is full of what might be called the authentic hybrid (Latour 1993) that is commercial cultures. By subjecting a wide range of these commercial cultures to empirical analysis and theoretical interrogation, we aim to show the value of an approach that transcends conventional dualisms, bringing together 'the cultural' and 'the economic', for example by exploring the links between production and consumption, while simultaneously blurring the boundaries between academic disciplines.

This is more than a rhetorical gesture, an intellectual manoeuvre confined within the rarefied world of academic debate. Although we doubt that there ever was a clearly definable market framed against the rest of the world , the attempt to keep something called commerce apart is looking increasingly futile. This is evident in changes in commercial culture itself as shops spring up in airports and railway

1

stations, as theme parks promote a sanitised version of our industrial 'heritage', and as 'cultural industries quarters' appear at the heart of many cities' economic development plans. The mutual implication of culture and commerce is clearly grounded in changes in the material world as well as in scholarly fashion. Academic debate has, however, cleared the ground for this kind of endeavour, providing a conceptual language for thinking about the conversion of symbolic or cultural capital into a more commodified form of economic capital (Bourdieu 1984) or thinking about the objectification of social relations in the varied forms of material culture (Miller 1987, 1998).

The chapters that comprise this volume derive from an inter-disciplinary seminar series organised by the editors with support from the ESRC (award no. R45126458096). Over eighty people, including academics, students and practitioners from a wide range of disciplinary backgrounds, participated in the seminars. The contributors to this volume reflect that diversity, including historians and geographers, anthropologists and sociologists, as well as those from consumer/ retail studies and from media, museum and cultural studies. Other people who participated in the seminar series but whose work is not represented here have contributed further to our goal of transcending disciplinary and conceptual binaries. To take just three examples: Linda McDowell's (1997) study of 'gender at work' in the City of London represents a sustained attempt to explore the embedded and embodied character of merchant banking and financial services; Sharon Zukin's (1995) work on the 'cultures of cities' includes an analysis of the role of artists and immigrants in the New York City restaurant trade; while Paul du Gay's (1996) study of consumption and identity at work demystifies the concept of 'enterprise culture' through an exploration of the construction and contestation of new identities among retail workers and consumers. As with each of the following chapters, these studies confirm the validity of Lash and Urry's bold assertion that "the economy is increasingly culturally inflected and . . . culture is more and more economically inflected" (1994: 64).

We are able to sustain our argument about transcending dualisms not merely at the level of theory or polemic, however, but also through the range of empirical work that is reported here. One of the aims of our seminar series was to avoid the tendency of some recent work in cultural studies towards excessive abstraction and over-generalisation. Instead, each of the studies included here is based on detailed empirical work, drawing on ethnographic methods, on in-depth interviews and focus groups, on archival work and painstaking field research. Through such methods we are able to trace the links between commerce and culture not just at the level of representation, through discourse analysis and textual scrutiny, but also, in many cases, at the level of practice, from the social relations of production through into the cultures of consumption that characterise our everyday lives (cf. Mort 1996).

This volume is also different from many previous studies in attempting to 'ground' our ideas in the specific contexts of place and time. By 'grounding', we do not imply an attempt to distil fluid trends and meanings into a set of rigid interpretations or permanent answers. Our emphasis is rather on circuits and flows, on chains of connection and ambivalent meanings, theorising these connections not in linear terms of encoding/decoding but in terms of circuits of exchange, with permeable boundaries that are subject to all manner of creative leakages. Through such an understanding, we seek to gain intellectual purchase on our material by insisting on its historical and geographical particularity (or on specific links between places and times). It is through tracing the links between economies, practices and spaces, we argue, that our understanding of commercial cultures can be advanced.

This is particularly true of the first section on the historical development of commercial culture and the paths to mass consumption but it is no less relevant to subsequent chapters on the spaces of contemporary consumption or the current restructuring of commercial culture. One particular example concerns the extent to which British post-war culture has followed the trajectory of commercial developments in the United States. Rather than positing some over-generalised 'Americanization' thesis, contributors to this volume tease out the similarities and contrasts in a range of different commercial domains – in fashion, advertising and retail. The argument is followed through in later chapters on the development of out-of-town shopping where an 'American' future is often predicted for the British retail trade but where such an argument is easily over-stated. Here, as elsewhere, we aim to provide an understanding of the context-dependent links between commercial and personal identities as they are rooted in particular places (Miller et al., 1998), based on our understanding of the links between economic restructuring and changes in consumer culture (Wrigley & Lowe, 1996).

The book is also distinctive in refusing to elide the division between production and consumption with the division between economy and culture. Our arguments about the nature of 'value' in the world of second-hand exchange, about the attempt of mass marketing to get closer to their consumers (whether the product is frozen pizza, lifestyle magazines or middle-brow novels) or about the nature of consumer 'choice' in contemporary British and American supermarkets cannot be understood without moving backwards and forwards between culture and economy, production and consumption.

The following chapters are divided into four sections (each with its own editorial introduction), addressing respectively paths to mass consumption, the birth of value, the links between consumption and commercial culture, and the restructuring of contemporary commercial culture. Running through all the chapters, we hope to show that putting 'commercial culture' at the centre of our conceptual map encourages the kinds of holistic approach and contextual understanding that eludes more narrowly-defined disciplinary understandings.

3

Peter Jackson, Michelle Lowe, Daniel Miller and Frank Mort

References

Bourdieu, P. (1984), *Distinction: a Social Critique of the Judgement of Taste*, London: Routledge.

du Gay, P. (1996), *Consumption and Identity at Work*, London: Sage.

Lash, S. and Urry, J. (1994), *Economies of Signs and Space*, London: Sage.

Latour, B. (1993), *We Have Never Been Modern*, Hemel Hempstead: Harvester Wheatsheaf.

McDowell, L. (1997), *Capital Culture: Gender at Work in the City*, Oxford: Basil Blackwell.

Miller, D. (1987), *Material Culture and Mass Consumption*, Oxford: Basil Blackwell.

Miller, D. (ed.) (1998), *Material Cultures: Why Some Things Matter*, London: UCL Press.

Miller, D., Jackson, P., Thrift, N., Holbrook, B. and Rowlands, M. (1998), *Shopping, Place and Identity*, London: Routledge.

Mort, F. (1996), *Cultures of Consumption*, London: Routledge.

Wrigley, N. and Lowe, M. (eds) (1996), *Retailing, Consumption and Capital*, Harlow: Longman.

Zukin, S. (1995), *The Cultures of Cities*, Oxford: Basil Blackwell.

Part I

Introduction:
Paths to Mass Consumption:
Historical Perspectives

Frank Mort

Reviewing the history of the twentieth century in the *Age of Extremes* (1994) the marxist historian Eric Hobsbawm cites three factors which qualitatively distinguish the world at the end of the millenium from society in 1914. Along with the effects of globalisation and the decline of European hegemony, Hobsbawm highlights a profound and long-term shift in social life attendant on the expansion of the international economy in the 1950s and 1960s. These 'golden years', as he terms them, were not simply characterised by a massive expansion in the productive capacity and technology of post-war capitalism in the West, they were decades when the fruits of consumer abundance began to transform individuals' perceptions of themselves and their relationships with each other. Compared with this phenomenon, he observes, future historians will probably view the twentieth-century's dramatic confrontations between capitalism and socialism, or even the horrors of total war, as of lesser significance. At one level there is nothing exceptional about Hobsbawm's thesis, it is the most recent and the most grandiose in a long line of accounts of the post-war period which have identified the expansion of consumer society as central to the remaking of social experience and cultural life (Galbraith 1958; Bell 1974; Bourdieu 1984). Consumption has become one of the grand narratives of the second half of the twentieth century.

All three of the essays in this part of the collection acknowledge the historical centrality of the coming of mass consumer society; but their arguments are implicitly ranged against accounts like Hobsbawm's which deal in vast epochal sweeps of economic and cultural change. In that sense they can be seen as part of a growing revisionist strand in recent studies of consumption – and in social and cultural history in a wider sense – which have moved away from historical generality and towards specificity. The concern here is with commercial cultures explored not as a single, unified entity but as the product of distinctive and often competing technologies and knowledges. Moreover, each of the essays investigates the impact of the expanding world of goods on historically specific aspects of social identity and subjective experience. Over-generalised accounts have frequently produced an undifferentiated understanding of the relationship between commerce and projections of selfhood, as if consumers' experience of who they are is simply triggered by market mechanisms. An added complication here is that in an era of so-called mass consumption, commercial experts, together with social theorists and cultural critics, argued strongly that the industrial societies of Western Europe were experiencing an erasure of social difference based on the hierarchies of class and status. The world of goods was valorised as central to this process of social levelling, as Europe supposedly followed in the wake of an American model of material and cultural democracy. Yet as the social democratic theorist and Labour Party politician, Tony Crosland, was quick to point out in his reading of the impact of affluence on the class structures of British society in the 1950s, the coming of near universal provision for a wide variety of commodities did not mean that status divisions based on the symbolic meaning of goods had been erased. Crosland identified new lines of division and demarcation which were being written into the networks of perceived egalitarian affluence (Crosland 1956; Crosland 1962). Understanding the historical processes whereby older social hierarchies were transformed and newer ones created by the impact of the commercial domain remains an underdeveloped project for historians of Western Europe in the mid-twentieth century. In Britain during the 1960s this issue was the focus for a series of major academic studies around the theme of 'the affluent worker', an important initiative by empirical sociologists to understand the impact of affluence on the economic self-perceptions, class allegiances and the cultural world-view of the skilled, male worker and his family (Zweig 1961; Goldthorpe et al. 1968). Similar research was undertaken in West Germany and France during broadly the same period (see Carter 1997; Ross 1995). But what also characterised this tradition of sociological writing , together with much of the cultural analysis which accompanied it, was a relative disinterest in the actual commercial techniques which generated the new forms of consumerism. Affluence was taken as a given; different market sectors, commodities, systems of production and consumer knowledge were run together. The assumption was simply that the 'affluent society' had produced major changes in the social experience of young people, women and sections of the working class. What remains as an unfinished project is to analyse those transformations as part of a generative process, driven by specific forms of commerce and entrepreneurship.

A first stage is to produce a more subtly nuanced map of the ways in which the commercial industries conceptualised and reconceptualised the consumer during this period of mass provision. A singled unified chronology, which focuses exclusively on the post-war decades, is unhelpful in this respect. Janice Winship, following the work of other recent historians, emphasises the importance of the

1930s as a formative moment in the orchestration of mass-market provision (Alexander 1994; Nava 1995). Moreover, the work of building markets was not the same across national boundaries; advertisers and retailers working in different contexts displayed real disparities in their approach to consumers and in their understanding of what was permissible commercial strategy. The differences involved in marketing to customers in the United States, as opposed to selling in the countries of Western Europe, highlight these variations. Victoria de Grazia's recent pioneering research on the 'detergent wars' of the 1960s illustrates the difficulties which confronted American corporations as they prepared to enter European markets (de Grazia 1998). American detergent companies needed information about the consumption patterns of the European housewife. Yet unlike in the USA, direct access to the female consumer in bourgeois French households was extremely difficult, as doorstep contact by the marketer was often still mediated by servants. In this context barriers to market penetration were social and cultural in the most profound sense.

In Britain what occurred in the period from the late 1920s through to the early 1960s was both a greater specification of the personality and the motivations of consumers and an important shift in the dominant forms of knowledge responsible for mapping their behaviour. As I point out in my own study, during the inter-war years it was primarily economists who began to promote a greater intellectual interest in the mechanisms of consumption. Confronting the failure of classical political economy to adequately grasp the deficiencies in demand created by the depression of the 1930s, theorists of imperfect or monopolistic competition stressed the advantages to be gained from external interventions into the working of the market. It was here that the twin engines of advertising and marketing assumed a positive role in potentially stimulating demand and regularising many problematic aspects of the consumer cycle. The significance of this inter-war economic discourse lay in the fact that it provided a public forum for debate about modern consumer management. Yet on the role and motivations of consumers themselves, economists were silent, falling back on an image of *homo economicus*, familiar from nineteenth-century political economy – an ideal type who was always assumed to be rational and perfectly informed. Keynes himself, in the majority of his published writings, chose to take as given those 'subjective factors' influencing demand, suppressing the intrusions of psychology and culture, in the interests of developing a sophisticated economic theory about the relationship between employment, investment and consumption. This hole within demand economics was filled by an eclectic mixture of knowledges in post-war Britain, some scientific, some humanistic, all of them dedicated to the greater identification of the consumer. What was striking about that process was how conceptions of the human personality – which were themselves such an important part of the expanding welfare state – were comprehensively revised to include the consuming personality. Social

9

democratic politicians like Crosland and Harold Macmillan in Britain, liberal intellectuals like Daniel Bell and David Riesman in the USA, together with Western marxists such as Theodor Adorno and Max Horkheimer, were all forced to confront the overwhelming potential of this secular version of social selfhood. The rise of the totalitarian dictatorships and the onset of the Cold War also meant that after 1945 the debate about consumer freedoms was driven by a sense of international political urgency.

There is, however, a enormous distance between these historical speculations about consumer motivation and the way in which individuals have actually participated in the world of goods. This gap is not simply due to the fact that consumers are naughty or resistant subjects, acting in ways which are irresponsible or irrational from the point of view of the commercial expert. It is in one sense inevitable, in as much as consumers are *always already acultured* when they participate in the specific practices of looking, shopping, purchasing and so on. Failure to acknowledge this basic fact is a form of denial which has produced both inadequate marketing knowledge and thin history. What are needed are more studies which situate particular objects, products and market sectors in their relationship to the lived reality of specific consumers. There is no one definitive approach to exploring these networks of commercial provision. One way forward is to demarcate a specific chain, running from production, distribution, marketing and the material culture surrounding commodities through to their social and symbolic use by consumers in particular environments and settings (Fine and Leopold 1993). Such an approach can deliver much in terms of concreteness, enabling meaningful comparisons to be made across different sectors and between different types of consumers. The difficulty is that such consumption chains have proved to be extremely 'leaky' (Glennie and Thrift 1993). There is strong historical evidence to suggest that consumers themselves have rarely viewed their participation in the marketplace as an isolated activity. The story of consumer modernity is precisely about the ways in which the display of goods – on the body, in the street or in the household – collides with other fields of social action, especially in the rituals of everyday life. It is not accidental that some of the most significant studies of consumer society have been those which have investigated consumption as part of a broader project of cultural history: Simon Schama's panorama of the world of goods at the founding moment of the seventeenth-century Dutch republic, John Brewer's studies of consuming sensibilities and the pleasures of the imagination within English eighteenth-century polite society or, closer to our own period, Carolyn Steedman's autobiographical narrative of class, gender and culture, shaped by a longing for the material fruits of 1950s affluence which were denied to those not living in 'normal' households (Schama 1987; Brewer 1997; Steedman 1985). All of these histories testify to the fact that commerce and entrepreneurship has had wide-ranging effects both on the formation of national cultures and on more intimate aspirations.

This issue of the relationship between particular structures of consumption and broader landscapes of power and personhood is central to Winship's study of the rise of the chain store during the 1930s. In charting the development of this specific form of retailing, Winship begins to map the relatively undocumented history of the taste patterns of the English lower-middle class during the inter-war years. Central to her argument is that the chain store's reach of mass provision was specifically, though not uniquely, to that class fraction which had not been addressed either by the nineteenth-century department store, or by the working-class communitarian traditions of the co-operative movement. English chains such as Marks and Spencer encoded a distinctive cultural repertoire into their shopping environments, which was organised around the themes of prettiness and neatness, transparency, cleanliness and uniformity. This was a marketing discourse of pleasurable but restrained consumption, which fed into and reshaped some of the existing routines of the petty bourgeoisie. It spoke most directly to women newly 'enfranchised' by their participation in the 'clean' and 'efficient' consumer industries of the 1920s and 1930s, or who were empowered by the styles of modern household management promoted in contemporary women's magazines. The presentation of the body, the cultivation of aesthetic sensibilities, as well as important aspects of these women's mental horizons were transformed by the consumerisation of personal and domestic life. Contained within Winship's story of the chain store is a key aspect of modern English suburban taste, as it was crystallised in the first part of this century.

Subjectivity has not only been assembled by addressing the consumer, the identities of those commercial intellectuals responsible for driving the demand cycle have been shaped by this process as well. In the mid-twentieth century the professional image of the advertising man loomed large in the social imagination in both Britain and the USA. Reviled as the harbinger of Mammon, or celebrated as the steward of a new secular science, the idea of the advertiser was over-determined by both disquiet and optimism about the progress of secular society. Sean Nixon's study of the unstable forms of professional identity inherent in the British advertising industry, at a key moment of its expansion during the 1950s, probes beyond these public myths. One of the difficulties confronting the historian charting the status of advertising is that the dominant model of expertise has been derived not from the sphere of commerce, but from the genteel and public service professions. Consolidated in the eighteenth and nineteenth centuries, the law and medicine stand as paradigmatic examples of the professional ethos. Consequently, newer *arrivistes* are always found to be wanting when measured against this established hierarchy. Along with Nixon's focus on advertising, we might include many other examples of status uncertainty in the commercial sphere, such as accountants, estate agents and journalists. In the 1950s advertisers and marketers displayed acute sensitivity to questions of professional competence. Such anxieties were dramatised as a concern about terminology and nomenclature: advertising as a 'profession' or an 'industry', advertising 'agents', with their implied subservience to the press, or the more independent concept of 'practitioners'. Nixon's encounter with the London advertising world reveals more than simply a compromised professional ethic. It points to the way in which for many men on the inside, a business or craft-based identification, with experience gained by doing and by practical example, made better sense than the achievement of formal professional status. The blurred social scripts surrounding the advertising professional also carried a series of competing versions of masculinity, which were themselves predicated on an implicitly homosocial environment and a continuing ideology of separate spheres for men and women within the professional classes. Genteel and responsible images of the advertising practitioner jostled for space with more explicitly careerist stories of ambition, profit and power. As Nixon indicates, such ambiguities have continued to influence the advertising world well beyond the 1950s.

The overall point about this emphasis on specificity is that it is only by drawing on the insights from grounded projects such as those included here that we can return productively to the grander narratives of consumption and the consumer society which have been the stock-in-trade of an earlier generation of historians. This turn to the concrete involves a necessary process of historical revision, but is not simply a descent into detail for detail's sake. Consumption is not some interesting but insignificant byway in the development of modern life, it is intrinsic to the dynamic organisation of economic society and to the human experience of being and becoming modern. Sociological and cultural theory has priviledged these aspects of consumer modernity, but has stopped short of refining their grandiose claims concretely at particular points in time and in delimited settings. A new type of cultural and economic history, which understands economics and culture as reflexively inter-related in ways which are neither predetermined nor monocausal, has the potential to transform our understanding of what commercial cultures have been and what they might become.

References

Alexander, S. (1994), *Becoming a Woman, and other Essays on 19th and 20th Century Feminist History*, London: Virago.

Bell, D. (1974), *The Coming of a Post-Industrial Society: A Venture in Social Forecasting*, London: Heinemann Educational.

Bourdieu, P. (1984), *Distinction: A Social Critique of the Judgement of Taste*, trans. R. Nice, London: Routledge & Kegan Paul, 1984.

Brewer, J. (1997), *The Pleasures of the Imagination: English Culture in the Eighteenth Century*, London: HarperCollins.

Carter, E. (1997), *How German Is She? Postwar West German Reconstruction and the Consuming Woman*, Ann Arbor: University of Michigan Press.

Crosland, T. (1956), *The Future of Socialism*, London: Jonathan Cape.

Crosland, T. (1962), *The Conservative Enemy: A Programme of Radical Reform for the 1960s*, London: Jonathan Cape.

de Grazia, V. (1998), 'The Great Detergent Wars of the 1960s: How American Multi-Nationals Stepped Over the Thresholds of European Households', unpublished paper presented to the Economic and Social Research Council's Research Seminar series, 'Commercial Cultures: Economies, Practices, Spaces'.

Fine, B. and Leopold, E. (1993), *The World of Consumption*, London and New York: Routledge.

Galbraith, J. (1958), *The Affluent Society*, Boston: Houghton Mifflin Co.

Glennie P. and Thrift, N. (1993), 'Modern Consumption', *Society and Space*, vol. 11, pp. 603–6.

Goldthorpe, J., Bechhofer, F., Lockwood, D., Platt, J. (1968), *The Affluent Worker: Political Attitudes and Behaviour*, Cambridge: Cambridge University Press.

Hobsbawm, E. (1994), *Age of Extremes: The Short Twentieth Century*, London: Abacus.

Nava, M. (1995), 'Modernity Tamed? Women Shoppers and the Rationalisation of Consumption in the Interwar Period', *Australian Journal of Communication*, vol. 22, no. 2, pp. 1–19.

Ross, K. (1995), *Fast Cars, Clean Bodies: Decolonization and the Reordering of French Culture*, Cambridge, Mass.: MIT Press.

Schama, S. (1987), *The Embarrassment of Riches: An Interpretation of Dutch Culture in the Golden Age*, London: Collins.

Steedman, C. (1985), *Landscape for a Good Woman: A Story of Two Lives*, London: Virago.

Zweig, F. (1961), *The Worker in an Affluent Society: Family Life and Industry*, London: Heinemann.

I

Culture of Restraint: The British Chain Store 1920–39

Janice Winship

Introduction

equally

By July 1999, at the end of its worst twelve months of retail trading in over a century, Marks and Spencer's hitherto majestic reputation had been badly dented. News reports of its AGM feasted on falling sales and delighted in the fifty something shareholder who 'climbed on to the stage . . . to berate the board about the unsexy knickers in its store' (*Daily Telegraph*, 16 July 1999: 1). This outburst only echoed the wider view that the store, best known for provisioning the nation with underwear, had fallen behind its competitors. As one commentator remarked: 'Can you think of a more unfashionable store?' (*Express*, 15 January 1999: 18). Outdated and overpriced, M&S was not appealing to the 'younger, label-conscious generation' (*Express*, 15 January 1999: 18), burying designer names beneath its M&S/St Michael label whilst other stores promoted them. The M&S brand, and consumers' immense trust in it, had been built on offering value for money, 'quality', but not cheap prices, and the company had adopted a low-key approach to advertising, store interiors and the pursuit of the customer. Against this background the announcement that, as a crisis-management strategy, M&S was almost doubling its ad budget for a national TV campaign and 'shock horror, finally conceded that it needs a unified marketing division', was newsworthy indeed (*Observer, Business*, 17 January 1999: 3).

Back at the AGM in response to another shareholder's question, the chairman was forced to engage with the almost unthinkable – a takeover – a discussion precipitated by the unexpected merger between US retailing giant Wal-Mart and the supermarket chain ASDA. Newspaper reports of this event played on the twin emotions of desire and fear. One set of accounts drew on a vocabulary of 'flirtation' and 'seduction', in what was described as 'a transatlantic romance': 'The world's largest retailer could have been in no doubt: Asda wanted to be wooed' (*Observer, Business*, 20 June 1999: 5). Another represented the takeover as an 'enemy' advancing: 'Uncle Sam invades' (*Guardian, G2*, 15 June 1999: 2). The image of

Wal-Mart was in stark contrast to the values allegedly embodied by M&S, whom over the years the press have affirmed for handsome treatment of their workforce, good relations with suppliers, to say nothing of their role in shoring up town centres and maintaining the British textile industry.[1] Wal-Mart was represented as ruthlessly exploiting sweatshop labour abroad and inventing the 'disposable workforce' at home (*Observer, Business*, 20 June 1999: 5) such that, 'by the middle of 1996 some 45 towns across the country had found Wal-Mart distasteful enough to keep it out' (*Guardian, G2*, 15 June 1999: 2). Wal-Mart 'greeters' might flatter shoppers with a 'syrupy southern friendliness' (*Guardian, G2*, 15 June 1999: 2) but the store expounded price not quality. As an American observer observed, 'it panders to my nastiest desire for Cheap and Plenty' (*Observer, Business*, 20 June 1999: 5).

There are echoes here of the 'invasion' ninety years ago when F.W. Woolworth's first shop opened in Liverpool to intense press hostility. Yet it was not long before Woolworth's 'three-and-sixes wedge[d] their way into British life', and Britons travelling to the US for the first time 'would note the familiar red front and exclaim: "Oh, you have Woolworth in the United States, also!"'(Winkler 1940: 161). The response to Wal-Mart's and Woolworth's arrival exemplifies the wider ambivalence towards American popular culture in Britain that tends to be orchestrated across a class divide: the working classes wanting to be wooed or enticed, revelling in the delights which the transatlantic romance offers, whilst a more puritan middle class denounces its cheapness and the seductive artifice thought only to be achievable through an ungentlemanly (unBritish) Barnum chicanery. The fear is of a loss of British cultural values as well as of an economic imperialism.

I am not wanting to suggest here that Wal-Mart, like Woolworth earlier, will necessarily wedge itself into the affections of the British nation, though it may, but to use this incident as a way into exploring some key aspects of the relation between British and American retailing cultures during the inter-war years. Whilst the term 'chain store' is American, established in the United States by the turn of the century and initially used in Britain to refer to the 'variety chain stores' like Woolworth and M&S, it soon became the popular term for the UK multiples. However, notwithstanding this borrowed terminology, the historical development of the British multiples has been distinctive. The antagonism towards Wal-Mart's takeover of ASDA, and to Woolworth's earlier arrival in Britain, highlights the perceived gap between the retail cultures of the two countries. Moreover, M&S's recent announcement of its intention to rely more heavily on advertising points to an important tension, somewhat hidden in recent commercial relations but evident in the earlier part of the twentieth century, between advertising-led and retail-led strategies of marketing. Manufacturers adopted brand advertising to develop a relationship of trust with consumers and thus shift goods off shelves, without the

1. A more critical account of M&S, as a company squeezing its suppliers, also prevails.

problematic intervention of a retailer shaping shoppers' selection. Multiple retailers adopted a competing strategy which relied more on the quality of their premises, their own-brand goods and keen pricing in order to win and sustain custom. If the former was perfected in the US, the latter was pioneered by nineteenth century co-operatives and early multiples in the UK and was reconfigured in the 1920s, partly under the influence of US retailers, including Woolworths in Britain.

Focusing on the inter-war years in Britain when the chain stores[2] expanded into a nationally important retailing form, I first examine the new 'landscape of power' of which these stores were a part. I go on to examine the trajectories by which the chain store form emerged differently in the US than in Britain, where 'restraint of trade' prevailed.[3] Finally, I consider the chain store's contribution to a 'culture of restraint', catering especially to the emerging lifestyle of the lower middle class and especially serving women and their social needs.[4]

'The New Post-war England, Belonging Far More to the Age Itself Than to This Particular Island' (Priestley 1934: 401)

On the last leg of his *English Journey* (1934), crawling into London through thick fog, J.B. Priestley invoked the landscape ahead:

This is the England of arterial and by-pass roads, of filling stations and factories that look like exhibition buildings, of giant cinemas and dance-halls and cafes, bungalows with tiny garages, cocktail bars, Woolworths, motor-coaches, wireless, hiking, factory girls looking like actresses, greyhound racing and dirt tracks, swimming pools, and everything given away for cigarette coupons . . . the smooth wide road passes between miles of semi-detached bungalows, all with their little garages, their wireless sets, their periodicals about film stars, their swimming costumes and tennis rackets and dancing shoes (p. 401).

Priestley was clearly uncertain about this new England – 'unfortunately it is a bit too cheap' (p. 403), he meant, of course, too American – but nonetheless appreciated its democratic appeal. In suggesting that it belonged 'far more to the age than to this particular island' (p. 401) Priestley's description prefigures Sharon Zukin's more recent observation that the market constantly opposes and undercuts place

2. I use the term 'multiple' when discussing nineteenth-century retailing, 'chain store' thereafter.
3. Following the title of a Report from a Committee appointed by the Board of Trade, *Report on Restraint of Trade* (1931), this phrase refers to the various anti-competitive mechanisms operating within British business (cited in Levy 1942: 3).
4. This strand is elaborated in Winship 2000.

in a process of creative destruction to form new 'landscapes of power' (1991: 5)
His landscape involves 'chaining' the nation in new ways: giant cinemas, wireless
masts, overhead power cables and of course Woolworths, and as he travelled around
England by the new transport of coach and motor car, Priestley pointed to the
trope integral to the undercutting of place – increased mobility. The playwright
John Osborne also identifies such a change, as he recalls the London suburb of
Ewell:

> In 1938 [Ewell] had few remnants of charm, but the 406 bus to Kingston every twenty
> minutes and the frequent Green Line to Morden had ended its life as a village. It had
> become *a timetable on a bus shelter, not lived in so much as passed through* (Osborne
> 1981: 58, my emphasis).

The new factories of the growth industries – synthetic fibres, electrical goods,
motor-manufacture, food-processing – were also less tied to place than the
traditional and declining heavy industries, they were in Sydney Pollard's phrase,
'more footloose' (1983: 79). They utilised electricity – an increasingly reliable
source once the Central Electricity Board was established in 1926 and the National
Grid completed by 1933 – and transporting less bulky raw materials and goods,
relied less on rail and canal than on the expanding road network, signalled in the
new road classification and vocabulary of trunk roads, by-passes and arterial roads[5]
(Jackson 1973: 112–13). Osborne, again:

> The 406 stopped outside [Ewell Parade where he lived] on its way to the by-pass and to
> Epsom. Epsom had only recently been widened, scythed through and turned from a
> pokey country town into a municipal concourse able to accommodate traffic, with a new
> Woolworth's, pubs and a brand new Odeon (1981: 59).

'Widened, scythed through' encapsulates the undercutting of place by market and
the changing landscape of chain stores (chain cinemas, chain pubs, chain teashops)
which dramatically pushed their way into British high streets in the 1930s.

Along with a new infrastructure and migration of investment went a mass
migration of people, from north to south, and from inner city to suburbs, shifting
the country's centre of gravity from the traditional manufacturing areas of Scotland,
south Wales and the north, to the midlands, and especially to London and the
south-east where there was expanding employment (Abrams 1946, Glynn and

---

5. More significant than the two million cars in Britain between the wars, was the mushrooming
of bus, and London underground, services for workers and shoppers from the suburbs, and the lorry
and the delivery van, on which retailing increasingly depended (Miller and Church 1979).

Oxborrow 1976, Beddoe 1989). Describing the consequent 'nationalisation' of the middle class, Harold Perkin refers to the mobility of the new 'spiralists', who unlike the 'burgesses' (the traditional local business and self-employed men), rooted in place, were 'career professionals who ... move up by moving round' (1989: 266–7). But mobility was also embodied in the figure of the young woman, 'the young working girl – lipsticked, silk-stockinged', who, in Sally Alexander's characterisation of Britain's two nations (south and north, suburb and inner city, in work and out of work, well off and poor), was set against 'the cloth cap and spare frame of the unemployed man' (1994: 103). Priestley, too, as he observed English life from the new social space of a cinema cafe in Boston, noted that with the influence of Hollywood stars, the young were no longer marked by their market town roots. But 'it was only the girls ... who had this cosmopolitan appearance; the young men looked their honest, broad, red-faced East Anglian selves', tied still to class and place (1934: 376).

I want to argue that this landscape, observed by Priestley and others, was the result of a ratcheting up of circulation, a process which was more effectively executed in the United States but also witnessed in Britain. It is not just that distribution of commodities was extended geographically, or that a wider class grouping was more firmly embraced within 'consumption communities' (Boorstin 1973: 89), or even that the process of circulation was speeded up, though it was, but that the character of goods *as* goods was pushed further.[6] From the mid-nineteenth century, the price tag as the measure of a commodity's exchange value, was institutionally set in place by the department store, and commodities simultaneously gained an aesthetic 'aura' through the dream-world ambience of store interiors (Williams 1982, Leach 1994). During the inter-war years a commodity aesthetic was more securely fixed by branding, and the associated processes of standardisation, packaging, and national advertising. On the one hand the communication of a twentieth-century brand advertisement was 'public and general', providing 'a form of insurance to the consumer that by buying this commodity, by smoking this brand of cigarette ... *he would not find himself alone*' (Boorstin 1973: 145–6, my emphasis). On the other hand, its representation of 'imaginary elsewheres' (Friedberg 1993: 2) fed into consumers' private flights of fantasy. Allowing 'the world *to flow*' (Boorstin 1973: 138, my emphasis), advertising contributed to the wider set of practices Raymond Williams refers to as 'mobile privatisation' (1990: 26). Yet in Britain this undercutting of place by market, the development of goods '*as* goods', was more limited and compromised than in the United States.

6. This argument borrows from Schivelbusch's analysis of nineteenth-century developments in the circulation of commodities (1980).

Janice Winship

The Middle Way

By 1939 in Britain the chain stores had carved out a market alongside, and in competition with, the department and co-operative stores, and were particularly noted for their own-brand goods. Their standardised fascias jostled for prime place in the redeveloped high streets and their mass-marketing strategies increasingly squeezed out the small, but still significant, independent trader. Their particular development was the consequence not only of Britain's compact geography and early industrialisation, but also of the political and cultural support for trade restraints, which were furthered by the retention of family influence in companies and by an ethos of business leadership as public service. At the heart of such practices were the class dynamics of British society. Under this regime, and seemingly paradoxical, the chain stores developed a national reach and a centralised organisation. In the United States, the co-operative movement was never significant but by 1939 the chain stores competed with the giant mail order houses and city department stores (both of which were pushed into chain development), and came under pressure from supermarkets. Selling only branded goods, the latter set up outside urban areas on tracts of cheap land with extensive parking lots. Compared to Britain, chain stores were less national, but the process of decentralised retailing was more advanced. This trajectory was shaped by the competitive intensity of the much later industrial expansion in the United States, where the larger land mass posed communication and distributional problems. Such intensity engendered both a more thorough incorporation of companies and development of managerial capitalism and, at various moments, resistance to monopolistic tendencies, including those of chain stores. At the heart of these processes was a class dynamic inflected by immigrant and ethnic cultures.

In both countries chain store development was marked by contestation: between different retailing forms for market share, between manufacturers, wholesalers and retailers over the distribution process, and between different modes of commercial expertise which established distinctive relationships with consumers. The outcome of these contestations was that wholesalers were largely squeezed out. Knowledge about goods – their selection, presentation and packaging – once the responsibility of the productive shopkeeper, was pushed back up the hierarchy, either to manufacturers and their advertising agencies, or to chain store head offices. At the same time, shop work was transferred from retailer to consumer by the introduction of more open display and self-service, a process Ursula Huws refers to as 'the externalisation of labour' (1988: 34). Rather than an assistant serving unpackaged and unbranded goods to the *customer*, the *consumer* directly confronts commodities, mediated by price, display, packaging and advertising's pre-selling.

Given that such battles to control the market aimed to offer a resolution to the crises of overproduction periodically wracking capitalism, it was ironic that the original mass retailer, creating the first British multiples, was the co-operative movement, providing an alternative to a 'market-oriented and competitive mode of production/consumption' (Gurney 1996: 11–12). Significantly, co-operative stores were set up to provide *pure* rather than cheap food, in a context where the increasingly urban working class were unable to produce their own food and the abysmal quality and adulteration of bought comestibles was commonplace (Burnett 1966). Through their wholesale societies (the Co-operative Wholesale Society in England, 1863; the Scottish Wholesale Society in Scotland, 1868), the co-operatives developed vertical integration – involving themselves in production as well as retailing – and set up branch stores (Davis 1966: 280). In this way their customer-members (those in regular employment, not the poor, whose precarious household economies relied heavily on credit from small shopkeepers) were supplied with a limited range of basic foodstuffs, footwear and hosiery. By 1905 the CWS was the sixteenth largest company in Britain, 'way ahead of Lever Brothers [soap], Huntley and Palmers [biscuits] and Brunner Mond[7] [chemicals]' (Gurney 1996: 20).

Whilst there is no evidence to suggest that the entrepreneurial multiples directly copied the co-op's modern organisational methods, the impact of this moral discourse of retailing on working-class culture was profound. Most of the founders of the multiples were working class and often, like Michael Marks and Meshe Osinsky (Montague Burton) Jewish émigrés (Aris 1970, Sigsworth 1990). Some, like Jesse Boot (Boots the Chemist), brought up as a Wesleyan in Nottingham, and his friend James Duckworth, who built up a chain of grocers around Rochdale, genuinely admired the co-op movement (Chapman 1974: 53, 130). Such men, who were well placed to appreciate the growing needs and desires of their customers, took quick advantage of new retailing opportunities. W.H. Smith gained railway contracts in 1848 and their bookstalls spread across the network in England, while John Menzies established a similar monopoly in Scotland. Thomas Lipton's shops in Glasgow (1872) were built on the back of fast new steamships importing cheap Empire butter, cheese, ham and bacon when the standard of living, and thus food consumption, was rising. Sometimes it was manufacturers who integrated forward into retail. The (US) Singer Sewing Machine Company (1856) had factories in Glasgow, and sold and serviced machines too expensive for traditional shops to stock, whilst the footwear manufacturers, such as J. Sears, the Trueform Boot Co retailed an output that the craftsman cobbler-retailer decried (Jefferys 1954, Mathias 1967, Fraser 1981).

The trajectories of the early multiples varied, but their origins were in family businesses painstakingly built up, first locally, then regionally, with expansion

---

7. In 1926 Brunner Mond became one of the four constituent companies of ICI (Hannah 1983: 109).

initially financed from profits, and incorporation and property development raising the larger capital needed for a national push (Scott 1994). They traded in a few basic lines, enabling vertical integration (or in the case of the Penny Bazaars like M&S, many lines for the same price), in rented and crudely fitted-out premises on the edge of high-density housing. Cash only and no deliveries meant they were not dependent on customers' loyalty and regular advertising pushed through the necessary high volume of goods. These were 'frontier conditions' when 'roguery was rampant' and 'advertisements relied for their attraction on tricks and sensationalism' (Harris and Seldon 1962: 18). As well as posters and inserts in the local press, the early multiples engaged in publicity stunts in town streets and used 'barkers' to entice those who dallied on the threshold. Early in the twentieth century, however, as sights were set on the national market, they exploited space in the new popular press, with Boots buying the whole front page of the lower middle class *Daily Mail* for 'ten consecutive days' during Christmas 1904, as well as '8 full-page insertions in *The Times*' (Chapman 1974: 85). Yet emphasis was also placed on the stores as their own best advertisement, with observers in 1878 noting that the Dundee branch of Lipton's 'was brilliantly illuminated by sixty jets' and marked by 'an air of smartness and cleanliness calculated to win over the most demanding housewife' (Mathias 1967: 46–7). What is important here is that chain stores and (own-brand) goods were promoted as one.

In the US, mass-marketing methods did not emerge from retailing in industrial working-class communities, but from mail-order selling to a predominantly rural population, and from the city department store selling to a more sophisticated urban market (Boorstin 1973). Such 'consumption communities' demanded different retailing strategies than in Britain. In the US, enticement and the awakening of desire were critical. In their different ways, brand advertising, the commercial aesthetic of the department store, created from 'facades of color, glass, and light' (Leach 1994: 39), and the illustrated mail order catalogue (the Sears, Roebuck catalogue was already running to over five hundred pages in 1894) all offered immense possibilities for consumer *imagining and longing* (Emmet and Jeuck 1950, Ohmann 1996).

US chain stores were established in this commercial and cultural context. As in Britain, they were initially 'shops with no frills, but where the (lower) middle class customer could save money' (Boorstin 1973: 109). Their rapid expansion occurred from 1910 when communication and transport links opened up the country, the population rapidly urbanised and the US market became the largest in the world (Chandler and Tedlow 1985, Tedlow 1990). They set up in small and medium-sized towns, keeping away from 'down town' city areas. In contrast to Britain, the US food chains had difficulty attracting working-class shoppers, since local stores served as social centres for immigrant communities and were 'the means through which they perpetuated the foodways that remained the core of 'ethnic culture' (Cohen 1990: 140). By the depression of the 1930s, however, with the chains squeezing out local outlets, and with state relief channelling unemployed welfare claimants into cheaper shops, working-class immigrant shoppers found themselves switching stores, if not allegiances. Consequently, the chains extended their class reach downwards (Cohen 1990, 1993).

The years of laissez-faire capitalism in America during the 1920s granted the chains certain financial advantages over small traders, but during the depression years when the chains had gained an oligopolistic position in some market sectors, anti-chain actions escalated, endorsed by Roosevelt's New Deal administration, which legitimated intervention into business practice. State legislation imposed taxes on chains, whilst at the federal level the Robinson-Patman Act in 1936 prevented chains buying goods at cheaper prices than small traders, and the Miller-Tydings Act in 1937 sanctioned price maintenance by manufactures (Lebhar 1959, Strasser 1989, Tedlow 1990). Whilst not seriously thwarted by the attacks, the chains adjusted their practices. One strategy was to pursue own-brand (ironically stimulating vertical integration and further entrenching their power), another was to quell criticism from the small trader by allowing prices to float upwards. The chains also improved their corporate image, pursuing the farm lobby, wooing unions and energising local managers to take part in local community affairs to promote good citizenship, and thereby mimicking the role independent merchants played in civic life (Raucher 1991, Ewen 1996). In the US trading environment, however, 'printed salesmanship', or brand advertising, which was strengthened by the consolidation of a commercialised radio from the late 1920s, developed as the acceptable means of market control (Levy 1942).[8] During the depression, as economic hardship hit consumers, the challenge to the chain stores from the large-scale supermarkets depended on taking advantage of manufacturers' brand advertising. Adopting a strategy of high volume and fast turnover, they offered cut-price packaged foodstuffs to the newly mobile car owner (Strasser 1989, Bowlby 1997).[9]

The field of struggle in Britain by the inter-war period was rather different. From the 1890s the leading form of mass retailing, the co-operatives, were increasingly attacked for poaching the custom of the better-off, on whom private traders depended. In the ensuing trade wars the co-operative stores were boycotted and demands made that their 'profits' be taxed (Gurney 1996: 199).[10] With the

8. Raymond Williams rightly comments that advertising is one means of control which in its 'full development, includes the growth of tariffs...cartel-quotas...price-fixing by manufacturers and that form of economic imperialism which assured certain markets overseas by political control of their territories' (Williams 1980: 178).

9. With this competion the US chain stores quickly copied the supermarkets.

10. These demands largely failed but in 1930 the Labour Party, fearful of its weak position politically, failed to step in to support the co-operative movement and in 1933 their reserves were taxed (Gurney 1996: 230).

rise of the multiples, the key means of defence for traders became the trade association, not legislation as in other European countries (Jefferys and Knee 1962). The British trade associations persuaded manufacturers to establish resale price maintenance (RPM) in order to guarantee profits, so that by 1938 27–35 per cent of all goods were sold at fixed prices (Yamey 1966). Though the initiative was of some benefit to small traders, increasingly it was the financially strong companies, including the chains, which played key roles in trade associations and reinforced their monopolistic position (Hilton 1998). Further, anyone not belonging to a trade association was regarded as a villain and price-maintenance was the '"moral" price to which every ethically-minded member of the association should willingly adhere' (Levy 1942: 117). For the chains RPM pushed the development of own-brands further than in the US, in order that prices for value goods could be lowered.

Trade associations, ranking alongside 'pools, cartels, trusts, combines (Levy 1942: 4), found favour within British economic and political life, where ideas to moderate competition were summed up in the title of Harold Macmillan's book *The Middle Way* (1938). Supporting the 'mixed economy', Macmillan was a progressive Conservative and a prime mover in cross-party debates from the 1930s to regulate capitalism's worst excesses, symbolised for the British by American practices.[11] As he put it: 'Britain has been moving along the road towards economic planning for many years now *in accordance with the traditional English principles of compromise and adjustment*' (1938: 186, my emphasis). Attempting to understand this compromise culture, the historian Martin Wiener has argued that the more gradualist nature of Britain's transition to a mature industrial society led to both a humanising vision of urban life and to a form of economic retardation. Capitalism was tempered. Wiener has emphasised that by 1939 the prevalent form of organisation in the British economy was 'uncompetitive private enterprise in partnership with the state' (1981: 109). Others have shown how the capital controlled by various public bodies or non-profit-making organisations (including the co-op and building societies) was 'of the same order of magnitude as the aggregate capital of all joint-stock companies' (Pollard 1983). Whether the Post Office, the BBC, the National Grid for electricity or the chain stores, these endeavours were conceived as 'public utilities' involving universal and standardised provision across the country.

With service valued over goods production, family control of companies over greater efficiency, 'the entrepreneurial class turned its energies to reshaping itself in the image of the [aristocratic] class it was supplanting' (Wiener 1981: 14).[12]

---

11. Such moves had been evident earlier when the Institute of Industrial Management, founded in 1920, 'propagated a "higher" conception of management than that coming over from the US' (Wiener 1981: 143).

12. Other historians offer different explanations but largely do not disagree with Wiener's thesis that British capitalism was retarded and compromised.

However, Wiener has suggested that outsiders, including Jews and Quakers, were 'less prone to such sentiments' and enjoyed a disproportionate success in British business' (p. 203). Chain stores like Burton, M&S and Tesco together with Lyons' chain of tea shops and Oscar Deutsch's chain of Odeon cinemas, were certainly led by successful Jewish outsiders (Aris 1970). Nevertheless, viewed as a whole the chain stores, both Jewish and gentile, also represented precisely the conservative culture of compromise and of public service more widely supported in Britain: these were anti-competitive companies.

At the same time, the chain stores were dedicated to implementing American managerial strategies in ways some industries were not.[13] From the US, the importance of store siting was emphasised, so too was the ambience of interiors, as the chains moved onto high streets, expanded store size and often their range of goods, increased their level of service and attracted a broader social market. There was a change of emphasis from 'large-scale and expert buying' to securing gains on the selling side by 'expert planning and standardisation of methods of property acquisition' as well as of 'shop layout', together with improved control of price, stock and distribution (Jefferys 1954: 89). Implementing such ideas depended on the chains adopting a divisional structure, each with specialised responsibilities, as is illustrated by Burton's attention to detail over transport. As the key link between their 'meticulously worked-out processes of production' and their means of 'satisfying customers in the shops', care was taken not to damage garments in transit (Sigsworth 1990: 84; Mort and Thompson 1994). Vans were built to the firm's design and supported a scarlet and gold livery with 'the green neon name-sign on the front of each vehicle above the cab' (Sigsworth 1990: 84).

Boots was even taken over and rationalised by a US company in 1920, United Drug, before returning to the control of the Boot family in 1933 (Chapman 1974). For Simon Marks and Israel Sieff, Chairman and Vice-Chairman of M&S, lessons learnt from retailing trips to the US were crucial to their transformation of the company's network of 'Penny Bazaars' into modern chain store enterprises, based on the idea that 'each counter-foot of space had to pay wages, rent, overhead expenses and earn a profit' (Marks cited in Sieff 1970: 142). These processes included simple pricing and regular stock checking to regulate the production and flow of goods. Alert to the competition of Woolworth, M&S slimmed its catalogue to the fastest-selling goods, upped its price limit and improved the store image (Briggs 1984, Rees 1969, Shaw et al. 1998).

Though modernists in their commitment to harnessing technology and adopting rational systems, the chain stores also domesticated these impulses by emphasising

---

13. Chandler indicates the limits of the British managerial process compared to the US, pursuing economies more through scale than scope, and with the management remaining more personal (Chandler 1990: 261).

a rhetoric of serving the common good, in ways which echoed the public service ethos of figures like John Reith, the first director general of the BBC (Scannell and Cardiff 1991). In particular the chains' concern about their working-class consumers, together with their investment in employee welfare at a time when the reputation of retailers as employers was poor, reflected their ties to a wider business and political ethic during the inter-war years. In M&S's case Israel Sieff was involved in PEP (Political and Economic Planning), which according to Arthur Marwick was one of the 'most enduring of the [1930s'] "planning" groups' (Marwick 1964: p 287). Promoting a politics of the 'middle way', Macmillan and Basil Blackett, director of the Bank of England, also played leading roles. Sieff's long-term friend was Aneurin Bevan, the left-wing minister responsible for overseeing the council housing programme and the National Health Service in the 1945 Labour administration, and Simon Marks had personal ties with Sir Harry, later Lord McGowan, chairman of ICI, a core supplier, whose paternalistic welfare schemes were intended to deflect militant trade unionism (Jones 1983: 64).

As befitted Britain's industrial culture of compromise and its upholding of the commercial value of 'restraint of trade', chain stores tempered the development of goods '*as* goods' more than their American counterparts. Not only did store and brand not compete in Britain, but in-store there was not the ferocious competition between brands fuelled by the pre-selling of advertising, where each brand demanded of the consumer 'buy me (not that other brand)!' Vertical integration eliminated wholesalers and competition between producers was controlled by the (producer)-retailer. If, as Boorstin maintains, brand advertising 'allow[ed] the world to *flow*', one literal flow was the potential global distribution of a brand via an array of retail outlets, while another was the 'imaginary elsewheres' offered by commodity-packaging and advertising. But with chain store own-brands, the goods could not be distributed independently of the chain and the 'imaginary elsewheres' they conjured up were always compromised by store-image. In these ways the retailer retained the paternalistic power to define, authenticate and evaluate goods on behalf of customers, much like traditional traders. At the same time a culture of restraint was important to those who were the stores' main customers. The chain stores had grown up with the working class, and as a proportion of that class adopted new ways of living and became part of an expanding fraction of the lower middle class, so the stores met their 'social needs' and fitted into their routines.

New Routines and the Performative Space of the Chain Store

An emergent class fraction in Britain during the inter-war years was characterised by the figure of the young working girl, lipsticked and silk-stockinged, referred to earlier. The new Fordist light industry recruited cheap, mostly non-unionised, female labour and the expansion of white collar workers in 'retail distribution, local government, transport and entertainments' increasingly relied on women (Pollard 1983: 184–5). The term 'white collar' graphically points to *dress*, invoking both the appearance of this worker and the worker s/he definitely is not. The *Marks and Spencer Magazine* showed a model standing primly for the camera and captioned, 'This neat and attractively dressed girl bought her clothes at a Marks and Spencer Store' (Summer 1932: 16). But the women assembling valves for wireless sets also have bobbed hair, white, low-belted overalls, probably art silk stockings (they have a shiny look) and heeled shoes with ankle straps. Miriam Glucksmann describes how such women took on the qualities of the work they performed: 'clean, neat and tidy workers', in contrast to workers in the older heavy industries who were seen as 'large, strong, untidy and bawdy' (1990: 216). Tensions around feminine status were played out through the body during the inter-war period, with dress being the visible embodiment of respectability and class aspiration.

In the celebratory book *Dunroamin*, a popular house name for new suburban owners, Paul Oliver suggests that the semi's predominant aesthetic was organised around a combination of 'pretty' and 'nice'. Whereas 'pretty' was 'full of charm, sentiment and sweetness', 'nice' was 'orderly and controlled' (1981: 181–2). 'Nice and clean, nice and neat, nice and tidy, nice and smart, nice and bright' also codes the outcome of new self-disciplines for women, tied to changed work practices and nurtured by a shift of routines at home and at leisure – all served by consumption. Above all 'nice and neat' connotes the culture of restraint, which sets this class fraction apart from the more expansive culture of the working class. During the inter-war period the expanding lower middle class curbed family size and 'kept themselves to themselves' (Giles 1995: 94), their emotional thriftiness matching a bodily demeanour of 'nice and neat' or, in Pierre Bourdieu's description of the petit bourgeois man, who makes himself 'small to pass through the strait gate which leads to the bourgeoisie: strict and sober, discreet and severe . . . he always lacks something in stature, breadth, substance, largesse' (1984: 338).

For young women across the classes, the shift from the fashionable Edwardian body – '"*raide*": taut, stiff, tight' – to the 'modernist' body of the 1920s – 'healthy, intelligible and progressive . . . functioning like an efficient, smoothly running machine' (Wollen 1993: 20–1) – involved practising new internal disciplines: 'exercise, sports and diet rather than the corset and the stays' (p. 20–1). However, the lower middle class attachment to the 'nice and neat' version of the modernist body demanded a particular inflection of new routines, including chain store shopping. Without servants or extended family support, managing a tight budget and upholding appearances, the lower middle class wife was a promising target for the magazine advice from 'scientific management' experts on running a rational home (White 1970). Advertising fed such routines, but it also offered respite: 'Salmon? that's a treat!' Husband enjoys the treat, (house)wife enjoys minimal preparation (advertisement for Sailor Salmon Slice, Brighton *Evening Argus*, 13 September 1931: 8). Alongside tinned peaches and evaporated milk, this treat-for-family/ reprieve-for-mum itself became a routine: Sunday tea after the rigours of preparing/eating the Sunday roast. Children were also caught up in such regimes proposed by experts like Truby King, who advocated no emotional pampering and feeding baby at regular intervals, never on demand (Hardyment 1983). Training, combined with doses of syrup of figs, encouraged the self-discipline of obligatory daily bowel movements. As Jackson Lears graphically describes US laxative advertising from the period: 'the pitch for occasional heroic purgation was being streamlined into an emphasis on "regularity" – a more methodical regime better suited to the emerging rhythms of modern life' (1994: 165).

Both the idea of the treat and the respectable routine were encouraged by the expansion of suburban supercinemas: 'going to the pictures' and enjoying 'luncheon or tea' in the cafe offered a 'brief escape from dull routine at low cost' (Jackson 1973: 176), while 'listening-in' to the wireless (affordable by the 1930s), offered entertainment and access to music, plays and discussions. As a key institution regularising daily life, the wireless schedule soon fitted around, and consolidated, women's domestic day-time duties and men's evening return from work, with the added 'convenience' of enabling women simultaneously to 'relax' and 'work' – listening in whilst ironing or darning (Pegg 1983, Scannel 1988).

The meaning of 'convenience', as saving labour and time when the latter has become a scarce commodity, might seem obvious enough, but in his analysis of women's new-found habit of smoking cigarettes in the inter-war period, Michael Schudson suggests a cluster of attributes. From the producer's point of view, the mildness of 'convenience' products means that they will appeal to a wide market. From the consumer's point of view, mild goods are easier to use but also 'do not offend' (Schudson 1993: 202). The development of a 'mass, British *middle-brow* culture', epitomised in the BBC's light entertainment output offering 'balanced' programmes that were relaxing, 'guaranteed soothing ("wholesome") by . . . exclusion of all excesses' (Frith 1983: 121), can be considered in this context of a culture of convenience. Such programming possessed what Schudson refers to as 'suitability', which helps facilitate 'social circulation' and mobility, and thus also contributes to democratisation.

A range of such convenience products were introduced into women's lives in the inter-war period. The newly developed 'roll-on', shaping the body with elastic instead of whalebone, steel and lacings, was easier to put on and more comfortable for the younger and lighter figure, and the unpopular word 'corset' was erased (Ewing 1978: 147). Similarly, the mass fashion for make-up – no longer the distinguishing sign of the prostitute – was worn and frequently renewed in public:

'Lipstick . . . marks were seen everywhere on cups and handkerchieves' (Jackson 1991: 146). This repetition was echoed in routines associated with hair that was regularly cut and washed, compared to long, pinned-up tresses. As the fondly remembered tag line from a shampoo ad declared: 'Friday night is Amami night' (*Woman's Own*, 5 November 1938: 60).

Chain stores variously catered to these new routines. In the 1920s, Etam opened branches in the City of London specifically to sell stockings to office girls (*The Times*, 21 March 1966: 13). Revealed by the shorter length skirt, these cheap rayon stockings were easily laddered, but not easily darned, and had routinely to be replaced to maintain respectability. Whether selling clothes or food, the chain store catered to a different rhythm. The image of the independent grocer continued to be that of the retailer who dropped round to consume a leisurely cup of tea while the mistress of the house decided on her weekly requirements. Her order would be delivered and she might enjoy considerable credit. Chain store shoppers did their own shopping, regularly, for cash. Often travelling by bus, purchases were in pounds and dozens, and goods were likely to be packaged and branded. Shopping was thus neither the bulk buying of grander households, nor was it the daily ounces and single items resorted to by the poor from nearby corner shops.

Suburban women, uprooted from their old ties with inner-city shops, became a natural constituency for the expanding chains (Blake 1936). The new 'simplicity' of women's clothes and the standardisation of men's shirts, were partly economies made by the retailer, a means of providing reasonable quality at a cheap price. But such clothes also allowed the consumer to blend in, not stand out from the crowd. As Oliver comments, the ethos in the new suburbs was '"keeping up with" not "*beating*" the Joneses' (1981: 191). A magazine article in which 'Mrs. Goodwife goes out shopping', vividly illustrates how chain stores facilitated a class mobility and suburban taste. Joining the tennis club ('the principal summer recreation in our suburb') was seen as a necessary but hardly an affordable expense, only managed by prudent purchases at M&S. Yet as the copy stressed: 'It was not a question of buying cheap clothes at low prices, all the things I purchased are in excellent taste' (*Marks and Spencer Magazine*, Summer 1932).

The space of the inter-war chain store 'superstore', was similarly distinctive. The 'chaotic-exotic' atmosphere (Williams 1982: 71), typical of earlier arcades and department stores which borrowed from the promiscuous mix of a market culture containing and rendering it safe for shoppers (Slater 1993), was almost wholly absent. Instead of this stimulating visual register contributing to the 'ambiguity of space' (Frisby 1985: 241) there was now the illusion of transparency. To cross the chain store threshold from the bustle and heterogeneity of the street was to step into another plane. Inside, stores were brightly and uniformly lit (resembling daylight as near as possible), while functional signage, indicating the type of good and price, 'Wool jumpers 2/11', was prominent, and placed at eye height. A limited range of goods were piled up, in an abundance (evidently mass produced but offering, for example, a range of colours or fabrics) on counters laid out in a symmetrical grid pattern. Goods were displayed at waist height (easy to look at and handle without the intervention of an assistant) with nothing to distract the customer from finding and contemplating the goods she was interested in. The space was ordered, hygienically clean and visible, spacious but not that imposing or spread across different floors. The whole retailing space could be immediately grasped. Hiding nothing and throwing up no surprises, its transparency communicated the accessibility of goods. There was the illusion that the barriers to consumption, for those who had hitherto consumed relatively little, had been removed. The lower middle class were *arrivistes* but only just. If consumption was crucial to their lifestyle it was not to be engaged in lightly and correspondingly their shops were relatively austere spaces. Nevertheless, in their uniformity and predictability, chain stores and their own-brand goods represented 'oases of order' in a notoriously uncertain world (Sigsworth on the Montagu Burton Chain, 1990: 53). Such order, such restraint, was a quality keenly appreciated by the insecure 'lower middles' (Jackson 1991).

Conclusion

In its magazine in 1932 M&S intimated to customers that it introduced 'the girl who makes the stockings to the girls who wears them' (*Marks Spencer Magazine*, Summer 1932), concisely pointing to how 'the sales effort' was the means by which production and daily life were ideally unified (Ohmann 1996: 74). Managing this 'sales effort' – the battle to build a relationship with the 'unmanageable consumer' (Gabriel and Lang 1995) – has become a lynchpin of capitalism's development in the twentieth century, with manufacturers and retailers often in competition with each other to control this process. Writing about the US, Susan Strasser has suggested that 'the manufacturers . . . won the turn-of-the-century battle . . . they held the power . . . by virtue of their advertised trademarks. Over the course of the twentieth century, those trademarks have become even more powerful' (1989: 285).[14] But in Britain the outcome of this battle has been less clear cut. In the first half of the century the forces which contributed to 'restraint on trade' lessened the pressure on manufacturers and small retailers to rationalise, but forced efficiencies on chains and contributed to a pre-eminence only fully realised in the post-Second World War period.

14. Indeed the world's most valuable brands are, with the exception of Sony, all American (Lury: 1998: 113).

Thus I have argued that the development of goods *as* goods, with brand advertising a lubricant enabling 'the world to flow', was partly checked in Britain by the practices of chain stores. Despite their admiration and imitation of American chains, especially from the 1920s, the particularity of their history differentiated them. Their profile in Britain derived as much from their relation to the culture of the new lower middle class, as from politico-economic relations shaping the retail environment. In granting this class fraction prime place within an expanding commercial and consumer culture, and suggesting their active role on the historical stage, my argument departs from those accounts which sideline this group. Some historians have not continued the story of the lower middle class beyond the First World War (Crossick 1977), others have focused on them in a middle-class context (Light 1991), or slipped the new lower middle class into the more heroic, working class (Giles 1995). Their story and far-reaching contribution to British culture, for better or worse, has yet to be fully told. As the twenty-first century has arrived it is an interesting question whether the 'culture of restraint', is being more exhaustively dismantled in Britain. The country may not yet be a US-style 'land of desire' (Leach 1994) but much has changed. M&S's fall from grace and Wal-Mart's challenge to the British supermarkets might usefully be viewed in this cultural context. It is then perhaps fitting that M&S should appoint as their first ever marketing director, Alan McWalter, 'the man who revamped the dowdy image of retail chain Woolworths' (*Guardian*, 24 September 1999: 27). After all, it was from the American chain that M&S learnt so much in the 1920s.

References

Abrams, Mark (1946), *The Condition of the British People 1911–1945*, London: Victor Gollancz.

Alexander, Sally (1994), *Becoming a Woman and Other Essays in 19th and 20th Century Feminist History*, London: Virago.

Aris, Stephen (1970), *Jews in Business*, London: Jonathan Cape.

Beddoe, Deirdre (1989), *Back to Home and Duty: Women Between the Wars 1918–1939*, London: Pandora.

Blake, A.E. (1936), *Planned Retail Advertising*, London: Blandford Press.

Boorstin, Daniel (1973), *The Americans: The Democratic Experience*, New York: Random House.

Bourdieu, Pierre (1984), *Distinction: A Social Critique of the Judgement of Taste*, London: Routledge.

Bowlby, Rachel (1997), 'Supermarket futures' in Pasi Falk and Colin Campbell (eds), *The Shopping Experience*, London: Sage.

Briggs, Asa (1984), *Marks and Spencer 1884–1984*, London: Octopus.

Burnett, John (1966), *Plenty and Want: A Social History of Diet in England from 1815 to the Present Day*, London: Scolar Press.

Chandler, Alfred D. (1990), *Scale and Scope: The Dynamics of Industrial Capitalism*, Cambridge, Mass.: Harvard University Press.

Chandler, Alfred D. and Tedlow, Richard S. (1985), *The Coming of Managerial Capitalism: A Casebook on the History of American Economic Institutions*, Homewood, Illinois: Richard Irwin.

Chapman, Sydney (1974), *Jesse Boot of Boots the Chemists*, London: Hodder and Stoughton.

Cohen, Lizabeth (1990), *Making a New Deal: Industrial Workers in Chicago 1919–1939*, Cambridge: Cambridge University Press.

Cohen, Lizabeth (1993), 'The class experience of mass consumption: workers as consumers in inter war America' in Richard Wightman Fox and T.J. Lears (eds), *The Power of Culture: Critical Essays in American History*, Chicago: University of Chicago Press.

Crossick, Geoffrey (ed.) (1977), *The Lower Middle Class in Britain 1870–1914*, London: Croom Helm.

Davis, Dorothy (1966), *A History of Shopping*, London: Routledge and Kegan Paul.

Emmet, Boris and Jeuck, John E. (1950), *Catalogues and Counters: A History of Sears, Roebuck and Company*, Chicago and London: The University of Chicago Press.

Ewen, Stuart (1996), *PR!: A Social History of Spin*, New York: Basic Books.

Ewing, Elizabeth (1978), *Dress and Undress: A History of Women's Underwear*, London: B.T. Batsford.

Fraser, W. Hamish (1981), *The Coming of the Mass Market, 1850–1914*, Basingstoke: Macmillan.

Friedberg, Anne (1993), *Window Shopping: Cinema and the Postmodern*, Berkeley and Los Angeles: University of California Press.

Frisby, David (1985), *Fragments of Modernity: Theories of Modernity in the Work of Simmel, Kracauer and Benjamin*, Cambridge, Polity.

Frith, Simon (1983), 'The pleasures of the hearth' in *Formations of Pleasure*, London: Routledge and Kegan Paul.

Gabriel, Yiannis and Lang, Tim (1995), *The Unmanageable Consumer: Contemporary Consumption and its Fragmentations*, London: Sage.

Giles, Judy (1995), *Women, Identity and Private Life in Britain, 1900–1950*, Basingstoke: Macmillan.

Glucksmann, Miriam (1990), *Women Assemble: Women Workers and the New Industries in Inter-war Britain*, London: Routledge.

Glynn, Sean and Oxborrow, John (1976), *Interwar Britain: A Social and Economic History*, London: George Allen and Unwin.

Gurney, Peter (1996), *Co-operative Culture and the Politics of Consumption in England 1870–1930*, Manchester: Manchester University Press.

Hannah, Leslie (2nd edn 1983), *The Rise of the Corporate Economy*, London: Methuen.

Hardyment, Christina (1983), *Dream Babies: Childcare from Locke to Spock*, London: Cape.

Harris, Ralph and Seldon, Arthur (1962), *Advertising and the Public*, London: Andre Deutsch.

Hilton, Matthew (1998), 'Retailing history as economic and cultural history: strategies of survival by specialist tobacconists in the mass market', *Business History*, Vol. 40, No. 4, pp. 115–37.

Huws, Ursula (1988), 'Consuming fashions' *New Statesman and Society*, 19 August, pp. 31–4.

Jackson, Alan A. (1973), *Semi-detached London: Suburban Development, Life and Transport, 1900–39*, London: George Allen and Unwin.

Jackson, Alan A. (1991), *The Middle Classes 1900–1950*, Nairn: David St. John Thomas .

Jefferys, James B. (1954), *Retailing in Britain 1850–1950*, Cambridge: Cambridge University Press.

Jefferys, James B. and Knee, D. (1962), *Retailing in Europe*, London: Macmillan.

Jones, Helen (1983), 'Employers' welfare schemes and industrial relations in Britain in inter-war Britain', *Business History*, Vol. 25, No. 1, pp. 61–75.

Leach, William (1994), *Landscape of Desire: Merchants, Power and the Rise of a New Americn Culture*, New York: Vintage Books.

Lears, Jackson (1994), *Fables of Abundance: A Cultural History of Advertising in America*, New York: Basic Books/HarperCollins.

Lebhar, Godfrey (1959), *Chain Stores in America 1859–1959*, New York: Chain Store Publishing.

Levy, Hermann (1942), *Retail Trade Associations: A New Form of Monopolist Organisation in Britain: A Report to the Fabian Society*, London: Kegan Paul, Trench, Trubner.

Light, Alison (1991), *Forever England: Femininity, Literature and Conservatism Between the Wars*, London: Routledge.

Lury, Giles (1998), *Brand Watching: Lifting the Lid on the Phenomenon of Branding*, Dublin: Blackhall Publishing.

Macmillan, Harold (1966 2nd edn, 1st edn 1938), *The Middle Way: A Study of the Problem of Economic and Social Progress in a Free and Democratic Society*, London: Macmillan.

Marwick, Arthur (1964), 'Middle opinion in the Thirties: Planning, progress and political "agreement"', in *English Historical Review*, April, pp. 285–98.

Mathias, Peter (1967), *Retailing Revolution*, London: Longmans.

Miller, M. and Church, R.A. (1979), 'Growth and instability in the British motor industry between the wars' in D.H. Aldcroft and C. Buxton (eds), *British Industry Between the Wars: Instability and Industrial Development, 1919–1939*, London: Scolar Press, pp. 179–215.

Mort, Frank and Thompson, Peter (1994), 'Retailing, commercial culture and masculinity in 1950s Britain: The case of Montague Burton, the "Tailor of taste"', *History Workshop Journal*, No.38, pp. 106–27.

Ohmann, Richard (1996), *Selling Culture: Magazines, Markets, and Class at the Turn of the Century*, London: Verso.

Oliver, Paul, Davis, Ian, Bentley, Ian (1981), *Dunroamin: The Suburban Semi and its Enemies*, London: Barrie Jenkins.

Osborne, John (1981), *A Better Class of Person*, London: Faber and Faber.

Pegg, Mark (1983), *Broadcasting and Society 1918–1939*, London: Croom Helm.

Perkin, Harold (1989), *The Rise of Professional Society: England since 1880*, London: Routledge.

Pollard, Sydney (1983 third edition), *The Development of the British Economy 1914–1980*, London: Edward Arnold.

Priestley, J.B. (1934), *An English Journey*, London: Heinemann and Victor Gollancz.

Raucher, Alan R. (1991), 'Dime store chains: the making of organization men, 1880–1940', *Business History Review*, Vol. 65, No. 1. pp. 130–63.

Rees, Goronwy (1969), *St. Michael: A History of Marks and Spencer*, London: Weidenfeld and Nicolson.

Scannell, Paddy (1988), 'Radio Times: The temporal arrangements of broadcasting in the modern world' in Philip Drummond and Richard Paterson (eds), *Television and its Audiences: International research perspectives*, London: BFI.

Scannell, Paddy and Cardiff, David (1991), *A Social History of Broadcasting: Volume One 1922–1939 Serving the Nation*, Oxford, Basil Blackwell.

Schivelbusch, Wolfgang (1980), *The Railway Journey: Trains and Travel in the 19th Century*, Translated by Anselm Hollo, Oxford: Basil Blackwell.

Schudson, Michael (1993), *Advertising, the Uneasy Persuasion*, London: Routledge.

Scott, Peter (1994), ' Learning to multiply: the property market and the growth of multiple retailing in Britain, 1919–39', *Business History*, Vol. 36, No. 3, pp. 1–28.

Shaw, Gareth, Alexander, Andrew, Benson, John and Jones, John (1998), 'Structural and spatial trends in British retailing: The importance of firm-level studies', *Business History*, Vol. 40, No. 4, pp. 79–93.

Sieff, Israel (1970), *Memoirs*, London: Weidenfeld and Nicolson.

Sigsworth, Eric M. (1990), *Montague Burton: The Tailor of Taste*, Manchester: Manchester University Press.

Slater, Don (1993), 'Going shopping: Markets, crowds and consumption' in Chris Jenks (ed.), *Cultural Reproduction*, London: Routledge.

Strasser, Susan (1989), *Satisfaction Guaranteed: The Making of the American Mass Market*, New York: Pantheon.

Tedlow, Richard S. (1990), *New and Improved: The Story of Mass Marketing in America*, New York: Basic Books.

White, Cynthia (1970), *Women's Magazines 1693–1968*, London: Michael Joseph.

Wiener, Martin (1981), *English Culture and the Decline of the Industrial Spirit 1850–1980*, London: Penguin.

Williams, Raymond (1980), 'Advertising: the magic system', in *Problems in Materialism and Culture*, London: New Left Books, pp. 170–95.

—— (1990), *Television, Technology and Cultural Form*, London: Routlege.

Williams, Rosalind (1982), *Dream Worlds: Mass Consumption in Late Nineteenth Century France*, Berkeley: University of California Press.

Winkler, John (1940), *Five and Ten: The Fabulous Life of F.W. Woolworth*, New York: Robert M. McBride.

Winship, Janice (2000), 'New disciplines for women and the rise of the chain store in the 1930s' in Mary Talbot and Maggie Andrews (eds) (1999), *'All the World and Her Husband': Women in Twentieth-century Consumer Culture*, London: Cassell.

Wollen, Peter (1993), *Raiding the Icebox: Reflections on Twentieth-century Culture*, London: Verso.

Yamey, B.S. (ed.) (1966), *Resale Price Maintenance*, London: Weidenfeld and Nicolson.

Zukin, Sharon (1991), *Landscapes of Power: From Detroit to Disney World*, Berkeley: University of California.

2

The Commercial Domain: Advertising and the Cultural Management of Demand

Frank Mort

In *The General Theory of Employment, Interest and Money* (1964), in a passage shortly before his famous formula specifying the relationship between employment, investment and consumption, Keynes reviewed both the 'objective' and the 'subjective' factors which influenced the propensity to consume. Under the rubric of objective influences Keynes listed a familiar range of economic variables. But his consideration of subjective factors influencing demand tempted him for a brief moment onto cultural territory and specifically onto the field of human motivations:

> There remain the second category of factors which affect the amount of consumption out of a given income – namely, those subjective and social incentives which determine how much is spent . . . These eight motives might be called the motives of Precaution, Foresight, Calculation, Improvement, Independence, Enterprise, Pride and Avarice; and we could also draw up a corresponding list of motives to consumption such as Enjoyment, Shortsightedness, Generosity, Miscalculation, Ostentation and Extravagance . . . Now the strength of these motives will vary enormously according to the habits formed by race, education, convention, religion and current morals . . . In the argument of this book, however, we shall not concern ourselves . . . with the results of far-reaching social changes or with the slow effects of secular progress. We shall . . . take as given the main background of subjective motives to saving and consumption respectively. (Keynes 1964: 107–10)

Keynes here suppressed the field of social and cultural change, and the vagaries of the human personality, in the interests of economic theory. Yet the relations he articulated at this point in one of the classic accounts of modern economics – about the connections between economic progress, secular ethics and the cultural and psychological motivations of individuality – were issues which resonated throughout the post-war period. A characteristic development across the industrial societies of Europe and North America in the mid-twentieth century was the proliferation of knowledges and technologies for connecting the world of economic activity with the field of culture and human relations. Both the advocates and the opponents of this strategy highlighted a vision of modern industrial society in which commerce and culture were now inextricably linked. Anthony Giddens and Zygmunt Bauman have argued that a defining feature of 'mature' or 'late' modernity was the new equilibrium forged between the economic and the cultural domains. This relationship had far-reaching effects, not simply on what was written and spoken about in official public culture, but on the ways in which modern subjects lived out a sense of who and what they were (Giddens 1991; Bauman 1987).

Historians have documented these changes via the concept which lies at the heart of Keynes' own theory – the idea of consumption. In a British context the intensified impact of consumption has become enshrined as one of the master-narratives of the 1950s and early 1960s. Together with economic growth, full employment, political consensus and the rise of the welfare state, it has been used as one of the basic building blocs to tell the story of post-war society. Yet inasmuch as the term is liminal, crossing the boundaries between economics and culture, between material life and the moulding of human wants, arguments about the precise significance of consumption have varied enormously. Economists and economic historians have foregrounded the impact of Keynes' own strategy of demand management, understood in the context of the offensive against socialist versions of the command economy, the move to fiscal regulation and the stabilisation of post-war international trade (Worswick and Ady 1962; Alford 1988; Cairncross 1992). Business historians have highlighted the shifts in productive organisation and output which underpinned the upsurge of consumer demand. Flow-line assembly, deskilling and standardised product design have been understood to provide the infrastructure of that quintessentially modern form for the dissemination of goods – the mass market. In Britain, arguments about the coming of mature consumer society, or the society of affluence, have often been tied to a still broader polemic about the impact of 'Americanisation'. There has been a widespread assumption that during the 1950s British business increasingly looked towards the advanced techniques of selling derived from the United States. The growing role of advertising and marketing – those twin engines of modern consumerism – has been at the heart of such accounts; commercial culture has been identified with a distinctive secular ethic which achieved its most developed forms in North America. A generation of political historians (often themselves part of the culture of post-war social democracy) have pointed to the ways in which formal politics defined consumption as part of the new post-war settlement, via a focus on rising living standards and the achievements of consensus and social progress (Crosland 1956; Bogdanor and Skidelsky 1970). Finally, sociologists and cultural historians, during the period and since, have examined the impact of changing consumption patterns on key groups targeted by the consumer industries. The relationship of affluence to regional and generational change within working-class communities, its effects on women's roles and experience and on the crystallisation of new youth identities has been studied almost obsessively (Abrams 1959; Willmott and Young 1960; Goldthorpe et al. 1968; Hebdige 1979; Wilson 1980; Steedman 1985). Taken together, these histories have embraced a general, thesis; namely that from the early 1950s British society entered a new phase of economic organisation and management which had far reaching effects on social and cultural life (Hobsbawm 1994).

The purpose of rehearsing such widely differing accounts is not to engage in a detailed appraisal of their approaches. It is rather to emphasise the point which Keynes touched on but drew back from elaborating; that the story of post-war consumption in Britain has been a multiple history which has ranged across the fields of economic policy, political calculation and the social and psychological management of the secular self. Yet therein lies an acute historical problem. This has been the persistent tendency to over-generalisation. At once part of a thesis on industrial and commercial restructuring, about the character of a new political settlement and the recomposition of class, gender and generational identities, consumption has been mobilised as a composite and synthetic term. It has been used to tell multiple stories about the nature of change in post-war Britain.

Faced with this burden of over-generality, recent work on consumption has moved towards a more concrete and grounded focus (Fine 1993; Mort 1996). Such an approach has treated consumption practices as sectorally specific. It has also distinguished between different moments in the consumer cycle and between different levels of knowledge and experience: commodity manufacture and product design, advertising and marketing, together with the projections of selfhood and social fantasy which have been seen as such a central feature of the post-war cultural landscape. Tracing the various practices which shaped the circulation of goods has enabled more meaningful comparisons to be made across different sectors of the consumer economy. It has also projected more complex patterns of historical change than those presented under the rubric of post-war affluence or the coming of the 'consumer society'.

The story charted here confronts three interlinked themes which have dominated debate about British consumption in the 1950s and 1960s: the crystallisation of a mass market in goods, the impact of American methods of entrepreneurship on British business and the professional culture and social imagery of the advertising industry. These are not simply issues of economic development, they also chart the cultural history of commerce during these years. In so doing, they have the potential to historicise grandiose sociological claims made about the connection between consumption and modernity. The cultural ramifications of bulk methods of selling, the international flows of commodities produced by the expansion of world trade and the versions of subjectivity carried by commerce – such questions need to be investigated concretely as well as philosophically, at particular points in time and in more historically nuanced settings.

The Coming of a Mass Market?

'Mass distribution marts, the logical outcome of machine and mass production, are a boon and a blessing to the people.' This was the claim made by Montague Burton, chairman of the largest British menswear clothing multiple in 1935 (M. Burton 1935: 13). In their heyday, from the 1930s to the early 1960s, such firms displayed many of the characteristic features of Fordist enterprise, embracing batch production which provided the infrastructure for the crystallisation of mass consumption. Household names such as Burton's, Hepworth's and the Fifty Shilling Tailor dealt in huge runs of standardised products, apparently serving a uniform market. Backed by a hierarchical and centralised business culture, these companies organised their retailing on a national scale. The quintessential product of the menswear sector, the suit, has been read as an emblem of mass society, projecting an image of collective masculinity which paralleled all of those other representations of gendered culture during the period: workers at the factory gate, the trade-union meeting, the football crowd (Gosling 1992; Mort and Thompson 1994).

However, on closer inspection menswear retailing provides an eloquent testimony to the partial and extremely uneven character of the British transition to mass consumption. Though Montague Burton lauded the arrival of the mass market, the picture inside his firm told a different story. Size, scale and nationwide coverage were certainly characteristic features of Burton's performance. The company's precise market share is not recorded, but from the 1930s Burton's was the largest manufacturer and retailer of tailored menswear in Britain (Monopolies Commission 1967; Honeyman 1993). Even as late as 1961, in the opinion of the Economist Intelligence Unit, Burton's remained the 'biggest brand name in men's suits' (Economist Intelligence Unit 1961: 26). In terms of market position the 'tailor of taste' lay almost in the dead centre of men's clothing retailing. Obviously distanced from the genuine bespoke trade of London's Savile Row and upmarket competitors like Aquascutum or Simpson's, Burton's claims to taste and affordable elegance also differentiated it from firms such as the Fifty Shilling Tailor, where the emphasis was almost exclusively on price. Occupying prominent sites, with over 600 branches across Britain, Burton's shops were landmarks in town and city centres during the post-war years. With characteristic fittings in marble, oak and bronze, designed to connote quality and solid worth, the atmosphere of a Burton's shop was unmistakable (Sigsworth 1990; Honeyman 1993). Such local details were centrally controlled from head office in Leeds, where business managers and even the chairman himself paid minute attention to window displays, opening hours and the routine of the working day.

Yet underpinning this form of retailing were a series of commercial arrangements which cut against the corporate model. These were to be found both within the manufacturing process itself and in Burton's approach to the consumer. During the inter-war years menswear had become increasingly dominated by two inter-related changes: the growth of large-scale factory production and an increasing number of branch tailors retailing their own product – what was known in the trade as 'multiple tailors' selling 'wholesale bespoke' (Board of Trade 1947). In reality, Burton's suits were factory made under strictly standardised procedures. Customers' individual measurements were fitted to pre-determined shapes and sizes: long-thin, medium, short portly, etc. These were produced as templates for cutters, to facilitate batch production. There was no direct personal contact between tailor and customer, no hand finishing, nor was a Burton's suit truly made-to-measure. Consequently, the taste leaders of Savile Row never tired of pointing out that Burton's was in fact a counterfeit tailors (*Mens' Wear* 1962). Yet the firm continued to imitate the genuine bespoke trade, especially in its approach to customers. 'Sir' was measured by Burton's salesmen with all of the ritual to be found in a traditional tailoring establishment. This ideal of dignity and decorum was epitomised in the preferred profile of the company's salesmen. The art of salesmanship was to be approached with high seriousness. All excess was to be avoided through restraint and quiet good manners. As Burton's famous memo-randum to staff counselled: 'Avoid the severe style of the income tax collector and the smooth tongue of the fortune teller. Cultivate the dignified style of the "Quaker tea blender" which is a happy medium' (Sigsworth 1990: 51; Burton's 1952).

It was this personalised stance which also guided Burton's policy on advertising. A company which was dedicated to mass retailing clung steadfastly to a local strategy for advertising and marketing as the most effective way of reaching its customers. This stance flew in the face of contemporary business philosophy, which underlined the importance of mass selling techniques for goods produced in bulk, on the grounds of cost effectiveness and national coverage (Bishop 1949; Institute of Practitioners in Advertising 1956). Until well into the 1950s, Burton's attitude to commercial communications was overwhelmingly local, with advertising positioned as close to the point of sale as possible. The window display, the role of the salesman, the location of the store on the high street, together with announcements in the regional press, these were seen as the most effective forms of promotional culture. Guidelines issued from head office to the branches repeated this formula endlessly. The impression made on customers by a well-dressed shop window could not be matched:

A well-dressed window is a greater selling force than a newspaper and other forms of publicity combined. To neglect the greatest selling asset . . . is unworthy of a progressive businessman . . . the shop window is better than a picture, for the prospective customer sees the original. Ten thousand words could not convey the same description that a good window does. (Burton's 1953: 55)

What was emphasised was the superiority of direct techniques of selling over national publicity. The shop front conveyed an immediate sense of visual excitement, an atmosphere of variety and an invitation to purchase, which advertising could not hope to match. Burton's argument was that adverts only created verisimilitude; it was the tangible reality of commodities on display which was the major selling asset. The point is important because the composite blueprint of national advertising, as the medium disseminating commercial information under the conditions of mass consumption, has oversimplified the structure of British business. Traditional techniques of retailing remained central for many firms during a period which witnessed a large-scale expansion of their market share.

The varied dynamics of so-called mass consumption become even more apparent when they are read alongside the promotional imagery which was circulated in the menswear market. From the 1930s to the mid-1950s selling techniques relied on one clearly identifiable icon. This was the image of the gentleman. The emblem dominated the advertising of the clothing multiples and also shaped the approach to customers on the shop floor. The gentleman represented the peculiarly negotiated discourse of modernity preferred by many British entrepreneurs. At Burton's he was a hybrid; a retailing compromise between traditional codes of social honour and more up-to-date, democratising influences. The gentlemanly conception of masculinity was formal and fixed. The ideal was of full adult manhood, indeterminate in age, but secure in position. In press advertising and pattern books Burton's gentleman appeared in a variety of milieus – about town, as well as on the way to the office – but his standard pose was always upright, if not stiff. He was depicted either solo or in dialogue with other men, linked by the bonds of a shared masculine culture. In manners and self-presentation this was a decidedly English world-view. It was taken as given that the gentleman always appeared correctly dressed, for clothes were a public sign of social esteem.

Burton's gentlemanly type was in part the legacy of nineteenth-century languages of class. Clothes as an expression of status, manners as visible markers of distinction, these rituals were grounded in a vertical model of class relations. After 1945 there was a more democratic tinge to the marketing of men's clothes. Burton's gentleman was now projected as a variant of 'John Citizen'. Depicted serving in the armed forces, or against the municipal landscape of the town hall, he was quite literally 'everyman', demanding clothes for his particular role in life (Burton's undated). In menswear at least the coming of mass retailing drew on forms of aristocratic symbolism, reworking them for a general public. Historians investigating commodity culture in West Germany and Italy during the same period have identified similar compromise patterns of commercial modernisation (Carter 1996; Piccone Stella 1994). What they point to is the fact that the so-called paths to mass-consumption were plural and diverse and that the pace of transformation was often extremely uneven. There was no single model of change.

The Americanisation Thesis

Arguments surrounding the advent of modern consumer society in Britain have revolved not only around blueprints of economic development, but also around an even more grandiose thesis. This has charted the impact of American business methods and their related forms of commercial culture. Variants of the so-called 'Americanisation thesis' exercised a paradigmatic function for entrepreneurs, as well as for intellectual critics of commercial culture, for much of the 1950s and 1960s. The United States introduced many of the major technological innovations associated with the mass market in goods and was also cast as the centre of diffusion for some typically modern consumer products. In the aftermath of the Second World War almost all of Western Europe took American mass society as a major point of reference – either to provide a positive vision of the future, or against which to define alternatives. By the mid-1950s in Britain these debates revolved around one specific medium – the power of advertising.

In the spring of 1956 Lieutenant Colonel Alan Wilkinson led the British delegation to the '4A's' Advertising convention held in Sulphur Springs, West Virginia. A doyen of the British profession and an ex-president of the Institute of Practitioners in Advertising (IPA), Wilkinson made frequent trips to the United States. He was continually impressed with the 'powerful and all-pervading influence of advertising on the American scene' (Wilkinson 1956: 1). During his visit he noted how every American, from President Eisenhower down, was advertising conscious. The industry had helped to shape the American national character and had made a major contribution to the country's very high standard of living. Advertising was central to the American vision of the future, Wilkinson continued, encouraging an immense vitality and a dynamic urge 'to go forward – to improve – to extend and enlarge' (Wilkinson 1956: 1). No visitor could help but benefit from a fortnight in the company of the United States' advertising élite. Wilkinson's advice to British colleagues was that they should visit the USA as soon as possible, and that they should visit it often.

Wilkinson's panegyric was a characteristic expression of British advertising professionals' pro-American stance during the post-war period. More often than not such sentiments were bound up with a positive commitment to the progressive forces of modernity, and especially to a secular ethic of material progress. In the years during and immediately after the War British advertisers weighed into the debate over economic and social reconstruction, offering their own vision of a dynamic future. Invariably, their language took its cue from American cultural symbolism. Countering socialist visions of the planned economy, the young agency man, Robert Brandon, believed that the post-war growth of British advertising, along similar lines to that experienced in North America between the wars, was critical for the economic modernisation of Britain (Brandon 1949). Frank Bishop, assistant general manger of *The Times*, writing in *The Ethics of Advertising*, looked forward to the expansion of the industry as part of a future utopia, in which for the first time in human history 'material needs may be adequately met for all mankind' (Bishop 1949: 35). Once again, Bishop's prototype for this revolution was the United States. In the 1950s, with the growing impact of psychological theories of consumer motivation, American advertising was endowed with an even greater power – to reshape human character. The most notorious of these interventions was made by the Austrian émigré, Ernest Dichter, who led his own Institute for Motivational Research in New York and who believed that contemporary American advertising was leading the way in the progressive modernisation of human nature. Frequently, such arguments were shot through with a free-market defence of commercial techniques of persuasion, in the face of what Dichter himself claimed was the 'present historical struggle between free-enterprise and communism (Dichter 1960: 178). As Dichter saw it, the battle for American hegemony lay not in the field of missiles and the conquest of space, but in the conquest of the emotions of the people of the world (Dichter 1960: 280). Though Dichter's theories were never adopted in Britain, his emphasis on the political and psychological power of advertising frequently was taken up.

The reverse of these optimistic visions of an American future were the periodic critiques of consumerism launched by British and other European intellectuals. Such assaults had already crystallised during the inter-war period, with the affirmation of a distinctive tradition of Englishness in the face of the perceived invasion of American popular culture. They had been spearheaded by the intellectual forces of English literary criticism, represented by figures such as T.S. Eliot and Frank and Queenie Leavis. Denys Thompson, himself a member of the Leavisite Scrutiny movement, in his polemic against the excesses of press advertising, *Voice of Civilization* (1943), set the tone for post-war critiques of American commercialisation. Making a familiar ethical distinction between real and false needs, Thompson singled-out advertising for stimulating artificial wants and for creating illusion rather than providing information (Thompson 1943: 21–2). American-style advertising was in danger of replacing literature as the formative influence on British culture, Thompson argued. Paraphrasing D.H. Lawrence, he noted that the great mass of the population was now 'living according to the picture', rather than being guided by more sustained intellectual influences (Thompson 1943: 108). Reversing the arguments disseminated by the industry, Thompson concluded that so-called democratic advertising was dangerously close to the propaganda of the dictators.

These essentially liberal critiques of advertising formed the mainstay of the counter-attack against consumerism throughout the 1950s and early 1960s. J.B. Priestley and Jacquetta Hawkes' travelogue to Texas and New Mexico, *Journey Down a Rainbow* (1955), exposed the 'American style of urban life'. For Priestley in particular, the United States was 'now the great invader' – the country which for most of Western Europe 'pays the piper and calls for most of the tunes' (Priestley and Hawkes 1955: ix). His famous characterisation of the American society of 'Admass' – 'my name for a whole system of increasing productivity, plus inflation, plus a rising standard of material living, plus high-pressure advertising and salesmanship, plus mass communications, plus cultural democracy and the creation of the mass mind' – resonated on both sides of the Atlantic. There was a working alliance between such critiques and blueprints for the reform of consumer culture emanating from the Labour Party in the 1950s, especially from its Fabian and Co-operative wings. Fabian proposals for a tax on advertising and measures for greater consumer protection continued to weld together ethical and moral critiques of American-led consumption with attacks on the economics of waste (Corden 1961; E. Burton 1955). It was this double set of arguments which provided the rationale for the new consumer rights groups emerging from the mid-1950s.

British responses to American forms of modern consumerism should not simply be read as negative critiques. Placed alongside the enthusiastic commercial endorsements of material culture, they are best understood as part of an extended discourse on the dynamics of mass society – its systems of provision, its mobilisation of wants and the mechanisms for constituting social relations. In Britain, this discourse was usually given a national inflection; fixed as part of a commentary on the American way of life. The difficulty is that such cultural commentaries appear myopic when they are read against the actual business relations developing between Britain and the United States during the post-war period. Closer inspection of this dialogue points to an altogether more complex relationship between British and American understandings of consumer society. The history of British television advertising in the 1950s provides a striking case in point.

The arrival of commercial television in Britain, in September 1955, brought to a head an already heated debate among political and cultural commentators about the creeping effects of consumerism. Television advertising was viewed by its opponents as ushering in an American culture of mediocrity, hidden costs and sinister methods of persuasion. Anxieties were compounded by the aggressive expansion of American-owned multinational advertising agencies in Britain, via a series of acquisitions, mergers and takeovers (West 1988). Vance Packard's exposé of American selling methods in *The Hidden Persuaders* (1957) seemed to confirm existing apprehensions about the new commercial medium.

Yet as reviewers were quick to note, the first night of commercial television in England was a modicum of decorum and restraint. Scenes from the inaugural ceremony at London's Guildhall were followed by Sir John Barbirolli and the Hallé Orchestra playing Elgar's *Cockaigne* Overture. There were speeches from Dr Charles Hill, the Postmaster-General, and from the quintessentially establishment figure of Sir Kenneth Clark. At 8.00 p.m. the cameras visited Associated Broadcasting's own television theatre for variety, featuring established music hall and television personalities such as Reg Dixon, Billy Cotton and Elizabeth Allen. It was during this programme that viewers saw their first commercial. As the young Bernard Levin described it for the *Manchester Guardian*: 'A charming young lady brushed her teeth, while a charming young gentleman told us the benefits of the toothpaste with which she was doing it' (Levin 1955: 1).

On the whole, British advertisers remained sceptical of techniques imported from New York's Madison Avenue, not on account of any cultural hostility, but for sound business reasons. John Hobson, founder of the influential John Hobson and Partners agency and later President of the IPA, noted how the producers of early television commercials quickly grasped that British audiences demanded a style of advertisement which was not provided by the American 'hard-sell' model. Hobson observed that: 'American experience and examples were not altogether helpful ... the hammer blow commercials of [their] Agency men were not considered suitable for the British public, who, it was thought, would not welcome this degree of hard sell in their living rooms' (Hobson 1986: 432). This acknowledgement of cultural specificity – that markets could not be treated entirely as multinational entities – had already been taken up by the Conservative MP Ian Harvey in his free-market defence of advertising, *The Technique of Persuasion* (1951). Harvey observed that advertising was international only in principle and artistic form; national and local characteristics made it essential to vary the appeal and the methods in which the appeal was made (Harvey 1951). According to the British agency, Crawford's, a company with a reputation for a stylish, art-directed approach in the 1950s, it was precisely the mismatch between American selling methods and the British character which drove domestic agencies to develop their own approach to commercial communications. Aggressive selling shifted goods for a time, Crawford's remarked, but ultimately such methods set up their own forms of resistance in the minds of many consumers. As Crawford's pontificated, this was because to Europeans American commercials lacked good taste (Crawford's International 1965: 3).

This emphasis on the distinctiveness of the UK market was upheld by many British businessmen who admired American commercial methods. Montague Burton travelled widely throughout North America in the immediate post-war years, assiduously noting the benefits delivered by modern consumer society (M. Burton 1943). But, as we have seen, his own firm retained selling techniques which were unlike American approaches. His successor at Burton's, Lionel Jacobson, concluded in 1957 that American systems would not work easily in British markets (Jacobson 1957).

There is a further difficulty in portraying the international dimensions of British business during these years simply in terms of an Anglo-American dialogue. This is the continuing importance of the Commonwealth. Commonwealth markets accounted for the largest proportion of Britain's export trade until well into the 1960s. Such exports included not only key consumer durables, but also commercial forms of knowledge. It was British expertise which was instrumental in setting up the Australian television network in Sydney in 1957, while many of the leading British advertising agencies established bases in the white Dominions (Perkins 1962; Madden and Morris Jones 1980; Whitwell 1989). The reverse of this dialogue was the image Australia and Canada occupied (quite as much as the United States) in the imagination of a generation of post-war working-class migrants, as lands of democratic plenty and consumer abundance.

What this story reveals is a more complex pattern of international business than that suggested by the simple idea of American hegemony in world markets. Though the United States loomed large in the imagination of domestic entrepreneurs and cultural critics, what was also stressed was the distinctiveness of the British economy and its forms of commercial culture, together with the continuing importance of imperial preference. In this context the British advertising industry emerged as a new expert grouping, claiming not only the ability to read the dynamics of consumption, but also the psychological dimensions of national character.

Advertising and the Reflexive Self

Anthony Giddens, addressing the characteristics of late modernity, has identified a significant recent shift within Western societies around the changing conception of identity. For Giddens this sea change has essentially involved a movement from the external projection of character, operating in the public world, to the idea of the self as constituted inside the personality with internal referents. The net effect of this process has been to produce social selfhood as a reflexively organised endeavour, which extends deep into the individual (Giddens 1991). A key mechanism for connecting the self-reflexive individual to society has been the growing impact of styles of life, or lifestyles. Giddens' concept of lifestyles has been more broadly conceived than its understanding by the post-war consumer professionals; it has embraced all those spheres of everyday life in which individual appraisal has displaced more external rules of authority. This idea of the reflexive self is important for understanding how the expansion of commercial advertising in the 1950s was conceived as a modernising project, whose ultimate aim was the reshaping of human character.

Institutionally, British advertising grew rapidly in the early 1950s. But professional discussion about its importance had preceded the expansion of the industry by more than a decade. Emerging out of political economy, this earlier debate had produced a cultural reading of economic life which was dedicated to a new form of governing and imagining the self. Unlike the expanding theories of maternalism, child welfare and social deviance, the classic terrain for this development was not the state but commercial society.

Economic theorists, such as Marshall and Pigou, had denounced advertising as a misuse of productive resources, because it introduced an added burden of hidden costs for manufacturers and consumers alike (Marshall 1927; Pigou 1929; Braithwaite 1928). But during the 1930s and early 1940s a new breed of economic commentator, influenced by theories of imperfect or monopolistic competition, focused on the advantages to be gained from extraneous interventions into the market. Advertising's role in stimulating demand for consumption goods, in regularising output and flattening the booms and slumps of the trade cycle, thereby contributing to a general lowering of prices and an increase in quality, were among the standard themes announced by the new apologists for promotional culture. The majority of these writers were influenced by Keynesian critiques of the deficiencies of demand and its effects on the real economy during the inter-war years (Courtauld 1942; Rothschild 1942; Laver 1947).

The point about these economic commentaries was that they pointed inexorably to issues which classical economics could not or would not answer. Almost imperceptibly, they moved into the domain of culture and psychology. As Bishop saw it in 1944, the products of one manufacturer were never quite the same as those of another (Bishop 1944). Variations in taste and subjective preference drew the consumer into complicated decisions of discrimination and choice. Such an acknowledgement led to an even more significant point which implicitly refuted one of the basic tenets of economic theory. It appeared that where consumption was concerned the concept of *homo economicus* – rational, calculating and always perfectly informed – was far from true (Robinson 1942). Consumers were usually equipped with very imperfect knowledge of the market-place and were easily influenced and persuaded. Writing at the height of the Labour government's austerity programme, the young economist Edward Laver concluded in 1947 that even for those on small incomes 'biological necessities' (such as food, clothing and shelter) accounted for only a portion of their incomes. With the rest consumers invariably sought to buy 'psychological satisfaction' and to express their personalities (Laver 1947: 14–15). From an economic standpoint advertising could be seen to create utility by 'moving and arranging minds' (Laver 1947: 49).

It was this questioning of some of the basic tenets of economic theory which opened the space for an expanded reading of consumer behaviour. In the marketing discourse of the 1950s the consumer emerged as a highly complex entity, by no means the passive tool of the advertisers (Miller and Rose 1997). Consumers needed to be mobilised, their tastes and desires mapped and future wants predicted. Here psychological theories loomed large. In 1958 British advertising and marketing came out strongly critical of the excesses of the American methods of subliminal advertising, on the grounds both of their suspected ineffectiveness and their immorality (Institute of Practitioners in Advertising 1958; Harris and Seldon 1962). But this injunction did not involve any wholesale jettisoning of the psychology of consumer behaviour. Advertising and marketing in the late 1950s were a promiscuous mixture of expert knowledge derived from sociology, literary criticism, psychoanalysis and the burgeoning field of market research.

Hobson's own company was at the forefront of efforts to match advertising's message to the social transformations which he believed had been set in train by the post-war upsurge in demand. Hobson himself was a gentleman player in the industry. A Cambridge English graduate, he was fully aware of the aesthetic potential of advertising. His influential text, *The Selection of Advertising Media*, first published in 1955, acknowledged that the profession was 'still an inexact science'. Hobson believed that in addition to a battery of quantifiable data on markets and audiences, agencies also needed much 'more complete knowledge on the workings of the mind and the emotions' (Hobson 1961: 12). The critical element here was what he termed the 'atmosphere' of the message. Atmosphere essentially involved subjective indicators, such as judging the mood of consumers and their emotional response to products. While other features could be measured, 'atmosphere' demanded a more 'intuitive and perceptive' approach. Such arguments opened the space for an enhanced role for creative artists, especially for copywriters and art directors, within commercial processes (Havinden 1956).

Attempts to read the psychology of consumers were given a more comprehensive and scientific gloss in the pioneering work of 'motivation research'. This was a characteristically British response to the excesses of American consumer psychology as represented by figures such as Dichter. Rather than pronouncing on the cultural future, motivation researchers insisted that their aims were much more prosaic: to supplement the knowledge of the manufacturer and the advertiser in their task of selling goods. According to Harry Henry, research director of McCann Erickson's European arm and a pioneer of motivational techniques in Britain, this approach was not an attempt to dupe the consumer, but to understand more fully the 'why' of consumer choice. Like Hobson, Henry was a characteristically hybrid intellectual. A pre-war graduate of the London School of Economics, he had served Montgomery during the War as a Statistical Staff Officer. Responsible for the Hulton Readership surveys from 1947 to 1953, he entered commercial market research in 1954. Henry was keen to emphasise that his methods did not champion one single social philosophy. Eclectic in form, they borrowed from clinical psychology and the other social sciences, as well as from behaviourism. Such techniques – which might include group discussions, in-depth interviews, as well as more specific tests to measure the personality – were especially important for gauging the impact of branded products, where the image or the personality of the commodity was all-important. Henry believed that the impact of television advertising was creating a situation in which image rather than reality was critical to purchasing choice (Henry 1961: 5).

A spate of celebrated television and press campaigns, for commodities as diverse as cars, cigarettes, food products and lager beers, testified to the impact of the new formula. Running through them were three themes which dominated commercial advertising in the late 1950s and early 1960s. These were the triple utopias of modernity, sex and status, expressed through an expanded conception of the personality of key groups of consumers. Advertisements designed by the London Press Exchange for cars and motor fuels were characteristic early examples of this genre. Their 1963 account, 'Getaway People', for National Benzole, carried the message of 'petrol for the with-it people', the 'people who did good things' (Pearson and Turner 1965: 42). While their vision of the new Ford Anglia car, produced in the same year, was anchored by the caption 'Beauty with Long Legs', accompanied by an image of a veiled and aloof woman, with bare midriff. A different language of modernisation, which was driven by changing patterns of class and family life, was evident in J. Walter Thompson's long-running narrative about 'Katie and the Cube' for Oxo Ltd. Beginning in 1958, the agency told an ongoing tale about the domestic adventures of a young modern housewife and her husband Philip – individuals on the lower rungs of the executive ladder, who were decidedly 'semi-detached people'. (Pearson and Turner, 1965: 79) While each of these campaigns was different, what characterised all of them were their efforts to suggest associations between modern people, commodities and a distinctive quality or style of life.

Among Hobson's contribution to this genre of adverts were two commercials addressed to younger men. His company's acquisition of Ind Coope's Double Diamond pale ale account from the London Press Exchange in 1963 involved an upgrading of the product. The traditional format of beer advertising (what was dubbed the masculinity of the saloon bar) was displaced by more modern codes of manliness. 'Double Diamond – the Beer the Men Drink', pictured men in a world of 'affluence and jet-age leisure': surfing, parachuting, water-skiing and mountaineering (Pearson and Turner 1965: 149). A different variation on contemporary masculinity was adopted in the agency's Strand cigarette advertising for W.D. and H.O. Wills which appeared three years earlier. Here, the individuality of the 'youth generation' was captured by an atmosphere of 'loneliness'. What John

May, a member of Hobson's team, who coined the successful slogan 'You're never alone with a Strand', suggested was a 'hyperconsciousness', an 'entirely independent way of living' among the young (Pearson and Turner 1965: 163). Drawing on the 'loner' theme pioneered by Hollywood cult figures such as Marlon Brando and James Dean, the actor in these cigarette commercials was shot in a variety of states of solitude. In one Strand advert he was filmed leaning against the wall of London's Chelsea Embankment, in another standing on a deserted Brighton beach. In both cases the settings reinforced what May termed a symbolic style of independence.

Atmospheric advertisements of this type reflected the soundings taken by market researchers about the shifts in post-war consumption patterns. Here we confront the wider cultural factors which were shaping the advertising industry's modernising project. Hobson's own musings on the marketing criteria used to analyse social class were informative in this respect. Acknowledging that the conventional five status graduations, A to E, remained a touchstone for the industry, he nevertheless insisted that class categories were in urgent need of revision. Hobson was emphatic that class now needed to be understood not simply as an economic indicator, but as a cultural variable, involving ways of life or 'lifestyles' (Hobson 1961: 22). Moreover, markets and consumer preferences were complicated by the emergence of what he termed 'special-interest groups', defined by age or by leadership position within the community. Hobson's point was reinforced in a report issued by the Market Research Society's working party in 1963, which concluded that growing professional confusion about the issue of class was also the result of its ever-expanding reference points within the social sciences (Tunstall 1964). Such findings paralleled the work of New Left thinkers like Raymond Williams and Edward Thompson on the cultural ramifications of class. But these commercial pronouncements probably had a closer affinity with liberal sociology and social democratic politics on both sides of the Atlantic. David Riesman's writing on the contradictions between forms of the 'outer directed' as opposed to the 'inner directed' self, Daniel Bell's fascination with an economy which had produced display as a critical marker of personal esteem, and Tony Crosland's efforts to reshape the culture and psychology of the British Labour Party in line with post-war affluence – taken together these projects marked attempts to confront the new relationship between culture and commerce (Riesman 1951; Bell 1956; Crosland 1956a). In all of them an expanded sense of personal selfhood was acknowledged as a necessary part of the future.

Conclusion

This movement towards an enhanced role for individuality under the conditions of post-war demand was not the result of some smooth meta-logic of the late modern epoch. It was dependent on much more specific strategies. It is here that we return to the problems of over-generality attendant on many of the accounts of consumption and modernity with which we began. The management of post-war affluence was formed at the intersection of a number of commercial and intellectual systems of entrepreneurship. In Britain, as in the United States, this process was characterised by the growth of knowledge and expertise dedicated to understanding the modern consumer economy. Conducted on the terrain of commercial society rather through the state, this process was humanised and psychologised by the figure of the consumer, who represented an expanding bundle of motivations and aspirations. But British advertisers and retailers were characteristically eclectic and pluralist in their epistemologies. Their acknowledgement of national markets and psychology, as well as the international dimensions of trade, makes any simple appeal to the Americanisation of British economic or cultural life during the 1950s appear misplaced. Moreover, our excursion into the organisation of the clothing sector revealed how much the process of modernisation was piecemeal and ad hoc. Methods for producing and circulating key consumer goods, together with their attendant cultural symbolism, rested as much on traditional technologies as on any coherent blueprint for the future. The paths to mass consumption need to be rethought in the light of these particularities.

In conclusion we might do well to return to Keynes' own speculations about the dynamics of the modern economy. As Keynes was well aware, 'demand management' (the term favoured by his own disciples, the post-war politicians and policy makers) was much more than a process of macro-economic regulation. Essentially it involved the construction of a set of programmes for orchestrating the fields of economics and culture. This is an ensemble which I would provisionally classify as the commercial domain. Less systematised than the traditional public sphere of government and social administration, it focused on the management of persons and families and, crucially, on the cultivation of the secular self. British liberal intellectual traditions and social democratic politics in the mid-twentieth century were reformulated in a forced dialogue with this commercial project. It represents a modernising impulse in which economics, culture and conceptions of the human personality were deeply inter-twined.

Note

An earlier version of this chapter was published in B. Conekin, F. Mort and C. Waters (eds) (1999), *Moments of Modernity: Reconstructing Britain 1945–64*, London and New York, Rivers Oram Press/New York University Press.

References

Abrams, M. (1959), *The Teenage Consumer*, London: London Press Exchange.

Alford, B. (1988), *British Economic Performance 1945–75*, Basingstoke: Macmillan.

Bauman, Z. (1987), *On Modernity, Post-Modernity and Intellectuals*, Cambridge: Polity Press.

Bell, D. (1956), 'Advertising and the Impact on Society', *The Listener*, 27 December, pp. 1069–72.

Bishop, F.P. (1944), *The Economics of Advertising*, Chicago: Richard D. Irwin.

—— (1949), *The Ethics of Advertising*, London: Robert Hale.

Board of Trade (1947), *Working Party Reports on Heavy Clothing*, London: HMSO.

Bogdanor V. and Skidelsky R. (eds) (1970), *The Age of Affluence, 1951–1964*, London: Macmillan.

Braithwaite, D. (1928), 'The Economic Effects of Advertisement', *Economic Journal* XXXVIII, pp. 16–37.

Brandon, R. (1949), *The Truth About Advertising*, London: Chapman and Hall.

Burton's (1952), 'Circular Letter to Branch Managers', Burton's Archives, Box 136, West Yorkshire Archive Service, Leeds.

—— (1953), *Manager's Guide*, Leeds: Petty and Sons.

—— (undated, 1940s , or early 1950s), *Pattern Books*, Burton's Archives, Box 136, West Yorkshire Archive Service, Leeds.

Burton, E. (1955), *The Battle of the Consumer*, London: The Labour Party.

Burton, M. (1935), *Globe Girdling: Being the Impressions of an Amateur Observer*, Vol. 1, Leeds: Petty and Sons.

—— (1943), *The Middle Path: Talks on Collective Security, Arbitration and other Aspects of International and Industrial Relations*, London: Petty and Sons.

Cairncross, A. (1992), *The British Economy since 1945: Economic Policy and Performance*, Oxford: Blackwell.

Carter, E. (1996), *How German is She? National Reconstruction and the Consuming Woman in the FRG and West Berlin 1945–60*, Ann Arbor: University of Michigan Press.

Corden, M. (1961), *A Tax on Advertising?* London: Fabian Society research series, no. 222.

Courtauld, S. (1942), 'An Industrialist's Reflections on the Future Relations of Government and Industry', *Economic Journal* L II, pp. 1–17.

Crawford's International (1965), *How to Break into World Markets*, London: W.S. Crawford Ltd.

Crosland, C. A. (1956), *The Future of Socialism*, London: Jonathan Cape.

—— (1956a), 'Advertising: Is It Worth It?', *The Listener*, 13 December, pp. 976–7.

Dichter, E. (1960), *The Strategy of Desire*, London: T.V. Boardman and Co.

Economist Intelligence Unit (1961), 'Men's Suits', *Retail Business* 4 (46), p. 26.

Fine, B. (1993), 'Modernity, Urbanism and Modern Consumption', *Society and Space* 11, pp. 599–601.

Giddens, A. (1991), *Modernity and Self-Identity: Self and Society in the Late Modern Age*, Cambridge: Polity Press.

Goldthorpe, J., Bechhofer, F., Lockwood, D., Platt, J. (1968), *The Affluent Worker: Political Attitudes and Behaviour*, Cambridge: Cambridge University Press.

Gosling, R. (1992), 'Gosling on the High Street', Radio 4, 10 July.

Harris, R. and Seldon, A. (1962), *Advertising and the Public*, London, André Deutsch.

Harvey, I. (1951), *The Technique of Persuasion: An Essay in Human Relationships*, London: The Falcon Press.

Havinden, A. (1956), *Advertising and the Artist*, London: The Studio Publications.

Hebdige, D. (1979), *Subculture, the Meaning of Style*, London: Methuen.

Henry, H. (1961), *Motivation Research and the Television Commercial*, London: ATV.

Hobsbawm, E. (1994), *Age of Extremes: The Short Twentieth Century 1914–1991*, London: Abacus.

Hobson, J. (1961), *The Selection of Advertising Media*, fourth edition, London: Business Publications Ltd.

—— (1986), 'The Agency Viewpoint 2', in H. Henry (ed.), *British Television Advertising: The First 30 Years*, London: Century Benham, pp. 423–35.

Honeyman, K. (1993), 'Montague Burton Ltd: The Creators of Well-Dressed Men', in K. Honeyman and J. Chartres (eds) (1993), *Leeds City Business 1893–1993: Essays Marking the Centenary of the Incorporation*, Leeds: privately printed, pp. 186–217.

Institute of Practitioners in Advertising (1956), *Development of the Service Advertising Agency*, Occasional Paper no. 2, London: Institute of Practitioners in Advertising.

—— (1958), *Subliminal Communication*, London: Institute of Practitioners in Advertising.

Jacobson, L. (1957), 'Comments', in file marked 'Tip Top Tailors', Burton's Archives, Box 182, West Yorkshire Archive Service, Leeds.

Keynes, J.M. (1964), *The General Theory of Employment, Interest and Money*, San Diego: Harcourt, Brace, Jovanovitch.

Laver, E.A. (1947), *Advertising and Economic Theory*, London, Oxford University Press.

Levin, B. (1955), 'ITV Makes its Bow – Polished and on Time', *Manchester Guardian*, 23 September, p. 1.

Madden, A.F. and Morris Jones, W.H. (1980), *Australia and Britain: Studies in a Changing Relationship*, London, Institute of Commonwealth Studies.

Marshall, A. (1927), *Industry and Trade: A Study of Industrial Technique and Business Organisation; and Their Influence on the Conditions of Various Classes and Nations*, London: Macmillan, 1927.

Miller, P. and Rose, N. (1997), 'Mobilising the Consumer: Assembling the Subject of Consumption', *Theory Culture and Society*, 14(1), pp. 1–36.

Monopolies Commission (1967), *United Drapery Stores Ltd: A Report on the Proposed Merger*, Cmnd. 3397, London: HMSO.

Mort, F. (1996), *Cultures of Consumption: Masculinities and Social Space in late Twentieth-Century Britain*, London: Routledge.

Mort, F. and Thompson, P. (1994), 'Retailing, Commercial Culture and Masculinity in 1950s Britain: The Case of Montague Burton, the "Tailor of Taste"', *History Workshop Journal* 38, pp. 106–27.

Packard, V. (1957), *The Hidden Persuaders*, London: Longmans, Green & Co.

Pearson, J. and Turner G. (1965), *The Persuasion Industry*, London: Eyre and Spottiswoode.

Perkins, J.O. (1962), *Britain and Australia: Economic Relationships in the 1950s*, Melbourne: Melbourne University Press.

Piccone Stella, S. (1994), '"Rebels Without a Cause": Male Youth in Italy around 1960', *History Workshop Journal* 38, pp. 157–78.

Pigou, A. (1929), *The Economics of Welfare*, third edition, London: Macmillan.

Priestley, J. B. and Hawkes, J. (1955), *Journey Down a Rainbow*, London: Heinemann Cresset.

'Pseudo Bespoke by Multiple Shops' (1962), *Men's Wear*, 10 December, p. 7.

Riesman, D. (1951), *The Lonely Crowd: A Study of the Changing American Character*, New Haven: Yale University Press.

Robinson, J. (1942), 'The Economic Effects of Advertising', *Economica*, new series IX, p. 294.

Rothschild, K.W. (1942), 'A Note on Advertising', *Economic Journal* LII, pp. 112–21.

Sigsworth, E. (1990), *Montague Burton: The Tailor of Taste*, Manchester: Manchester University Press.

Steedman, C. (1985), *Landscape for a Good Woman: A Story of Two Lives*, London: Virago.

Thompson, D. (1943), *Voice of Civilization: An Enquiry into Advertising*, London: Frederick Muller.

Tunstall, J. (1964), *The Advertising Man in London Advertising Agencies*, London: Chapman and Hall.

West, D. (1988), 'Multinational Competition in the British Advertising Agency Business, 1936–1987', *Business History Review* 62, pp. 467–501.

Whitwell, G. (1989), *Making the Market: The Rise of Consumer Society*, Melbourne: McPhee Gribble.

Wilkinson, A. (1956), 'Reflections on the 4As Convention', Institute of Practitioners in Advertising, *Institute Information* 3(120), p. 1.

Willmott, P. and Young M. (1960), *Family and Class in A London Suburb*, London: Routledge & Kegan Paul.

Wilson, E. (1980), *Only Half Way to Paradise: Women in Postwar Britain*, London: Tavistock.

Worswick, G. and Ady, P. (eds) (1962), *The British Economy in the Nineteen Fifties*, Oxford: Clarendon.

3

In Pursuit of the Professional Ideal: Advertising and the Construction of Commercial Expertise in Britain 1953–64

Sean Nixon

Introduction

One serious weakness in our professional front is the position of the advertising practitioner – or advertising agent as he is generally called by the public. This term advertising agent covers a multitude of sinners. As far as I can make out, anybody can call himself an advertising agent. I think we should drop the name altogether and establish the title advertising practitioner exclusively and clearly as the title solicitor, barrister, physician and surgeon are established. We owe it to the public and to ourselves. Advertising practitioner should mean a recognized professional, not a vague somebody who has something to do with publicity.

> John B. Nicholas, Advertising Club's Conference, Harrogate, 26 September 1953
> (*Institute Information*, Vol. 1, No.2, p. 8)

John B. Nicholas's intervention at the Advertising Club's Conference was reprinted in the September 1953 edition of *Institute Information*, the recently launched publication of the Institute of Incorporated Practitioners in Advertising (IIPA). Reproduced on the back page of the newsheet, his comments nestled amidst the typical range of miscellaneous information: a list of activities of the Institute's seven standing committees, a news piece on the Institute's Mansion House dinner and a programme of up-and-coming events for the autumn and winter of 1953. Nicholas's comments, however, addressed an issue which went well beyond these run-of-the-mill matters of business news. In raising the issue of the title used to describe those who worked in advertising, he touched on a theme which was to preoccupy the Institute during the mid-1950s and early 1960s. This was the question of the professional status of advertising. Although not a new concern – the rationale for the establishment of the IIPA as the corporate body of advertising agencies in 1927 had been to promote professionalism – the years between 1953–64 witnessed a renewed and extensive push to consolidate professional standards of conduct within the industry. Thus, by March 1957, the concerns expressed by Nicholas about the professional authority of those working in advertising had moved from the back page to the leader article in *Institute Information*. It's bold headline: 'Practitioners, Agents – or What?', reiterated the terms of Nicholas's earlier intervention and signalled the extent to which debate about the status and public standing of advertising people had moved centre stage in the concerns of the now renamed Institute of Practitioners in Advertising (IPA). Over the next seven years, *Institute Information*, together with its successors *IPA News* and *IPA Forum*, returned time and again to this issue. What emerged across these publications was an emotionally charged campaign to promote the professional standing of those working in advertising; a campaign which centred upon the erasure of the term advertising agent and its replacement by the idea of the 'practitioner'.

In this article, I want to reflect on the debate within the IPA about the identification of those working in advertising as agents or practitioners and to explore the ways in which the Institute attempted to resolve the question of professionalism within the industry. In doing so, I engage with, and partly challenge, some of the established ways advertising has been written into post-war histories of consumption. These histories have taken the expansion of private sector consumption during the decades immediately following the Second World War as central to understandings of social and political change during this period. As Frank Mort has pointed out: 'together with economic growth, full employment, political consensus and the rise of the Welfare State', the intensified impact of consumption 'has been used as one of the building blocks to tell the story of post-war society' (Mort 1999: 56). The problem with such accounts is that advertising has tended to be subsumed into a more general idea of consumption and has found itself lost amidst broader narratives dealing with the coming of the mass market. As a consequence, the specific contributions of advertising to the social and cultural transformations associated with the expansion of consumption have been obscured. In particular, a detailed sense of the advertising industry during this period, its institutional arrangements, forms of expertise and corporate and workplace cultures have been neglected. Opening up the debates within the IPA represents an attempt to address these concerns.

A further consequence of subsuming advertising under the more general rubric of consumption has been to produce a rather flat and untroubled picture of the economic and cultural rise of advertising practitioners. It is as if the place of advertising as one of the privileged engines of mass consumption was unproblematic and had a functional necessity about it. In setting out the debates about professionalism orchestrated by the IPA, I want to suggest that for industry insiders the position of advertising could not be assumed, nor was it in any sense guaranteed. As the debates within the IPA show, establishing the authority and status of advertising practitioners and advertising agencies was something to be achieved rather than taken for granted.

The exchanges within the IPA also force us to revise those accounts of advertising which have placed it rather too generously within the wider expansion of experts and expert knowledge seen to characterise the post-war years. While the authority of experts may have become central by the 1950s to: 'not only economic management and social policy, but also the areas of cultural taste, the urban and rural environments, consumer behaviour and the psychological well-being of communities' (Conekin et al. 1999: 15), the ability of different groups of experts to successfully exercise that authority was not equally shared. Economists, social policy advisors and planners, working largely within the state, may have enjoyed unparalleled faith in their abilities, but the same could not be said of advertising experts during the 1950s. My own account problematises the success of advertising people in securing their status as trusted professionals. Though there was a concerted move by the IPA to establish the authority of advertising practitioners as professionals, what is striking is the limited and partial success of their project. Advertising remained an aspiring or semi-profession. Viewed retrospectively, this failure is one of the most significant features in the history of post-war advertising. It has had long-term consequences for the sector, leaving the status of advertising agencies and practitioners unclear, caught between being suppliers or service providers to clients on the one hand, and being full-blown business partners offering expert advice and competencies on the other. This instability also had effects on the subjective identities of post-war advertising practitioners themselves. While often aspiring to the status of professional experts, they nonetheless found themselves caught between this and competing, non-professional identifications.

'Worthy of its Responsibility': Advertising in the Modern World

The eleven years between 1953 and 1964 represented a particularly buoyant period for the IPA. During these years its membership increased from 230 to 270 member agencies and the Institute held its first national conference at the Grand Hotel in Birmingham in 1954. The buoyancy of the Institute was also evident in the proliferation of publications which it produced during this period. The most significant of these were the Occasional Paper series, launched in 1955. These papers covered various aspects of the advertising business, ranging from a guide to members on overseas advertising to a report on the impact of commercial television. The IPA also produced a renewed statement of its aims and functions in 1956. There is a strong sense in the introduction to this concise but portentous

28-page pamphlet that the industry was entering on a new and expansive phase; a phase in which both the distinctive qualities (the 'special craft', as the publication put it) of advertising and its role in the 'modern world' were being increasingly recognised. The launch of the Institute's monthly newsheet, *Institute Information* in 1953 also formed part of this increased confidence and energy. The publication reveals an organisation keen to proselytise about the services which it offered to its members and to show itself off as a respectable professional body, especially in relation to key legislative issues effecting the industry. *Institute Information* reproduced photographs of the period interior of the IPA's impressive Belgrave Square building in London's Belgravia, together with photograph-led reports of the IPA's luminaries enjoying themselves at the annual dinner and dance or at social events and exhibitions. Accounts of the Institute's social calender, in fact, figured prominently in *Institute Information*. Coverage of the annual dinner and dance of 1960 noted how this event had seen the introduction of a little more informality. Black tie was allowed instead of the previous full evening dress, and there were no formal or policy speeches. The President's speech was described in the following terms: 'It was not really a speech – more a fireside chat to two or three friends, full of humour and sincerity.' This was followed by a speech from the actor Kenneth Horne, a cabaret from Ron Moody ('using an old and well-known act that is, nevertheless, still amusing') and dancing until 2 a.m. (*Institute Information*, Vol. 7, No. 8, 1960, p. 4). Through coverage of this sort, the Institute's newsheet offered a tantalising glimpse of scenes of informal social intercourse, showing an organisation bent on associating itself with all the signs of genteel respectability.

In the midst of its confident blossoming, the IPA was attempting to promote professionalism within a very particular kind of industry. Reflecting on the contemporary structure of British advertising gives a clearer sense of the context in which the IPA debate about the nomenclature of advertising people was taking place. Large-scale quantitative expansion of the industry was a key feature during this period and was evidenced by the fact that advertising expenditure had risen to £456 million in 1960. This amounted to 1.2 per cent of GDP, up from 0.71 per cent a decade earlier (Sampson 1962: 580; Jordons 1989). Despite this increase, a central characteristic of the industry remained its composition from a plethora of weakly-capitalised, privately owned enterprises. Established as partnerships, or more typically partnerships incorporated as limited companies, UK advertising agencies usually bore the name of their founding individuals or partners. These individuals often remained powerful presences within the company. Arthur Varley – or Colonel Arthur Noel Claude Varley CBE, MIPA, to give him his full title – a founding partner of Colman, Prentis and Varley – was one example of this type of influential personality. John Pearson and Graham Turner, writing in the early 1960s, suggested that on meeting Varley he appeared 'as an amiable, slightly portly, good-looking old Wykemist with a pipe and a tweed suit' (Pearson and Turner 1965: 107). They also described him not only as a businessmen but also as a shaman, 'a person who could arouse belief' (Pearson and Turner 1965: 108). Charismatic rather than bureaucratic authority, then, was a distinctive feature of these commercial enterprises.

Another noteworthy feature of the industry during this period was its weak geographical concentration in London and its lack of the equivalent of the American advertising industry's Madison Avenue (Pearson and Turner 1965: 16). The offices of the larger agencies ranged from Mayfair and Knightsbridge, through Holborn, the Tottenham Court and Euston Roads to the Strand. Fleet Street and its surrounding lanes also remained a key location for agencies – a legacy of the development of advertising agents in the mid-nineteenth century and their association with the popular press. The key point is that the agency sector was made up of a range of small, medium or largish privately-owned companies, with its key players scattered across the West End of London. These were also usually companies with a short history. As the IPA noted in 1956, the industry in its modern form had only really been established in the inter-war years (IPA 1956).

However, there are a number of important qualifications to add to this picture of advertising. The first concerns public flotation. During the post-war decades, a number of agencies floated on the stock exchange for the first time (Brunnings was the first to do so in 1961). The effect of these company flotations was to increase the amounts of capital circulating within the industry and, in so doing, signal the sector's growing financial maturity. A further issue was rather more significant. It concerned a phenomenon which became a strong theme in accounts of British modernity in the post-war years, the 'Americanisation' of British advertising (Mort 1999). Whilst American agencies had been based in Britain since the turn of the century, the late 1950s saw their renewed involvement through an intense period of acquisitions in London. Beginning with the takeover of Hobson, Bates and Partners by Ted Bates in 1959, the so-called 'American invasion' had a significant effect on the domestic industry. By 1964, eight of the top eighteen agencies in the UK were controlled by American agencies (Brierley 1994), while American commercial techniques and forms of organisational culture were making their presence felt in Britain. The 'American invasion' prompted a number of responses from within British advertising. These ranged from what Pearson and Turner termed the assertion of a 'mood of advertising nationalism', to a sympathetic reaction to mergers (or takeovers) by agency bosses, stemming from a recognition of the increasing need for size in winning the big accounts of international clients. For the IPA, there was certainly a concern to engage with American commercial knowledges and forms of expertise. What is clear is that the IPA's renewed push to promote professionalism was in part shaped by this encounter with American knowledge and practice. The presence of the advanced managerial styles and techniques of American advertising in the heartlands of the domestic industry, prompted a reflection on the status of the British adperson (or the 'adman', as he was more usually termed) and in doing so fed into the debates about professional standards.

The American invasion was not the only contemporary factor shaping this renewed debate about professional authority. Two further conjunctural issues were influential in the debate about the nomenclature and status of advertising folk. The first of these revolved around the intensive critique of advertising which emerged during this period. Vance Packard's *The Hidden Persuaders* (Packard 1957) still stands out as the book which most successfully carried this critique to a wider public. First published in Britain by Longmans, and then reprinted as a Penguin Special in 1960 and as a Pelican Book in 1962, *The Hidden Persuaders* took to task advertising agencies for deploying a range of insidious techniques, drawn from psychiatry, to influence and manipulate the mind of the consumer. The power of the book's argument stemmed in part from the way it successfully drew on wider Cold War anxieties about brainwashing and subliminal messages and from its strong appeal to a moral order which protected the 'privacy of our minds' from commercial manipulation. Critiques of this sort were registered almost obsessively in the IPA's Council Reports between 1958 and 1964 and it is clear that they constituted an important spur for the industry to establish its status as a respectable occupation.

The other significant factor shaping the debates about professionalism in the 1950s and early 1960s sprung from the increasing recognition on the part of industry insiders of advertising's growing economic significance. Essentially, this was an acknowledgement of 'advertising's significant contribution to Britain's impressive economic recovery', as the *Investors' Chronicle* put it in January 1960 (*Investors' Chronicle*, January 1960, p. 11). It is important to note the way in which this economic recovery was represented. Echoing popular commentaries, what loomed large was a construction of a boom around the burgeoning consumer sectors of the economy and the associated expansion in the circulation of consumer goods. This representation of economic prosperity was significant. Its ordering of the signs of recovery enabled those inside the advertising industry to claim a central role in national economic regeneration, despite the fact that such a version of recovery was extremely attenuated. This positioning of advertising was also co-joined with a defence of the industry against its critics. Leading advertising people made much of the industry's contribution to economic prosperity, as a way of countering the charges made about advertising's promotion of false needs and its encouragement of wastefulness. Amongst these spirited defences was an emphasis on the value of advertising in making available a greater range of cheaper goods and as a guarantor of the freedoms inherent in liberal democracies (*Institute Information*, Vol. 4, No. 7, 1957, p. 5; *Institute Information*, Vol. 3, No. 10, 1956,

p. 4; IPA News, Vol. 9, No. 4, 1962; *Institute Information*, Vol. 7, No. 4, 1959, p. 8; *Institute Information*, Vol. 1, No. 11, 1954; *Institute Information*, Vol. 6, No. 3, 1958). It was through the promotion of professionalism that the IPA aimed to demonstrate its capacity to discharge these economic and political responsibilities. What, then, was the precise nature of the debate about professionalism and how did it impact on the industry? It is appropriate now to examine this in detail.

Standards of Professional Conduct

W.H Emmett (Overseas) Ltd., in liquidation, sued E.C. De Witt & Company (Australia) Proprietary Ltd., for £14,442 for newspaper and radio advertising. At the same time John Fairfax & Sons Proprietary Ltd. sued the same defendants for £324 in respect of advertising inserted in their newspapers, the Sydney Morning Herald and the Sunday Herald. Before payments had been made by the De Witt Company to Emmetts, Fairfax and other newspapers had claimed payment direct on the ground that Emmetts had acted as agents and that on their failure, recourse could be made to the advertiser as principal. De Witts did not deny that they were liable for payment to somebody and paid the whole amount due into Court at the beginning of the action in 1954. The action lasted five days and evidence was called by Emmetts to prove the custom of trade that advertising agencies contracted as principals or independent contractors . . . In giving judgment in favour of W.H Emmett (Overseas) Ltd., . . . Mr. Justice Gorman ruled that the plaintiffs (Emmetts) acted as principles both ways, that is in their relations with their client and with the newspaper. *The Judge stated that the custom alleged by the practitioners in advertising had been established.* The action brought by John Fairfax & Sons Proprietary Ltd. was dismissed with costs. (*Institute Information*, Vol. 4, No. 7, 1957, p. 1)

This apparently arcane legal ruling, with its insight into the colonial networks of commercial law, addresses the central theme of the debate over the naming of advertising people as agents or practitioners. As the report of the case emphatically noted, it focused on the legal definition of the advertising agency as principal. What this meant was that the advertising agency, in buying advertising space, acted not as the agent of the client but as an independent party in its own right. Thus it was to the agency and not the advertisers (the client) that media owners (in this case, Fairfax & Sons) had recourse if non-payment for the advertising space occurred. The ruling made clear that the definition of the agency as principal also applied in its relationship with media owners. In other words, agencies acted as an independent party in relation to newspaper publishers or television companies as well. In coming to his judgment, Mr Justice Gorman in the Queen's Bench Division, in fact, confirmed the custom of trade first established in the *Tranton* v. *Astor* case of 1917. In confirming this earlier decision, Mr Justice Gorman, however, was clearly troubled by the status of the plaintiffs Emmetts (the advertising agency). As *Institute Information* noted, 'he tried to avoid the use of the word "agency" and his references included "contractors", "independent contractors" and, as a last resort, "advertising people"' (*Institute Information* 1957, p. 1). *Institute Information* could but sympathise with his worship's lexical difficulties. It noted how the case 'emphasised once again the illogical and, at times, embarrassing nomenclature of the advertising agency.' The article went on, in an irritated tone, to suggest ways of resolving this difficulty. It suggested:

> Should we not, in fact, now consider trying to abolish altogether the term 'advertising agent'? The individual who engages in the practice of advertising is a 'practitioner' and the Institute, by its title, is the corporate body which represents its member-practitioners. Long though the word may be, it is accurate and has none of the anomalous and misleading connotations which the word 'agent' brings in train . . . If, in all literature, correspondence and conversation, Fellows, Members and Associate Members and qualified staff of member agencies would refer to themselves and their friends as practitioners in advertising, a great service would be done to the business. (*Institute Information*, Vol. 4, No. 7, 1957, p. 11)

This issue of the title used to describe advertising people was raised again two years later in another leader article in *Institute Information*. It reported the Trade Relations Committee's review of the contractual undertakings of agencies and its confirmation of the custom of defining the advertising agency as principal. On this occasion, *Institute Information* set out more fully the way in which agencies acted as a principal in their dealings with media owners and advertisers. It also included comments on how agencies should handle the relinquishing of an account and its transfer to another agency. Institute Information pointedly termed this a 'practitioner-practitioner' relationship (*Institute Information*, Vol. 6, No. 7, 1959, pp. 1,12). The misleading nature of the term advertising agent was also addressed in a third leader article in July 1962. This time *IPA News* reported that the principle of the advertising agency contracting as principal had been reaffirmed by the Lord Chancellor, Lord Shackleton, in a House of Lords discussion on broadcasting. This reaffirmation had been prompted by a question about the formal links between television companies and advertising agencies under the terms of the 1954 Television Act. This aspect of the custom of trade which defined the agency as principal in the relationship between agencies and media owners was, if anything, a more sensitive one than that which had been centrally at stake in the Emmetts, De Witt and Fairfax case (relating to agency-client relationships). Being able to demonstrate that its member agencies could offer (in the IPA's terms) independent and impartial advice to clients depended on breaking all associations with the origin of advertising agencies as agents of the press. These earlier practices – where enterprising agents would buy space in bulk from newspapers and then sell this space on to those wishing to advertise – were the guilty family secret which had to be buried in the promotion of professionalism.

In supporting the claims of agencies to be independent commercial entities, the IPA was keen to promote the status of the service advertising agency. The term had been first formally taken up by the Association of British Advertising Agencies, the IPA's predecessor, on its establishment in 1917. It was later incorporated as a central tenet of the IPA's founding constitution. A service advertising agency was one which could, in the view of the IPA, offer 'advice and assistance in the selection of advertising media, the preparation of adverts and the conduct of advertising and selling' (IPA 1956: 26). In practice this 'comprehensive and fully qualified service' implied an agency which could offer a range of specialised functions such as market research, media buying facilities, creative services and account management skills. The IPA put a high premium on this organisational form and its associated set of service competencies. In fact, the IPA explicitly saw itself as representing the interests of service agencies and together with the definition of the agency as principal, the organisational form of the service agency formed the conditions of IPA membership.

Promoting the service agency was clearly central to the IPA's ambition to establish the authority of its member agencies as autonomous professional experts and to distinguish them from 'mere' contractors who bought space for clients. Promoting service agencies also meant that the IPA became involved in trying to foster professional standards in the conduct of the business of advertising. In this respect, the bye-laws of the Institute are important for the way they attempted to formalise codes of professional conduct. The IPA viewed these bye-laws as a code of ethics, designed to raise the standards of behaviour of member agencies and through this increase the professional status of individual members (IPA 1956: 1). Aside from the initial bye-law, which rather anodynely emphasised the importance of upholding the 'dignity and interests of the Institute', the remaining seven rules centred upon the issue of speculative copy and attempted to regulate competition between member agencies. Speculative copy, or speculative briefs, referred to unsolicited approaches made by agencies to advertisers regarding their advertising. The IPA was adamant that such approaches were not only unsound in business terms, but went against principles of professional conduct. Thus, while the IPA assured potential clients that it was not against competition between agencies, it noted:

> no agency can prepare a worthwhile plan for a potential client until it has made an exhaustive study of the client's problems at first hand and in a manner that is incompatible with speculative effort. Speculative campaigns are, therefore, basically unsound, unethical, and not in the best interests of advertisers. (IPA 1956: 12)

The bye-laws relating to speculative briefs were binding and their breach represented grounds for expulsion from the Institute.

The IPA's concern to promote professionalism through its codes of practice was supplemented by a set of certifications relating to the conditions for individual membership. They formed the second way in which it attempted to establish a form of occupational closure in the delivery of advertising services. The Institute offered three categories of membership for individuals: Fellow, Member and Associate Member. Fellows were members or associate members who had rendered outstanding services to advertising. Each year a number of Fellows were elected by the Council of the IPA and it was the Fellows who dominated the Institute's standing committees. Membership itself, however, was by examination – both the joint intermediate examination and the final examination. Candidates for membership were usually required to have had five years experience with a recognised agency and to be able to 'satisfy the Institute's examiners that they have the ability to plan, organise and conduct a national advertising campaign . . . And are able to represent their advertising agency correctly and responsibly in relation to its clients' (IPA 1956: 18). The joint intermediate examination was run by the IPA and the Advertising Association (AA), and was held at technical schools and colleges across the country. Once this stage had been passed successfully, individuals could then proceed to sit the final exams for membership or associate membership. Tuition for these final exams took the form of a series of lectures given by established practitioners at Belgrave Square and was supported by weekend courses.

During the late 1950s and early 1960s the IPA was also concerned to extend the range of certificated education and training available to its members. In 1958 it set up a working party to discuss art training for advertising. More significantly, it gave strong support to the first full-time course in advertising studies established in 1960 and run by the Department of Advertising Studies at the London County Council College for the Distributive Trades. The course – which included classes in English, advertising administration, reproduction, design, economics, psychology, media, copywriting and law, together with visits to agencies and advertisers and practical work on advertising problems – was organised to fit in with the tuition required for the Institute's examinations. The IPA's greatest success in the extension of certificated advertising education, however, came with the establishment of the Higher National Certificate in Business Studies (HNC), agreed between the IPA, AA and the Department of Education and Science (DES) in 1964. The new qualification included advertising and marketing within its syllabus and courses were first held in the spring of 1967.

The moves to extend certificated advertising education during this period were complimented by a stepping up of recruitment initiatives. Paramount here was the establishment of the Institute's recruitment and training committee in the late 1950s and the forging of closer links with the University Appointments Board from 1959. Both initiatives put a premium on the recruitment of graduates, with the latter project involving second- and third-year undergraduates visiting agencies during the summer vacation. Other entrants were not overlooked however. As *Institute Information* noted, not only was it important to attract more graduates, but also 'public school boys and the cream of the secondary schools into advertising. There is a place, to, for the products of the modern schools and plans are afoot for producing an integrated pattern of recruitment' (*Institute Information*, Vol. 4, No. 12, 1957, p. 1).

These initiatives to formalise recruitment, taken together with developments in certificated advertising education, represented further signs of the IPA's ambition to promote professional standards amongst advertising agencies. The agreement reached with the DES over the HNC in Business Studies was particularly important. It marked the standardisation of advertising education under a national examination system whose qualifications were guaranteed by the state. The HNC also formalised advertising as a coherent body of expertise and a teachable set of competencies. Central to this process was the attempt to not only establish advertising practice as a set of specialised skills, but also the concern to set in place a theoretical grounding for this training. This grounding was important, since the predominance of trained expertise over practical experience formed a key tenet of professional status.

Through these initiatives the IPA played a key role in not only organising advertising people, but also in performing the role of a qualifying association. Both these functions were central to its attempts to control the market in advertising services. As we have seen, the promotion of the service agency loomed large in this strategy and formed part of the attempt by the IPA to establish the authority of its members as competent professionals. The conditions of membership to the Institute were an integral part of this form of occupational closure. They represented an attempt to create an artificial scarcity in advertising and marketing services. Overall, such developments marked a concerted attempt to professionalise advertising. The steady and inevitable march towards professionhood which the IPA spoke of during this period, however, ran up against a number of significant stumbling blocks. For the 1950s and early 1960s were more adequately character-ised as a period in which professionalisation was ultimately postponed.

The Limits of Professionalisation

The central limitation on these strategies of professionalisation was the weakness of the IPA in controlling the supply of advertising services. Despite the buoyancy of the organisation throughout the 1950s and early 1960s and the increase in its membership, by 1964 it could only claim just under half of the 550 agencies listed in the *Directory of Advertising Agencies and Personnel* as its members. The situation was even bleaker when it came to individual members. In this category, only one in ten advertising personnel were members (Millerson 1964; *Institute Information*, Vol. 8, No. 12, 1961, p. 1). Unsurprisingly, the IPA was keen to put a positive spin on these figures. It could claim with some justification that they did under-represent its successes as a corporate body, particularly in terms of the fact that it could count as its members all of the big London-based agencies. The IPA also made much of figures which suggested that its members were responsible for handling 80 to 85 per cent of the total business dealt with by agencies. This figure requires some unpacking, however. It said more about the way the top agencies dominated the sector, particularly in relation to the big-spending clients, and the division between them and the rest of the industry, than it did about divisions between IPA and non-IPA member agencies.

Even when read in a sympathetic light the membership figures did not tell the whole story of the IPA's authority within the industry. John Mellors, whose was copy director at S.H. Benson Ltd. in the early 1960s, offered some dismissive words about the IPA in his retrospective account *Memoirs of an Advertising Man* (Mellors 1976). Describing those aspects of his working life which he disliked, he complained:

> One side of advertising which bored me stiff was anything to do with its trade association, the Institute of Practitioners in Advertising. Its name, I thought, reflected its pomposity . . . The Institute devised a series of examinations as part of its policy of promoting advertising as a profession rather than a business. Privately I didn't think it mattered which we were and what people wanted to call us. What the hell was wrong with being a business? Businesses employed our talents. Why weren't we content to be a business ourselves? (Mellors 1976: 97)

More seriously, even amongst those agencies which it could count as its members the IPA had a problem getting them to identify with their corporate vision. This difficulty was made explicit in an editorial in *Institute Information* setting out the rationale for the change in the Institute's name in 1954:

> It is interesting to note that . . . 15% of Incorporated Practitioners and 25% of Registered Practitioners fail to describe themselves as such on their letter headings and other printed matter. It is difficult to see how the Institute can truly justify a programme of external public relations on behalf of its members, until they are *all* prepared publicly to identify themselves with the Institute . . . It would add materially to the Institute's strength and standing if *all* members would show that they are proud to use the description to which their membership entitles them. (*Institute Information*, Vol. 2, No. 1, 1954, p. 1)

We can see in these comments a familiar theme in exchanges between professional associations and their members. The scenario of the professional body chastising its members for their lack of interest in its promotional activities and for their general passivity in relation to its aims is a stock-in-trade picture of organisation-member relationships. The grumblings of the IPA on this matter, however, clearly carried the weight of a more substantive anxiety. This had to do with its relative weakness as a corporate body in the advertising industry, but also on its perceived lack of recognition within the world of industry and British public life.

The failure of a significant minority of its members to fully identify with the Institute was not its only cause for concern. The second problem confronting it was the issue of the Institute's exams. Between 1953 and 1964, as the Institute took steps to bolster the place of certificated training in the industry, *Institute Information* came back time and again to the recidivism of agencies in the face of its initiatives. A leader article from January 1955 entitled 'Why Examinations?', urged greater awareness amongst member agencies of its exams and argued for greater weight to be given to them. It proposed that agencies should make 'tangible expressions of appreciation' to successful candidates and even went so far as to suggest that in recruiting staff agencies should – *ceteris paribus* – appoint applicants with the initials MIPA or AMIPA after their names. The editorial also suggested that agencies might offer promotion, salary increases or bonuses to IPA members. More practically, it encouraged agencies to appoint personnel officers to inform their staff about the examinations and to support them through the assessment process (*Institute Information*, Vol. 2, No. 5, 1955, p. 5).

Two months later, *Institute Information* returned to the same issue. On this occasion the tone of the editorial verged on the despairing. The focus of the article, pointedly entitled 'Education Apathy', was the recent weekend course for students preparing for the examinations. The weekend had clearly been something of a disaster, with only fifty students attending. *Institute Information* complained about the lack of interest displayed by senior agency executives in relation both to the course and its associated exams. Referring to a photograph taken of the participants at the weekend, the editorial acidly challenged agency heads to identify their staff amongst those represented. Like the earlier editorial, it encouraged agencies to appoint education or personnel officers to promote the exams within their agencies and, further, to act as a point of contact in educational matters. It saw this latter function as a way of preventing such issues finding their way straight to what it termed the 'W.P.B' – the waste paper bin (*Institute Information*, Vol. 2, No. 3, 1955, p. 1).

What lay behind these complaints from the IPA was the resistance of many agencies, and especially senior agency figures, to the IPA's initiatives to formalise education, training and staff development. This resistance sprung from a deep-rooted concern about the relative balance between the theoretical and practical learning required to make an effective advertising person. Against the IPA's attempts to formalise training, many advertising folk emphasized that an 'adman' could not be manufactured and that the craft was learned through practical experience of agency life. Such was the force of this counter argument, which predominated throughout the higher echelons of British business during the 1950s, that it produced the display of more than a little ambivalence by the IPA towards its own exams. Subsequently the IPA made much of its weekend courses as 'practical education', emphasising that: 'the examinations must be viewed more circumspectly – they are not ends in themselves and study for them should not be made a substitute for hard work within the agency, which is a severely practical necessity' (*Institute Information*, Vol. 4, No. 12, 1957, p. 1). A long article in *IPA Forum* in 1964, whilst restating the problem of the lack of recognition given to the courses and exams by agencies, also argued that 'it would be unthinkable to insist on qualifications as a condition of practicing . . . most of the leading figures in the industry learned the hard way, by practice not precept' (*IPA Forum*, No. 1, 1964, p. 4). The persistence of this notion of 'practical education' represented one of the major limitations to the professionalisation of advertising practice during the postwar years. Against the establishment of formal training in specialised skills associated with the drive to professionalise, many advertising people held onto a notion of learning by doing and practical experience.

The Professional Ideal

The years between 1953 and 1964 witnessed the IPA's concerted effort to professionalise advertising running aground principally upon the rocks of the industry's own indifference. The story about professionalisation in this period, however, does not end here. Despite its failure at an institutional level, the drive to professionalise threw up a diffuse set of cultural scripts about what it meant to be an advertising person. Looming large among these was the image of the advertising practitioner as a professional, shaped in the mould of the established professions.

The attempt to equate advertising people with doctors, lawyers and solicitors was evident in the introduction to the second impression of the IPA's *Aims and Functions* (IPA 1956). The introduction begin by quoting Francis Bacon's dictum: 'I hold each man a debtor to his profession.' It then proceeded to draw an equivalence between the incorporation of the IPA in 1927 and the guarantees to patients and to clients embodied in the formation of the established professions. This attempt to forge an image of the advertising practitioner as equivalent to a doctor or lawyer was evident again in a polemical piece by David Ogilvy, President of Ogilvy Benson Mather, reproduced in *Institute Information*. Setting out his unhappiness with the status of advertising, Ogilvy suggested that the only solution was to make advertising into a profession. Professionalisation was important, he suggested, because only then would clients award the same respect to the judgment of agencies as they did to that of 'their lawyer, or their doctor, or even their accountants' (*Institute Information*, Vol. 2, No. 5, 1955, p. 8). Setting out the debate about the identity of advertising folk as agents or practitioners a couple of years later, *Institute Information* also attempted to draw the same equivalence between advertising practitioners and doctors and lawyers:

> It might be recalled that most of the professional descriptions were coined in the reign of Elizabeth I, when the English language was bursting into full flower. Words like 'doctor', 'solicitor', 'barrister' came to denote individuals who practiced in medicine and the law. Perhaps the present Elizabethan age could produce a word which would be simple, practical and dignified and serve to describe the individual who practices . . . advertising. (*Institute Information*, Vol. 4, No. 7, 1957, p. 1)

What, though, did the image of the professional associated with law and medicine signify to advertising folk aspiring to this same status? What kind of cultural identity did it mark out? One way of exploring this is to see the identity condensed in the figure of the doctor or lawyer as an example of what Neil McKendrick has called the professional ideal. Focusing on literary representations, McKendrick has argued that the professional ideal forms one of three dominant ideals associated with representations of the world of business and commerce over the last 200 years (McKendrick 1986). He describes the other two as the gentlemanly ideal and the business ideal. In McKendrick's account these competing images are seen principally in class terms, as divisions between aristocratic values and those of the middle class and between the wealth-creating and professional middle classes. However, as Michael Roper has argued in the context of research on the post-war professionalisation of management, the ideals set out by McKendrick are also quite clearly gendered (Roper 1994, chapter 2) . The self-made man, the leisured gentleman and the cultured professional represented competing versions of masculinity. In terms of unpacking the meaning of the professional ideal, then, we can see that it has been powerfully linked since the end of the nineteenth century with a version of gentlemanly masculinity.

McKendrick's argument is instructive in thinking about the way the image of the established professions might have signified to advertising people during the post-war period. One way of reading the IPA's attempt to represent the advertising practitioner as a professional is to see it as an investment in a form of gentlemanly masculinity. We need to proceed cautiously on this point, however. Whilst in McKendrick's account there are clear, if unacknowledged, assumptions about the professional as a masculine identity, the gendering of the term within *Institute*

Information and the IPA publications was much less apparent. In many cases the invocation of the image of the professional advertising practitioner was not accompanied by any decisive or clear-cut representations of masculinity. The term was sometimes inclusive in its frame of reference, referring to men and women. More commonly, though, there was a tension played out between this inclusive reference and an implicit gendering of the term. This tension derived from the way the term professional was both non-gender specific and yet was associated with patterns of exclusive reference to men – patterns of reference underpinned by the dominance of men as the movers and shakers of the industry and by the wider forms of gender segregation which characterised advertising employment. Within the IPA's image of the world it was men – as authors, agency chiefs, experts, fellows, council members, the President – who were the visible social actors. In contrast, women usually appeared in highly circumscribed positions – as wives of members, or as the information officer at the Institute. This differentiation coded the discussions within the IPA as a dialogue between men and helped on many occasions to fix the exclusively masculine reference of the advertising practitioner as a (gentlemanly) professional.

If the image of the IPA as effectively a men's club helped to establish an association between the coding of professional advertising practice and gentlemanly masculinity, the representation of the advertising professional remained in general a decisively underwritten and unstable one, both in terms of its occupational and gendered meanings. This is a further key aspect of the cultural scripts embedded in the debates about professionalisation. Despite the attempts to forge a vision for advertising by drawing the equivalence with doctors and lawyers, this professional identity was never fully consolidated. In those places where one might have expected to find it – in the profiles of exemplary advertising practitioners – the qualities of professionalism jostled with other scripts. The example of Hubert Oughton, Chairman and Managing Director of W.S. Crawford Ltd, serves to illustrate this point.

Oughton was a ubiquitous presence on the pages of *Institute Information* in the 1950s. This high profile stemmed from his involvement in many aspects of the life of the Institute and from his association with other industry bodies during this period. Between 1951 and 1954 he was President of the IIPA and subsequently an ex officio vice-president. He was Honorary Treasurer of the Advertising Association from 1953 and then its President in 1959–60. He sat on seventeen committees, including chairing the National Readership Survey Controlling Committee and was a member of the Board of Trade Advisory Committee on Commercial Information Overseas. He also acted as treasurer to the National Advertising Benevolence Society. Underlying the breadth of Oughton's activities was his strong sense of both the value of advertising and his dedication to serving its corporate structures in order to promote the industry's interests. He was a man who was, as he himself once put it, proud of his calling and of the people in it (*Institute Information*, Vol. 2, No. 1, 1955, p. 2).

The highest levels of professional recognition flowed from Oughton's commitment to the corporate institutions of advertising. In 1954, he was the winner of the Advertising Association's MacKintosh Medal awarded for 'personal and public service on behalf of advertising'. A year later he won the Publicity Club of London cup for services to the industry and in 1960 he received the OBE in the New Year's Honours list. Oughton was in many ways the personification of the Institute and the archetypal committee man. He was strongly associated with the pursuit of respectability within the industry, which formed such a central element in the debate about professionalisation and with its implicit codes of gentlemanly masculinity. However, further exploration of Oughton's public perona begins to throw up other significant character traits. *Investors' Chronicle* described him as 'naturally creative' and as an artist (*Investors' Chronicle*, 8/1/1960, p. 102). The paper also suggested that he possessed 'two characteristics normally not present in an artist. They are flair for organisation and unerring ability to select the pre-eminent point from masses of apparently important data.' The organisational skills attributed to Oughton as an agency boss were underscored by the identification of a strongly ambitious streak in Oughton, which was coupled with more than a touch of the workaholic passions. The profile noted:

an early decision . . . was to indulge in a first-class season ticket for the daily train journeys to and from Town. He reasoned that physical and mental expansiveness would prove more conducive to days of achievement and fruitful work than the cramped irritating journeys of a straphanger. That this was not a form of self-aggrandisement was shown by his continuing to work ultra-long days broken only by snatched lunches of poached eggs on toast. . . . Like most busy people, he usually finds time for the extra duties nobody else wishes to shoulder (*Investors Chronicle*, 8/1/60, p. 102).

An heroic image of the advertising practitioner also surfaced in Oughton's own self-appraisal and sheds further light on his understanding of himself as an advertising man. In proposing a toast to the Lord Mayor and the Corporation of the City of London at the annual dinner of the Institute in 1953, this 'disciple of private enterprise' suggested:

[It is] a proud occasion for industry and the profession of British advertising to be within the famous walls of the Mansion House, the centre of a city which founded the world-wide trade of Country and Empire on what are now called 'Merchant Adventurers' in the century of the first Queen Elizabeth, and which, at the moment, now house[s] the modern equivalent of those Adventurers – the exponents of the craft of advertising. (*Institute Information*, Vol. 1, No. 2, 1953, p. 4)

Skillful and enterprising businessman, artist and gentlemanly professional, these were the central identifications which jostled together in representations of Hubert Oughton. Historians and sociologists of the post-war professions need to know much more about the cultural resources which shaped such social scripts. What these preliminary findings point to is the instability of the image of the advertising practitioner. It was the unholy trinity of terms used to describe advertising in this period (as an art, a craft and a business) which lay at the root of this instability; an instability which effected advertising's occupational image and the identities of the individuals who worked within it.

Conclusion

I have ended by pointing to the instability of the image of the advertising practitioner which was embedded in the debates about professionalism during the 1950s and early 1960s. As with the moves pursued by the IPA at an institutional level, the instability of this cultural script of the 'advertising man' pointed to the difficulty inherent in consolidating the professional status of advertising. Despite a concerted drive, the IPA ultimately failed in its task. In this sense, advertising cannot be neatly inserted into the larger story of the expansion of public and private sector professionals in the post-war years. It represents a failed process of occupational professionalisation. Ironically, the very commercial success of the agency sector during this period worked against professional consolidation. The ability of agencies to secure a certain amount of de facto legitimacy as the pre-eminent suppliers of advertising and marketing services amongst a range of clients effectively undermined the rationale for professionalisation pursued by the IPA. The logic was undeniable. If agencies were emerging as trusted service providers amongst the producers who constituted the expanding consumer goods sectors of the economy, then the guarantees to clients which the IPA felt were central to delivering this trust appeared unnecessary. The pull of the identity of the business-man was also an equally significant factor. It is likely that many advertising people felt comfortable with their identities as businesspeople. Achieving the status of a professional may not have been a high priority.

Significantly, however, the issue of professionalism has remained an important one for the advertising industry. It has lingered on most notably in the activities and ambitions of the IPA. Subsequent developments reveal how the Institute remains hypnotised – just as it was in the 1950s and 1960s – by the professional ideal embodied by medicine and the law. In this respect the IPA, and the industry it seeks to represent, remains the prisoner of a history which continues to unsettle the relations between clients and agencies. In opening up this history, my aim has been to contribute to a more complex account of the expansion of the commercial domain during a key period in the history of post-war British economic expansion. Such a project is important if historians and sociologists are to move beyond the over-general accounts of commercial and business practices which continue to dominate research on this field of cultural and economic endeavour.

Note

I am grateful to Stuart Hall, Frank Mort, Michael Roper and Bill Schwarz for their comments.

References

Brierly, S. (1994), *The Advertising Handbook*, London: Routledge.

Conekin, B., Mort, F. and Waters, C. (1999), 'Introduction', in *Moments of Modernity, Reconstructing Britain 1945–1964* , London: Rivers Oram Press, pp. 1–21.

Crompton, R. (1990), 'Professions in the current context', in *Work, Employment & Society* Special Issue, pp.147–66.

Directory of Advertising Agency Personnel and data (1961), London: World's Press News & Advertisers Review.

Institute of Practitioners in Advertising (1956), *Aims and Functions*, London: IPA.

Institute Information, 1953–62, London: IIPA/IPA.

Investors' Chronicle, 1960, London.

IPA Forum, 1964–, London: IPA.

IPA News, 1962–4, London: IPA.

Johnston, T. (1982), 'The State and the Professions:the peculiarities of the British', in A. Giddens and G. MacKenzie (eds), *Social Class and the Division of Labour*, Cambridge: CUP, p. 35–52.

Johnson, T. (1989), Review of A. Abbott, *The System of Professions* in *Work, Employment & Society* 3 (3), p. 413.

Jordons (1989), *Britain's Advertising Industry*, Bristol: Jordon & Son Ltd.

MacDonald, K. (1995), *The Sociology of the Professions*, London: Sage.

McKendrick, N. (1986), '"Gentleman and Players Revisisted": the Gentlemanly Ideal, the Business Ideal and the Professional Ideal in English literary culture', in N. McKendrick and R.B Outhwaite (eds), *Business Life and public policy:essays in honour of D.C. Coleman*, Cambridge: CUP, pp. 98–137.

Mellors, J. (1976), *Memoirs of an Advertising Man*, London: Magazine Editions.

Millerson, G. (1964), *The Qualifying Professions, a Study of Professionalization*, London: Routledge & Kegan Paul.

Mort, F. (1996), *Cultures of Consumption, Masculinities and Social Space in Late Twentieth Century Britain*, London: Routledge.

—— (1999), 'The Commercial Domain: Advertising and the Cultural Management of Demand', in B. Conekin, F. Mort and C. Waters (eds), *Moments of Modernity, Reconstructing Britain 1945–64* , Rivers Oram Press, pp. 55–75.

Nixon, S 1996 *Hard Looks: Masculinities, Spectatorship and Contemporary Consumption*, London: UCL Press.

Packard, V. (1957), *The Hidden Persuaders*, London: Longmans.

Pearson, J. & Turner, G. (1965), *The Persuasion Industry*, London: Eyre & Spottiswoode.

Perkin, H. (1989), *The Rise of a Professional Society, England since 1800*, London: Routledge.

Piggot, S. (1975), *OBM, a celebration*, London: Ogilvy, Benson & Mather.

Roper, M. (1994), *Masculinity and the British Organization Man since 1945*, Oxford: OUP.

Sampson, A. (1962), *Anatomy of Britain*, London: Hodder & Stoughton.

Saxon Mills, G. H. (1954), *There is a tide . . . the life and work of Sir William Crawford, K.B.E, Embodying an Historical Study of Modern British Advertising*, London: William Heinemann Ltd.

Steer, P. (1988), *The Business Studies Dictionary*, London: Macmillan.

Tiratsoo, N. (1999), 'Limits of Americanization: The United States Productivity Gospel in Britain', in B. Conekin, F. Mort, and C. Waters (eds), *Moments of Modernity, Reconstructing Britain 1945–64*, Rivers Oram Press, pp. 96–113.

Part II

Introduction:
The Birth of Value

Daniel Miller

The analysis of exchange, especially in anthropology but not only there, has tended to be driven by a rather simplistic contrast between two idealised extremes – the 'gift' and 'commodities' (or sometimes the 'market'), and the two distinct ways these are thought to constitute value. In the idealised pure market situation goods are completely stripped of the consequences of who is actually doing the buying and the selling, and money itself as an abstracted medium of exchange acts to preserve this decontextualised process. The ideal gift is constituted by the exact opposite. Things are regarded as inalienable, since the object is so tied to the social and religious context of its origin that it can never fully be given away but comes back as the ethos of reciprocity creating the relationship between giver and receiver. Much of this literature stems from the writings of Mauss (1954) and later commentary (e.g. Carrier 1995, Gregory 1982). Many anthropological works have also sought to challenge this dichotomous approach by looking at the embedded quality of the market and the strategic quality of gifts (e.g. Appadurai 1986, Bourdieu 1977, Gregory 1997 Thomas 1991; for debates see Schrift 1997)

In some ways this debate has run its course especially when the argument can be turned on its head (as in Gell 1992 and Miller in press). What is required is a new approach that does not evoke this dualistic perspective but suggests a route to transcend any such opposition. A candidate that is emerging through a similar anthropological grounding as a promising approach to the study of the embedded nature of economic action is that based upon the concept of value. It is worth considering the colloquial meaning of the term 'value'. On the one hand this is used in relation to many market variables such as price and equivalence where we talk of the 'value' of an object, but the very same term simultaneously evokes many of the attributes of the gift, when we talk about value as that which what really matters to us, and that which is not reducible to the market etc. Indeed on reflection the ability of this one word to cover a gamut of implications and if used ironically the contradictions between them are astonishing. The semantics of the term value are themselves curious and critical evidence for an alternative approach, since we seem quite happy to continue to use as a common term something that seems to have the specific role of mixing up and refuting any simple dualism of utility and the personal. This leads to the question as to how far it is the colloquial use of the term value as against the academic dualism that best describes our experience of exchange, and then to the further question of where does value come from, and how does it manage to transcend what seems like a common sense duality between these two forces of the disembedded market on the one hand and contextualised exchange on the other.

There are also found within anthropology arguments that lead towards a concern with exchange as a process that creates value. Much of the literature influenced by the work of Strathern (1988) is focused as much on how value is represented in exchange as on the people as agents carrying out the exchange. For example Foster (1990) argues in his study of exchanges in a Melanesia society that exchanges do not take place in order to create an equivalence between what is exchanged i.e. shell discs and pigs, but quite the opposite. What matters is the differences in the objects since by exchanging one quality for another they come to be an appropriate expression of, for example, the value that a funerary feast is intended to achieve. Value is not something that the exchanged objects are reduced to but something created by the act itself. The implication of such studies is that the definition of value varies according to the context of transaction.

Most of these anthropologists see such processes as pertinent to exchange in Melanesia and would not expect to find them in places such as Britain and the US. Yet anthropologists working in a variety of economic contexts have come to similar conclusions when confronted with the problem of locating the 'market'. More sociologically orientated approaches to the contemporary market such as Callon (1998) have recently attempted to in some ways protect the concept of the market by showing how it works as a frame in turn protecting itself from those 'cultural' factors that need to be kept extraneous to it. By contrast anthropologists such as the contributors to Carrier (1997) and Dilley (1992) have taken a more radical stance. Rather than suggesting that it is market relations that are protected by such framing, they imply that it is the ideological commitment to a discourse of the market that various powerful forces wish to keep unsullied. In short the very idea of a market is an attempt to create the normative concept and thereby to establish a regime of value.

In all of the three chapters that constitute this section of the book, there is a tension. But I want to suggest that collectively what they represent is not some simple trajectory from purely embedded to purely disembedded forms of value. Indeed it is vital to the overall purpose of this volume to point out that these chapters lend no support to the presupposition that we find out in the world, either a commercial world characterised as decontextualised or some force to be called 'culture' that represents the embedded context. Too often we view economics as though there was some inherent abstract economic force, a sort of wild beast of freedom, striving to be free of all constraint in its entrepeneurial drive, and straining at the leash to escape the social and moral restraints of culture as context. While culture appears as the kind of muddy bog that slows our horse to a walking pace as it negotiates a field that lacks all clarity and reason since culture is inherently messy and irreducible to any clear set of elements or attributes that comprise it.

These chapters help to show that this is nonsense. Instead of seeing culture as the context of commerce, or its constraint, what these chapters show clearly is something which I suspect is much more generally true which is that commerce is often itself the force and infrastructure which is used to create culture as normativity. So far from straining away from culture, commerce often gives birth to it. The implication of this section and perhaps of the book as a whole is that very often culture is itself the product of commerce. Indeed one of the reasons the term 'value' so well elides any simple distinction between market and gift is that the very thing that commerce most often creates is 'value' in its full and ambiguous colloquial sense.

The topic of all three chapters is exchange. In the perspectives I am resisting here it would be assumed that exchange is all about creating equivalence by abstracting from the particular nature of the things exchanged, so that they may be regarded for the purposes of exchange as commensurate and equivalent. By this process the possibility of exchange is facilitated. Exchange demands as of necessity a rise to the market. But these chapters show exchange as something quite different. What they reveal instead is a very different underlying process. It is a process of making objects appropriate to those involved in the exchange itself, and operates primarily through bringing together rather than separating the abstract and the particular.

The chapter by Clarke and that by Gregson, Brooks and Crewe both address what might be thought of as a nearly identical subject. They are both concerned with the second-hand exchange of clothing. What is so intriguing about reading them here in direct juxtaposition, is that from the analysis of these two examples of what might be thought of as the same subject they manage to come to diametrically opposite conclusions. In the first case Clarke shows that exchange is based on an ideal. An object that is exchanged as an item of second-hand baby clothes should continue to contain within itself enough of the history of its own prior experience of personal and social involvement to be appropriate to its destination. It works quite literally as an item of material culture. So an object that is too decontextualised, i.e. stripped of its prior social life, is not suitable for exchange. In the case analysed by Gregson, Brooks and Crewe we find exactly the opposite. The problem that must be overcome is precisely the degree to which there is too much of the previous body attached to the clothes so that it is important to remove this. We are used to thinking in terms of people taking their clothes off but here we have to get used to the idea of clothes taking their people off!

At first glance it seems as though the radical opposition between the two chapters might be equated with the fundamental opposition of gift and commodity in as much as one is looking to decontextualise and the other to re-affirm context. It might seem that the more exchange becomes a market like transaction the more abstracted, depersonalised and dehumanised is the commodity, as in the removing of the body from the clothing, while by contrast the more gift-like the exchange the more we acknowledge that it is an inalienable aspect of the person that is retained. But this does not work at all for these chapters. The stripping of the person from the clothes documented by Gregson, Brooks and Crewe is not an exemplification of a pure market at all. What is stripped away is only the particular body of the particular previous user. What the chapter makes clear, however, is that the value of the clothes (especially for the middle-class shopper) is still derived in large measure from the fact that they have been previously worn. Ideal second-hand clothes are ones that can represent a particular era such as Edwardian, or 1960s. The value of such clothes is that they are authentic, i.e. they really were actual 1960s clothes as opposed to the fake 1960s clothes one could buy in new clothing shops. It is their past which gives them authenticity which gives them value. So what the cleaning of the clothes produces is a switch from signifying some particular individual to signifying a more generic link with the people of that past of interest to the buyer. This is a process of re-contextualising, not one of de-contextualising.

With Clarke things work in the opposite way. Clothes that were too market-like were seen as unacceptable, e.g. putting prices actually on the clothes was a complete turn-off to potential buyers. But these items are no more the pure gift that the adult clothes are pure commodities. Baby clothes had to retain elements of the person, but they also had to demonstrate sufficient alienation from prior ownership to be partible. After all one didn't want to have one's own toddler running down someone else's toddler to insist on having back 'their' clothes (something I have certainly experienced for myself with considerable embarrassment!). Much of Clarke's chapter is concerned with the subtle negotiations involved in retaining the personality of the garments while making them appropriate to move on to a new stage in what might be seen as the clothes' own biography. It is this balance that gives value to the goods.

So instead of the older dichotomy we find that notwithstanding the total opposition of their perspectives both chapters contribute equally to the larger concern of how we can create value. This may range from the sense of obtaining value for money, to the struggle to turn money into value, but either way the idea is to create value in a form that could not be obtained from the ordinary purchase of first-hand clothes in a more conventional market-like setting. Whether one is cleaning an old item of clothing to make it look like a fine example of 1950s style, or whether one is noting the pedigree of a toddler's jumpsuit, the intention is to make the clothes into objects that we come to value in every sense of that term, which is one of the reasons, perhaps, we retain and use a term 'value' with such a diversity of meanings.

Having established the two polar positions which come together in the mutual task of creating value, we are in a better position to assess the chapter by Slater, since in many ways his chapter shows how the tension between these two routes to value can be found within one process of exchange. In the exchange of sex-pics we see on the one hand there is a fear of the rise of automated list servers that clearly have no person behind the screen. In this respect they appear like the characters in Clarke's chapter wanting to embed their exchange in a larger field of sociality. On the other hand they can also appear to follow the same concerns of Gregson, Brooks and Crewe's chapter in that they are quite prepared to strip their images of context to the degree that they can use them to formulate principles of exchange in and of themselves. These are not in this case prices but they are analogous to price in that they use devices such as exchange ratios, to produce formal modes of exchange. Either way the conclusion that follows from the observation of these exchanges follows in the same direction as both the previous chapters. What is produced through these transactions is value.

In one way Slater even more clearly than the other chapters demonstrates how it is exchange itself that is used for the creation of value where value stands for the normative basis of culture. We might think that people who swop pornography are following merely some libertarian opposition to normative and moral constraints. In his other writings on this topic Slater (1998) has shown just how untrue this is. These people are intensely concerned to establish a clear moral universe within which they participate in determining what is moral and what is immoral action. What is fascinating in the chapter included here is that this is not true just of what kind of sex pictures may be exchanged, but it is true equally for establishing the very rules of exchange. Thus the games people play of establishing exchange ratios, cheating on them, and then protecting them.

All three chapters suggest a certain amount of labour involved in making the objects appropriate to exchange. So we see with sex-pics some pride in collecting that lies behind the production of files filled with particular categories of sex-act or participant. With charity shops we see the workers labour and indeed the pride involved in the act of removing stains and secretions from the garments in preparation for their re-sale. Even with the baby clothes there is the labour of the market and the pride of parents in their children which seems to attach itself also to the children's clothes. In all three cases this labour leads on to acts of exchange which are 'proper', where participants can as it were feel good about the exchange in and of itself. Without this labour participants feel they may be sullied by the clothes. If the people selling baby things didn't care about them they are not worthy clothing, and even those exchanging sex pics feel cheated if their values expressed in proper exchange and collecting are violated. It is absolutely clear that the value being created and then threatened is not simply value for money or value equated with money, since after all money doesn't enter into the sex-pic exchange at all.

One of the reasons that these three chapters may usefully be generalised to much wider fields of exchange relates to this final point. The conclusions reached have not been based on chapters which discuss gifts in the conventional sense nor does it seem to make much difference to the conclusion whether or not the objects are actually sold for cash during the act of exchange. This is important since there are many exchanges that take place outside of market conditions such as party-plan selling, inheritance and craft work which would also act as examples of what has been discussed, but even more important there are many exchanges that take place for money in market-like conditions where the same would be true, and these may range from company mergers (e.g. Burrough and Helyar 1990) through to buying high fashion and stylish items where being seen to buy, and the place where it is bought can be just as important to the emergence of value, as the goods themselves. In a previous study of multinational and smaller firms (Miller 1997) I found it impossible to locate some case of pure market conditions which lie outside of this larger process where commerce is used to create value. The same applies also to the purchase of 'big-ticket' items – I was gratified last week to find that my advice to a friend to sell her house through showing prospective buyers around in person and with full details of how the property had played a part in her life, rather than leaving this to estate agents, once again proved profitable! To conclude, these chapters are not some aberrations on the fringes of the true economy, they are simply particular positions which clarify a foundational process which applies to most exchanges and most aspects of economic life. That is to say commerce is often the source not the opponent of value.

Having argued that these chapters relate to a much broader field of exchange and transactions, it is worth concluding with a reference also to their particularity. There is a feeling in all three cases of people developing exchange from scratch. They seem to have to establish anew the premises and principles by which they operate, and they then work on the goods concerned to make them appropriate. Perhaps it is in these situations where we seem to see again 'the birth of value' that the fundamental relationship between exchange and value is particularly apparent. What is striking in these chapters is the evidence that notwithstanding the sense that we live in highly developed if not over-developed economies, we can still see something of the raw creativity of social actors in inventing the conditions for the birth of value.

References

Appadurai, A. (ed.) (1986), *The Social Life of Things: Commodities in Cultural Perspective*, Cambridge: Cambridge University Press.

Bourdieu, P. (1977), *Outline of a Theory of Practice*, Cambridge: Cambridge University Press.

Burrough, B. and Helyar, J. (1990), *Barbarians at the Gate.* London: Arrow.

Callon, M. (1998), 'The Embeddedness of Economic Markets in Economics', in M. Callon (ed.), *The Laws of the Market*, Oxford: Blackwell.

Carrier, J. (1995), *Gifts and Commodities: Exchange and Western Capitalism since 1700*, London: Routledge.

Carrier, J. (ed.) (1997), *Meanings of the Market*, Oxford: Berg.

Dilley, R. (1992), *Contesting Markets*, Edinburgh: University of Edinburgh Press.

Foster, R. (1990), 'Value without equivalence: exchange and replacement in a melanesian society', *Man* 25: 54–69.

Gell, A. (1992), 'Inter-tribal commodity barter and reproductive gift-exchange in old Melanesia', pp. 142–68, in C. Humphrey and S. Hugh-Jones (eds), *Barter Exchange and Value: an Anthropological Approach*, Cambridge: Cambridge University Press, pp. 142–68.

Gregory, C. (1982), *Gifts and Commodities*, London: Academic Press.

—— (1997) *Savage Money*, Amsterdam: Harwood Academic Press.

Mauss, M. (1954), *The Gift*, London: Cohen and West.

Miller D. (1997), *Capitalism: An Ethnographic Approach*, Oxford: Berg.

—— (in press), 'Alienable gifts and inalienable commodities', in B. Kirschenblatt-Gimblett and F. Myers (eds), *Material Culture: Habitats and Values*, Sante Fe: School of American Research Press.

Schrift, A. (1997), *The Logic of the Gift*, London: Routledge.

Slater, D. (1998), 'Trading sexpics on IRC: embodiment and authenticity on the internet', *Body and Society* 4: 91–117.

Strathern, M. (1988), *The Gender of the Gift*, Berkeley: University of California Press.

Thomas, N. (1991), *Entangled Objects*, Cambridge, Mass.: Harvard University Press.

4

'Mother Swapping': the Trafficking of Nearly New Children's Wear

Alison Clarke

To the foreign eye, a mid-Eastern bazaar ... is a tumbling chaos: hundreds of men ... shouting in each others' faces, whispering in each others' ears, smothering each other in cascades of gestures, grimaces, glares – the whole enveloped in a smell of donkeys, a clatter of carts, and an accumulation of material objects God himself could not inventory, and some of which he could probably not identify ... sensory confusion brought to a majestic pitch. (Geertz 1979: 197)

The Lonsdale Mother's Group (LMG), North London, holds a nearly new sale of children's clothes, toys and equipment in a spacious church hall at 10 a.m. each alternate month. To the outsider's eye, with the exception of the 'enveloping smell of donkeys', LMG sales are not dissimilar to Geertz' description of a Moroccan *suq*, or eastern bazaar. They are hectic, noisy, excited events in which piles of assorted wares are tugged and tousled in the course of animated transactions between eager buyers and sellers. In contrast to the bazaars, however, LMG sales are organised solely by women, for women. Under the auspices of their roles as mothers, women are both the vendors and buyers at such events. This chapter explores how and why these unique sites of consumption arise in an urban environment with an array of easily accessible retail outlets for children's wear from catalogues, department stores to charity shops.

This chapter draws on broader ethnographic research concerning the provisioning of households in North London. The initial ethnography was shared with Daniel Miller (whose research dealt with formal modes of consumption such as supermarkets, shopping malls and high street outlets (Miller 1998), and combined preliminary interviews and participant observation involving seventy-six households. This section of the research revolves around twenty-five of these households and considers a range of informal, non-retail or alternative means of acquisition including mail order catalogue purchase, gift giving and the making of home-made goods. The ethnographic site in North London, a street referred to as Jay Road, consists of a cross-section of housing; 1960s blocks of council flats and maisonettes; semi-detached 1930s homes; Edwardian rented and owner-occupied maisonettes and larger Victorian family houses occupied predominantly by middle-class families on adjoining streets. The ethnic groups prominent in the area and included in the study range from those of Greek Cypriot, West African, Jewish, Asian, South American, West Indian and Irish origins. The core research for this chapter, empirical data of nearly new sales, deals ostensibly with women who live on low incomes but who define themselves as pursuing middle-class values and lifestyles.

Preliminary interviews used to assess types of provisioning encountered by households on the street failed to acknowledge 'hand-me-downs' and second-hand clothing exchanges as significant provisioning forms. Yet through participant observation it emerged as a prevalent form of alternative acquisition particularly in the homes of less affluent but consciously middle-class mothers. While certain households merely supplement formal retail acquisition with this trafficking of second-hand goods, others rely on it exclusively for the provisioning of their children. Jennifer, a mother of Southern Irish origins, depends entirely on second-hand children's clothes and toys as an everyday means of provisioning. As well as supplying her own children with clothing and toys, she regularly attends nearly new sales to find items for her extended kin in Ireland. The 'trafficking' in second-hand children's wares, then, is used in a variety of forms and at various levels of involvement but it forms a staple, yet formally unacknowledged, mode of alternative acquisition on the street in North London. Nearly new sales make visible the wider practice of 'hand-me-down' and intra-household provisioning. This chapter begins with an exploration of the particularity of a household's use of second-hand children's clothing and moves on to consider the implications of nearly new sales as unique urban consumption spaces.

'Hand-Me -Downs and 'Cast-offs': A Moral Economy of Clothing

It's a beautiful, gorgeous little white fur coat; real fur with mother-of-pearl buttons and a sweet little hood. But Sophie can't wear it – she loves it but she just can't wear it. People would probably throw tomatoes at her in the street and [laughing] they'd think I was Cruella Deville! But we still keep it in the wardrobe, it's too nice to hide away and charity shops around here probably wouldn't take it anyway. (Jane, 37, North London, discussing an item of 'hand-me-down' clothing received from relatives in the United States)

Every three months or so Jane receives a consignment of 'hand-me-down' children's clothing from relatives across the Atlantic. As a mother of four children, aged between eighteen months and six years, these parcels form an integral part of her household provisioning. The consignments of clothing arrive after a lengthy process of vetting undertaken by Cindy, Jane's American sister in-law, the mother of two girls aged four and eight years. Most of the items are the result of seasonal 'clear-outs' and have been set aside from other piles destined for neighbours' children, thrift shops and garage sales.

Jane considers her American sister-in-law Cindy as 'a bit of a smooth operator' who, despite her comparative wealth, is a particularly resourceful woman when it comes to the provisioning of children's clothes. According to Jane she effectively operates a 'racket' in cast-offs and hand-me-downs whereby she guiltlessly converts the copious and generous gifts of her children's grandparents into hard cash by selling the items (often scarcely worn before being outgrown) for a decent price at her 'nearly new' garage sales. Despite Cindy's apparent callousness in system-atically selling off the grandparents' gifts as profitable commodities Jane admires her gall and understands this as a legitimate way of recouping part of the cost of these beautiful, yet scarcely worn, clothes. There are certain items, however, which even the ever-resourceful Cindy deems too special to sell or profit or pass on to non-kin. Consequently, items such as the fur coat (mentioned in the above quotation) are reserved for the English nieces and nephews. Deemed special enough to warrant the cost of overland postage and packaging, they are sent off to England. Several weeks later they re-emerge as boxed-up consignments in a completely new North London context.

Despite the intimacy invoked by the practice of imagining your own child's clothing worn by someone else's offspring, and of receiving and deciphering the intimate material culture of another's household, prior to these exchanges Jane and Cindy rarely had contact with each other. They sustain a long-term transatlantic relationship through the exchange and sorting of thrice-yearly consignments of hand-me-down and nearly new clothes.

When the children's clothes, plucked from their American context, first arrive in North London they begin their journey into another network of exchanges between friends and relatives. Many articles undergo a process of 'de-acquisition' through which they are passed to neighbouring households or alternative arenas of provisioning (such as charity shops, nearly new sales, recycling centres, etc.) while others under go 're-acquisition' whereby motifs and labels are removed or patches added. In this process of 'de-acquisition' and 're-acquisition' articles such as a real fur coat (previously described) and an overly elaborate 'gaudy' sequinned party dress become displaced and problematised as the biographical trajectories of the commodities drastically change (Kopytoff 1986). Exported from the social relations of a suburb in Connecticut to an urban street in North London, in the processes of 'mother swapping' certain items are rendered distasteful, anomalous or impractical within their new context.

A polyester Disney nightdress with a *Beauty and the Beast* motif, for example, presents an inter-household dilemma which could either secure or undermine Jane and her daughter's valuable neighbourly relationships. The nightdress, sorted from the most recent American consignment of clothes, holds an unsurpassable appeal for Jane's six-year-old daughter, Sophie. In principle, Jane and her partner discourage their children's interest in Disney merchandise, which they consider as exploitative and non-educational. But Jane is fully aware of the desirability of the *Beauty and the Beast* nightdress amongst girls of Sophie's age group and for Sophie in particular it holds a special premium, operating, as it does, outside the rules that constitute the moral economy of this household. The dilemma of the Disney nightdress is further compounded by its dubious status as a 'synthetic' garment. As a compromise, Jane offers the nightdress to her daughter, not for her own use, but as a potential gift for her friend Rachel (a seven-year-old girl living next door but one). In this way the magical but problematic article can be experienced vicariously through Sophie's relationship with her friend Rachel; it can be kept while given. It also acts as a long-awaited reciprocation of Rachel (or her mother's) generosity towards Sophie who receives many of Rachel's cast-offs.

Unfortunately, allowing Sophie to present Rachel with a polyester Disney nightdress might be construed as insensitive or insulting to Rachel's mother; why would Jane try to pass off an item, deemed problematic within her own household, to another mother? Both mothers have frequented the local LMG nearly new sales and discussed at length their tastes and preferences and, in particular, their shared disinclination towards their children wearing synthetics. Over a cup of coffee later in the week Jane pre-empts the 'problem' of the contentious hand-me-down Disney nightdress by assuring Rachel's mother of her own ambiguity towards the item and explaining that if deemed unsuitable, despite its contemporary appeal, it 'can always be sent to Oxfam'.

The passages above offer glimpses into the particularity of a given household's use of second-hand children's clothing. Clearly it is a form of provisioning integral to everyday domestic activity. However, this example, despite its specificity, is by no means exceptional. The term 'trafficking' is used to denote a precarious activity in which goods are dealt with, not in one-off isolated acts of exchange, but within the ongoing, convoluted, contradictory and tentative world of 'mothering' and sociality. The provisioning of second-hand children's clothes is an integral part of the social process that might be described as 'mother swapping'; for entrenched in the transactions and material culture of the second-hand informal economy of children's wear are the identities, knowledges and formations of women as 'mothers'. A small amount of academic literature deals with the informal economies which operate around clothing; such as the stealing and borrowing of clothing within the household (Corrigan 1995) and the fashion-oriented acquisition of second-hand clothing through markets and thrift stores (McRobbie 1989). Such studies highlight this used or 'hand-me-down' clothing as a vital, but under-researched, facet of contemporary consumption.

Notably, a recent study, made by Gregson and Crewe, of British car boot sales points out that 'within the confines of car boot sales it is the buying and selling of children's clothing which comprises the single most important category of goods with which women, irrespective of class, are involved' (1998: 86). The comparative invisibility of this form of acquisition amongst informants themselves can perhaps be explained by what Devault describes as the 'naturalisation' of women's domestic work as carers and provisioners (Devault 1991). The day-to-day sorting, exchange and circulation of 'hand-me-downs' and 'cast offs' and the attendance of informal consumption spaces such as 'nearly new sales', belongs to the broader practice of caring in which arduous repetitive tasks and tacit skills are bound with emotional ties, intimate relations and anxieties. Activities such as straining the pips from the tomatoes of a 'fussy-eater', removing the labels from a child's clothing to prevent the scratching of over-sensitive skin, ensuring a two-year-old toddler's favourite dinosaur socks are washed and ready to wear are not only functional responses to ensure the 'smooth running' of a household, they are crucial acts of valorisation.

Through the trafficking of used children's clothes we see both the work of caring and the practice of valorisation. As mothers swap anecdotes about cast-off items, formerly intimate parts of the material culture of their everyday routines and social relations, they generate a unique form of sociality. 'Mother swapping' is taken from the domestic sphere, to inter-household relations and further valorised through the activities of the market place encapsulated in the nearly new sale. Here skills of dealership combined with cajolery, playfulness and intrigue (traditionally associated with the wily traders of street markets and the mythology of the eastern bazaar) are appropriated by women in the creation of a self-made and consensual market place.

The 'Nearly New Sale': Constructing a Utopian Market Place?

Nearly new sales are typically held on a weekday; they commence with a gathering of women, equipped with babies and buggies, in a long queue winding its way around the front of the church hall. As the sales are extremely popular, they form a common topic of conversation at the ethnographic site, Jay Road in North London. Several weeks prior to the sales taking place women discuss potential purchases, social encounters and donations to the event. This 'buildup' begins as soon as the sale dates are listed in the bi-monthly listings section of the LMG newsletter. While the newsletter formally advertises the sales events the crucial information, including speculation regarding the 'quality' and content of the next sale, circulate via word of mouth. Admission to the sale costs 20p with stall rental costing £4 for members and £8 for non-members. Around eighty women (and accompanying buggies and babies) are in the sale hall at any one time and there are typically around twenty-five stalls. A tea hatch to the rear of the hall serves refreshments and is the focal point for respite from the affray of the gathered crowd. It is here that mothers gather to swap details regarding purchases made or intended and where verdicts are reached regarding the comparative 'success' of the sale. Consensus forms around the gender bias of the goods on offer (is it a 'boy' sale or a 'girl' sale?) and whether prices are perceptibly lower or higher than previous events.

Formal mother's organisations are popularly recognised by women for their proselytising approach towards mothering. Advice meted out to women from organisations such as the Mother's Union, Women's Institute and the National Childbirth Trust (NCT) is historically located in a middle class discourse of social reform (Andrews 1997). While many mothers in the ethnographic study happily embrace the liberal endeavours of the NCT (Miller 1997) the legacy of formal mothering advice stands as an anathema to most women involved in the nearly new sales. As the Lonsdale Mothers Group is tied to a socio-geographically diverse London borough (referred to here as Lonsdale) and, unlike organisations such as the NCT does not advocate a formally prescribed approach to mothering, within the street it is generally considered as a liberal, or alternative, organisation. Many women involved in LMG activities are those who see themselves peripheral to mainstream mother's groups and who, in some cases, seek to disassociate themselves completely from what one informant described as the 'perfect mother syndrome'. One woman described the LMG in terms of a rite of passage into knowing-motherhood, 'the place where you come when you've outgrown the NCT, know what you're doing and have moved on from baby-talk'. Another informant from 'the street', named Anne, who was particularly critical of over-competitive mothers and what she described as a 'materialistic' southern English mentality in general, used the story of a local bring-and-buy sale to highlight the anti-social behaviour of most middle-class mothers. Notably this particular informant contrasted the horror of the 'bring n' buy' incident with her positive experience of the LMG sales. The bring-and-buy sale organised in support of a Blue Peter charity appeal was held in a mother's house situated towards the leafy and more affluent area of Ibis Pond. Anne parked her baby son safely in the corner of a room only to return minutes later to purportedly find him smothered by a fur coat; 'I just happened to turn round and see his legs sticking out from under a heap of fur, I couldn't believe it. She'd just dumped the thing on top of him and trotted off to look at the stalls. I asked her what she thought she was doing, and she said it wasn't her fault she didn't see him there! That's fairly typical of *them* [middle class London mothers].'

As a single mother in her forties, Anne had originally joined the NCT in an attempt to thwart the isolation of motherhood, but found herself marginalised by her single mother status and the fact that her frank and informal attitude seemed to cause offence; ' Oh, I remember trying to talk about relationships, you know, and that sort of thing, anything really except about babies and my gossip went down [at an NCT meeting] like a lead balloon. So me and some other mothers I'd seen at the nearly new [LMG sale] got together off our own backs and we have barbecues and things, you know it's really nice and we talk about everything.' Although backed by a formal newsletter and membership scheme the LMG nearly new sale operates as a distinct entity within and of itself; a space in which 'mothering' is defined through transactions and market relations in a localised setting.

LMG nearly new sales are ostensibly middle-class enterprises, as reflected in the profile and addresses of the key organisational members, but they attract a mixture of members and non-members alike from the local area. It is not the LMG as an organisation that constructs the aesthetics or practices of the nearly new sale. For many women their involvement with the organisation is confined to their attendance of the sales and they have no intention of supporting any other of its activities such as bonfire nights, picnic parties or policy meetings. Rather the sale has become a unique market place where talk and tactility, luck and kismet come together in a sensory world far removed from the nearby shopping malls or supermarkets of North London. For, amidst 'a jungle of price and a cacophony of goods' (Geertz et al. 1979: 217) women circulate around the hall stopping stall to stall, leaning over one another to fondle and scrutinise an array of miniature items: hand-knitted mittens, baby booties, shiny swimming costumes and tiny rain coats.

Sites such as department stores have been identified by numerous academics as vital facets in the construction of modern femininity that encode 'a masculine heterosexual gaze' in the promotion of commodities (Porter-Benson 1986, Reekie 1993, Winship 1985). Conversely, Gregson and Crewe (1997a) argue that the highly gendered but heterogeneous world of the car boot sale allows for multiple feminine identities through which women can exercise their skills as homemakers and carers as well as construct themselves in the context of the 'male gaze'. In the nearly new sale, liberated from the conventions of formal retail spaces, the scrutiny of shop assistants and male companions, women create a unique site of feminised sociality.

Although many women in this milieu recognise each other solely through acquaintances between each other's children, this distanced familiarity enables the gradual development of friendships. In discussions initiated by stallholders and purchasers regarding the history of particular garments and associated experiences, women use each other's households and family members as mutual reference points. Such conversations might concern seemingly practical issues, such as sizing, in which a whole group of women become involved as a typical taped conversation reveals: 'This label is Naf Naf supposedly age eight,' says one stall holder. 'But it's French so it's much smaller than it says and wouldn't fit my daughter,' comments another. However, despite the apparent functionalism of matching a garment with an absent child such exchanges are premised more on sociality than expedience. Most lengthy discussions end, not in a closed sale, but in a polite farewell gesture and a move to the next desirable stall.

Discussions combine with physical demonstration as the 'value' of specific items is determined. If a garment is hardly worn, its near mint condition might theoretically increase its worth but it might also raise questions about its usefulness or desirability; why didn't the child or mother like it? Is its design inappropriate for the age group concerned? Is it made from non-washable materials and therefore difficult to maintain? In other words the testament of the stallholder (as mother) proves vital to the validity of the object for sale. At one stall, a young mother Jane (balancing her baby in one arm and a large hold-all on the other) spots a pair of pink pyjamas decorated with gold sparkly inscriptions and cartoons. She immediately recognises the stallholder, a vendor with whom she associates some successful and 'quality' purchases. 'What age little girl are you looking for?' asks the stallholder, 'Oh, she's a big five-year-old' responds Jane; a typical conversation ensues in which the stallholder explains the size and age of her own children in relation to the garments offered for sale. In this case, Jane and the vendor laugh as

Figure 4.1   Second-hand Wellington boots 'collected' by a North London mother.

they describe the shift from pink to gold preferences in little girls and the stallholder warns 'wait until she gets to the black phase. It's all black now with my girl – she wouldn't be seen dead in pink.' The encounter closes with the purchase of several pink and sparkly items for Jane's daughter. At the following nearly new sale Jane identifies this mother as a sympathetic vendor and a potential friend.

Second-hand clothes and toys are not lamented as a poor alternative to shop-bought equivalents despite the fact that the majority of informants mentioned in this study live on severely restrictive budgets. Economic imperative alone does not explain why a busy mother with two toddlers to supervise would spend three-quarters of an hour scouring a crowded church hall sale on the off chance of finding a pair of second-hand, pink-elephant motif, Wellington boots (known colloquially as 'Ele boots') for her daughter. A functionally equivalent, brand-new pair could easily be purchased at the local department store for a similar price (so highly prized are the articles at nearly new sales). But the bazaar-like atmosphere of the sale is a unique arena of consumption bounded by friendship, ethics, expertise, solidarity and pleasure as much as thrift and prudence.

'Ele boots' and traditional 'educational' toys (such as wooden primary coloured building bricks) have particular kudos at the sales (see Figure 4.1). When publicly negotiating the purchase of a miniature 'play' kitchen (complete with toy pots and pans) for her two-year-old son the knowledges and values a mother is bringing to bear (in this case openly defying gender stereotypes) are at the core of the sale's market exchanges. To the outside observer, the nearly new sale seems to operate as a market in the classic sense of the term; through perfect competition it reaches equilibrium and by implication buyers and sellers are maximally satisfied. In the neo-classical model of market economy consumers and sellers are assumed to have full knowledge of the intentions of others. But, as Michael Stewart notes in his study of Hungarian horse fairs, such models do not easily lend themselves to empirical analysis of real markets: 'the market process rests, amongst other things, on the existence of actors' ignorance: it is precisely the uneven distribution of knowledge . . . between traders and peasants which allows profits to be made' (Stewart 1992: 99). In the case of North London mothers (who are both the traders and the buyers) this uneven distribution of knowledge generates an intense forum for the negotiation of knowledge and consensus.

Although several of the stallholders are regular traders (women who supplement their income on a casual basis through the sales) the majority of stalls are hired by mothers like Melanie. It is through the sociality of the exchanges at the sale that buyers ascertain trustworthiness of the sellers and the extent of their profit motive. In this sense Melanie would seem to be the ideally ethical stallholder, motivated by genuine circumstance to sell her child's high-quality wares at potentially bargain prices. After being persuaded by friends, she uses the sale to pass on an accumulated array of redundant clothes and artefacts related to a specific stage in her child's development. In this specific case holding a stall at the nearly new sale is an act of finality. Tired of being an isolated single mother in London, Melanie has decided to move 'back to her roots' in Scotland and before the move she is clearing out her two-year-old son's outgrown or rarely used items. Pricing up her son's clothes the evening before the sale, then, proved an emotive experience in that it signalled the demise of her London life and the precious few friendships formed at events such as the nearly new sales.

Initially Melanie attaches adhesive price labels to each of her child's items in preparation, within minutes of the sale's commencement she begins desperately to remove them. Despite extensive pre-sale inquiries (ringing around friends and nearly new initiates) her prices prove untenable. A particularly fraught incident, in which a potential buyer accuses Melanie of charging 'about a hundred times over the odds' for a pair of toddlers jeans, confirms to her that there can be no fixed prices attributed to her son's clothes; instead they were adapted to suit each trading encounter. Although reassured by other stallholders that the woman had 'been out of order' and that none of them 'recognised her anyway', Melanie amended her sales style and repartee accordingly. As women visited the stall she accumulated information from their responses towards items and from in-depth conversations appertaining to specific goods, often held simultaneously with up to four different women. Melanie also combined her sales banter with the news of her forthcoming move to Scotland. Prices were lowered and heightened in a seemingly erratic fashion over the course of the sale. On another occasion Melanie's original asking price of £1 for a 'pop-up' toy was lowered to 20p for a non-English speaking Asian mother with a disabled son in a wheelchair. Melanie had been happy to lower the price of her son's much-loved toy in exchange for seeing the pleasure it had brought to a truly deserving child. Prices, then, altered according to the timing and context of the buyer's interest, the attitude of the buyer towards her son's used clothes and demeanour conjured up in the transaction. Melanie enjoyed relaying information about sizes and the appeal of certain toys, and details about her own son to the other mothers. Profit came, not just in the form of the £70 put towards her son, Jeremy's, climbing frame fund but in the valorisation of her 'mothering' through knowledge/value swapping.

Many of the stalls borrow display techniques from formal retailing (colour co-ordination, arranging wares according to age or size groups, etc.). But the over-rationalisation of goods through indication of age range and gender suitability (using written labels or a sliding scale display) and the use of fixed pricing labels, according to informants' comments, proved the least appealing approach. Potential purchasers are more interested in the subjective opinions of the stallholder than objective labelling. The stories or 'biographies' of the goods do not just operate as forms of authentication but as insights into the knowledge and values of the previous owner. As Smith (1989) describes in his study of auction houses, price acts as a crucial means of constructing social value and consensus within the social relations of the sale. Crucially, the interaction between the women over potential exchanges at the nearly new sale creates a form of sociality and consensus making that ultimately feeds back into the inter-household informal economy of used children's clothing discussed at the beginning of this chapter.

Keeping While Giving: Protecting Inalienability and Constructing Value

Contrary to popular images of marauding women at jumble sales or housewifely bargain hunters eyeing up the best cut of meat, women at these nearly new sales adhere to a particular style of decorum. Like Smith's (1989) depiction of auctions, the actors of the nearly new sale exercise courtesies and allegiances in their trading community. Despite spending most of their time avidly concentrating on the wares set out before them, and on the method for best traversing a chaotic and crowded church hall turned market place, filled with the sound of impatient toddlers and excited transactions, the women dress as if for a social event. In the winter many sport fashionable hats and functional but trendy coats with bright lipstick. They are dressed in a fashion that would not easily translate to the formal shopping expedition of a West End high street but which, in its studied informality, is by no means thrown together or everyday. Leggings are worn with colourful baggy jumpers and scarves; hiking boots with woolly socks depict a kind of active urban woman rather than a provincial high street shopper. The nearly new sales shoppers are dressed for action as they move from stall to stall holding babies, bags and potential purchases simultaneously.

Amongst the chaos of the sale, informants frequently 'recalled' items on stalls that might be of relevance to other mothers as friends and acquaintances. Similarly, many attendees of the sales could not resist the temptation of purchasing goods for absent friends or women they had become familiar with through other mother-related activities (such as picking the children up from school). Sandra, for example, spotted a collection of children's books written in Finnish. As she remembered a certain mother (absent from the sale) had just employed a Finnish nanny she bought the whole lot, despite her own severely limited budget. She justified the purchase on the grounds of serendipity and an imagined scenario in which the absent mother's nanny might read bedtime stories to the children in a native language. It seems incongruous that a low-income mother (with two of her own young children to support) should chose to buy such an obscure but thoughtful gift for another considerably more affluent mother (apparently too busy with her career to attend the sale herself). Yet, in exercising such a finely honed expression of her con-sumptive skills and motherly imagination Sandra's monetary limitations were superseded by a form of sociality that stands for the nearly new sale as a whole.

Purchased from a formal retail outlet as a pre-meditated gift, the Finnish storybooks would have proved utterly inappropriate. But given to another absent mother as mementoes and trophies from a missed LMG nearly new sale, they increased Sandra's status as a mother and potential friend whilst reiterating the shared currency of the event.

Friendship is also commonly initiated directly through the transferral of second-hand wares. Several informants spoke of receiving bin liners full of baby clothes from female neighbours; comparative strangers previously unrecognisable to them except perhaps in passing on the street. The arrival of a new-born child prompted gestures of familiarity, manifest in the gifting of second-hand clothes, which many women had not previously or subsequently experienced. There was a blurred distinction drawn, however, between the 'lending' and the giving of clothes; a blurring which added to the precariousness of the second-hand trafficking process in general. Relatives, close friends or potential close friends might hand over a consignment of baby clothes on the premise that certain earmarked items were expected to be returned to their original donor after a certain stage of a baby's development. This arrangement was often based on an unspoken understanding that mothering, whilst temporal, could never be fully completed. Even women who openly discussed their resistance to having any further children expressed superstition in totally relinquishing their ownership of some of their baby-related wares. Obviously in some cases this was confined to articles of sentimental or familial value (hand-knitted cardigans or particularly memorable garments) but it also applied to more apparently functional wares.

Neither gifts nor commodities, used baby and children's clothes warrant a form of exchange closer to Weiner's (1992) theory of inalienable possessions (a paradox of 'keeping-while-giving' in which possessions must *not* be given, and if they are circulated, must be returned to the donor) than Herrmann's view of 'inalienable commodities' or Gregson and Crewe's 're-enchanted commodities'. The acquisition of such goods transcends the desire of the individual and notions of possession associated with other types of 'owned goods'. The transactions of the nearly new sales act as modes of exchange which perpetuate the status of used baby and children's clothing as a specific form of material culture associated with women's biological and cultural reproduction and ensuing social relations.

The creation of a market place in second-hand children's clothes, within an already established culture of clothing exchange, is obviously motivated neither by economic imperative or functional necessity alone. Rather, it operates as a public arena in which the 'trafficking' of the semi-devotional goods of babies and children is celebrated and the knowledges and skills of mothering practised. In relation to garage sales in contemporary United States Herrmann argues that their predominance is directly linked to the demise of 'earlier face-to-face means of distributing used goods to those who could most use them (e.g., clothing exchanges or extended kinship networks)' (1997: 916). Clearly, clothing exchanges thrive in the North London setting and nearly new sales have not merely arisen as a replacement for an authentic form of what Herrmann describes as 'social egalitarian' exchange. It is through this market place and its monetary transactions that the significance of caring and nurturing and the isolation of housework are countered by the significance of friendships and women's sociality. The perpetuation of this sociality relies on the status of the material culture and its relevance, not just to babies and children themselves, but to the social dimensions of women's identities as mothers.

Like other alternative arenas of consumption, such as car boot and garage sales, nearly new sales are defined by the face-to-face transactions between buyers and sellers (offering personal possessions as goods), the negotiation of a non-fixed pricing system and a heterogeneity of goods. As Gregson and Crewe (1997a) point out, in their study of car boot sales in Britain, the act of purchase is woefully over-simplified in consumption literature (tied as it is to assumptions regarding transactions in formal retail environments). Through interviews they contextualise the purchases of car boot consumers exploring the intended use of purchases as gifts, ornaments, renovated objects and potential commodities for further exchange arguing that the practices of acquisition and the meanings of goods are inseparable spheres.

Comparable approaches to alternative spaces of provisioning, such as Herr-mann's study of garage sales in the United States, self-avowedly 'emphasize the social relations of exchange rather than the items that change hands' (Herrmann 1997: 911). For Herrmann the material culture of garage sales is generalised as 'the manufactured effluvia of late 20th century American household' (1997: 916). It is gift giving, in the guise of market exchanges, which transforms these fungible goods into inalienable commodities. Rather than the invisible hand of the market place, it is the seller at the garage sale who controls the price and 'the social relations of the exchange' and these vary according to the face-to-face encounter of each transaction.

Similarly, according to Gregson and Crewe the act of purchase is the means by which goods are 're-enchanted'; through ritual and performance, they are divested of their original owner's associations, and re-invented as possessions by their purchasers. Despite the similarities between garage, car boot and nearly new sales both Herrmann and Gregson and Crewe's work emphasises the significance of face-to-face transactions in creating the meaning of 'possession' for the consumer in a way that is not easily equated with the practices of the nearly new sale. They talk, for example, of ridding objects of the 'contamination' of the previous owner and, whilst valuing the 'history' of second-hand goods, seeking to re-appropriate them through renovation, etc. Although children's clothes are bought and altered the material culture of the nearly new sales, I propose, is better understood as 'lent' rather than 'possessed'. Nearly new sales are understood as part of an ongoing trajectory, rather than as finite, singular events. Their objects are never fully divested of their original owner's associations for invested in them are the knowledges of 'mother swapping'.

Conclusion: Consensus and a Papoose Only Policy?

Apart from the occasional flare up over mis-pricing, nearly new sales are defined more by co-operation than the competition associated with popular notions of jumble sale bargain hunters. Buggies, however, and their increasingly impatient occupants have become an increasingly controversial issue at these events which has prompted discussion over a proposed 'Papoose Only Policy'.

Although the hall is relatively spacious, when filled with around twenty-five stalls, eighty women and thirty abandoned push-chairs freedom of movement to view the hall becomes restricted. For despite the apparent child-centred nature of the events women use various strategies to relieve themselves of the buggies and their children and so render themselves 'hands free' to scout around and circulate. One informant who regularly attends sales initially used to take her buggy to the far side of the hall and leave her sleeping toddler by the women at the tea stand, checking him at regular intervals. This ploy, however, required the child to be sleeping, a rare and luxurious treat. It also proved contentious since word of a number of regrettable 'incidents' involving unsupervised toddlers at the nearly new sales had been getting round. Several informants independently and un-prompted retold the story of a two-year-old found outside on the street unattended having wandered off from her mother who was happily engrossed in bargain hunting in the church hall sale. Although no one would name the mother of the child, this indicated, by consensus, that things were getting out of control and that the interests of children were no longer forming the focus of such gatherings. At another weekend sale a leading and admired Ibis Pond organiser (described by one informant as a 'big chief mother') condemned the use of buggies in the hall outright and the neglect of the children parked in them. She had reached the point of proposing a total ban on buggies and planned an announcement to appear in the next newsletter. This signalled a move towards a 'papoose only' policy in the future that would ensure women would not abandon their children in favour of bargain hunting. Obviously there were inherent contradictions in this debate – a mothers' group proposing to ban mothers with buggies would effectively preclude those women with children larger than 'papoose' carrying age or those without daytime childcare. Essentially this moral debate focused on whether or not children's needs were being neglected at such events; 'I think they're really awful places for children, really boring,' said one informant. Another, however, regaled at how much her little girl enjoyed playing with other toddlers in cardboard boxes amongst the stalls.

The 'papoose only policy' contention reveals the nearly new sale as a moral rather than merely economically motivated community. It also reveals the tension between women's roles as carers and provisioners and their desire for increased sociality. In transient urban populations, such as the street in North London, where women caring for children have limited access (due to restrictions of time, finances and social worlds) to places of sociality such as work, social clubs and other non-domestic activities (Allen 1996), 'community' is effectively built around children. The nearly new sales, the public spectacle of 'trafficking' in children's clothes as an alternative form of provisioning, brings the chaotic aesthetics of the bazaar to an urban North London setting. Through these events, their prices, transactions, exchanges and social relations, consensus around mothering is created. Like Smith's challenge to economic models of auctions (as expressions of rational economic man in the purest form), the transactions of nearly new sales 'are not exclusively or even primarily exchange processes. They are rather processes for managing the ambiguity and uncertainty of value by establishing social meanings and consensus' (Smith 1989: 163). Pricing at such events, unlike Herrmann's description of garage sales, is far from arbitrary. Rather it is the means of measuring shared knowledge and of amending and negotiating the social construction of value.

For some informants nearly new sales represent part of a broader move towards ethical forms of consumption, in which goods are recycled and the alienation of conventional retail outlets countered. Aside from this self-conscious and class-based understanding of second-hand consumption nearly new sales operate implicitly as alternative modes of consumption.

Through these sales with their 'mother swapping' transactions and entre-preneurial flourishes, women valorise, transform and contest their knowledge as mothers. The domestic work of women is taken through dealing, trafficking, talk and banter, into the public realm of the market and back in to the intra-household relations of the 'hand-me-down' clothing economy. Like the gypsy horse-traders of Hungary (Stewart 1992) who continue to sell horses at a loss in order to maintain their cultural advantage over the economically superior peasants with whom they trade, mothers, turned traders, 'traffic' their goods on the periphery of an otherwise hostile market (filled with over-priced Disney merchandise and Telly-Tubby jigsaw puzzles). The material culture of babies and children, its aesthetics, maintenance and acquisition constitutes the expertise of women's work and social relations as much as horses (as opposed to other forms of cattle) are linked to the cultural status of Hungarian gypsies. Although these entities are traded they are never, for the gypsies at the horse-fair or mothers at the nearly new sale, reduced to alienable commodities. For they are the means, through the market, by which a degree of control is exerted over the outside world. Such venues are used by women, not to perpetuate their work as mothers, carers and provisioners, but rather to invert such roles in the creation of an alternative commercial culture.

References

Allen, G. (1996), *Kinship and Friendship in Modern Britain*, Oxford: Oxford University Press.

Andrews, M. (1997), *The Acceptable Face of Feminism: The Women's Institute as a Social Movement*, London: Lawrence and Wishart.

Corrigan, P. (1995), 'Gender and the gift: The case of the family clothing economy' in S. Jackson and Moores (eds), *The Politics of Domestic Consumption*, Hemel Hempstead: Harvester Wheatsheaf.

Devault, M. (1991), *Feeding the Family*, Chicago: Chicago University Press.

Geertz, C., Geertz, H. & Rosen, L. (eds) (1979), *Meaning and Order in Moroccan Society*, Cambridge: Cambridge University Press.

Gregson, N. and Crewe, L. (1997a), The bargain, knowledge, and the spectacle: making sense of consumption in the space of the car-boot sale' *Environment and Planning: Society and Space*, Vol. 15, pp. 87–112.

—— (1997b) 'Performance and Possession: Rethinking the Act of Purchase in the Light of the Car Boot Sale' in *Journal of Material Culture*, Vol. 2, pp. 241–63.

—— (1998), 'Dusting Down *Second Hand Rose*: gendered identities and the world of second-hand goods in the space of the car boot sale' *Gender, Place and Culture*, 5, 1: 77–100.

Herrmann, G. (1997), 'Gift or Commodity: What Changes Hands in the U.S. Garage Sale?' *American Ethnologist*, 24 (4): 910–30.

Herrmann, G. and Soiffer, S. (1984), 'For Fun and profit: an anaylsis of the American garage sale', *Urban Life*, 12: 397–421.

Kopytoff, I. (1986), 'The Cultural Biography of Things: commoditization as process' in Appadurai, A. (ed.), *The Social Life of Things*, Cambridge: Cambridge University Press.

Miller, D. (1997), 'How infants grow mothers in North London', *Theory, Culture and Society*, 14(4): 67–87.

—— (1998) *A Theory of Shopping*, Cambridge: Polity Press.

Smith, C. (1989), *Auctions: The Social Construction of Value*, Hemel Hempstead: Harvester Wheatsheaf.

Stewart, M. (1992), 'Gypsies at the Horse-Fair: A Non-Market Model of Trade' in Dilley, R. (ed.), *Contesting Markets: Analyses of Ideology, Discourse and Practice*, Edinburgh: Edinburgh University Press.

Weiner, A. (1992), *Inalienable Possessions*, Berkeley: University of California Press.

5

Narratives of Consumption and the Body in the Space of the Charity/Shop

Nicky Gregson, Kate Brooks and *Louise Crewe*

This chapter presents some of the initial findings and formulations from an ongoing project on charity shops and retro shops as spaces of second-hand exchange and consumption, and is intrinsically linked to previous research on car boot sales (Gregson and Crewe 1997a, 1997b; Gregson, Crewe and Longstaff 1997; Crewe and Gregson 1998; Gregson and Crewe 1998). Briefly stated, our argument is that debates on second-hand exchange and consumption have much to contribute to furthering our theoretical and empirical knowledges of contemporary consumption. More specifically, we maintain that this investigation makes four significant interventions in these debates. First, the analysis of second hand enables us to extend existing, often rehearsed, arguments regarding the necessity of thinking in terms of chains of production and consumption to acknowledge that this is not simply about chains of production linked to an end point of first-cycle consumption (Jackson 1993; Jackson and Thrift 1995), but that these chains extend to encompass further cycles of exchange and consumption too. So, goods are not only potentially resaleable but are open to re-enchantment; they have consumption histories and geographies just as much as production histories and geographies, and such characteristics need recognition in our analyses (and see too Kopytoff 1986; Appadurai 1986). Secondly, an analysis of second hand forces us to think hard about spaces of exchange. As we have argued before, one of the features of contemporary research in the consumption field is its tendency to think not just in terms of discrete spaces, but to emphasise hegemonic spaces, notably the nineteenth-century department store and its late twentieth-century counterpart, the mega-mall (Blomley 1996; Chaney 1990; Domosh 1996; Dowling 1993; Goss 1993; Lancaster 1995; Morris 1991; Nava 1995; Porter-Benson 1986; Reekie 1993). Quite apart from re-inscribing their dominance, such foci also pose problems for thinking about other spaces of exchange. Indeed, they encourage us to think about these other spaces as in some way/s alternative to, counterposed to, these dominant spaces; as understood on their terms and in their terms. By contrast, in our research we prefer to think in terms of the relationality and simultaneity of second-hand and first-cycle spaces of exchange (Gregson and Crewe 1997a). Moreover, we argue that this relationality itself exposes to consumers the workings of power in consumption, and is suggestive of the potential of second hand for consumer resistance/s (Gregson and Rose 2000; Miller and Rose 1997). Thirdly, the analysis of second-hand exchange and consumption opens up an increasing depth of understanding of the complex motivations and imperatives at work within contemporary consumption and their negotiation by individuals. Empirically, for example, our previous work together with that of Alison Clarke on *Loot* (Clarke 1998) points to the importance and potency of the conjuncture of thrift and the bargain with fun, laughter and pleasure, and with the development of specialist, accumulated practical and localised knowledges which are a feature of various forms of second-hand exchange and consumption. Fourthly, and finally, we would point to the way in which the second-hand arena alerts us to the critical differences between commodities. So, for example, there are worlds of difference between goods such as uncooked foods on the one hand, which – whilst they might be capable of resale – are impossible to consume second hand, and second-hand clothing, books/magazines, furniture, household appliances and so on on the other, which are not only re-saleable but open to further and possibly different uses too. But there are other important differences between those goods which have potential consumption biographies, and these we maintain relate to their differential inscription with discourses of the body. Thus, whereas goods such as cookers, TVs, electrical appliances, books, CDs, records, tables and chairs may well have been subjected to highly personalised possession rituals, they remain relatively immune to bodily discourses. In comparison, second-hand clothing and key items of furniture, notably beds and bedding, are not. Instead, their consumption as second-hand goods requires the negotiation of their previous bodily associations and potential histories.

In this chapter our focus is on the last of these issues. Specifically, we confine our attentions to the purchase of second-hand adults' clothing within the space of the charity shop.[1] Drawing on a range of materials including extended periods of participant observation working in contrasting charity shops in Sheffield and Weston super Mare (one a large national organisation with numerous shops, the

---

1. As Alison Clarke's chapter in this volume, together with our research on car boot sales (Gregson and Crewe 1998) indicates, children's clothing is a different case altogether, interestingly relatively immune from the concerns of this chapter. We suspect that this has much to do with the provisional, pure, unsullied construction of the child's body in comparison to that of the adult, particularly with respect to leakiness. Indeed, we would suggest that, notwithstanding the frequent and often extreme leakiness of young children's bodies, this body remains unmediated by the (sexual) constructions which characterise the leaky adult body.

other a nationally based charity with one shop), as well as briefer periods of participant observation, interviews with charity shop management, volunteers and charity shoppers, we argue that charity shops are spaces of exchange inscribed with and constituted in part through narratives of the body, as well as spaces which work to recite normative constructions of the body (see Douglas 1966; Foucault 1977; Grosz 1994; Shildrick 1997). Thus, the sale, purchase and consumption of adult clothing through charity shops are all shown to require the negotiation of various constructs of the bodily; the body as leaky excess; as polluting, contaminating, threatening other; as material, subject to disease and death.[2] We conclude the chapter by reflecting on the distinctiveness of second-hand adult clothing purchased through charity shops, arguing that the recent wearing of so much of this clothing gives it a corporeal quality quite unlike that of older clothing sold for instance through retro/vintage outlets.

Exchanging the Body: Repackaging and Revalorising Second-hand Clothing in Charity Shop Space

I have to ask, twice, what to do – and am put onto emptying the green sacks which are the -gasp with excitement – retro sacks (blue for mixed stuff, and the stuff that goes back to the depot. Black for ragbags) . . . This begins a very frustrating morning: as soon as I start anything, Nagwa comes over and takes over – by at one point elbowing me out of the way to 'supervise' what I am doing (the highly tricky job of putting something on a hanger and checking it for stains and holes. Rather disgustingly, when I ask if there's a clothes brush to brush off dry stains, hair etc Nagwa tells me to "use my hands"! Bleughhh!!) (KB: Shop B)

Camilla and I come to the rescue of a fab fur collared coat which, if it was any other style, would have been immediately binned but although mucky (covered in oil with holes in, as if bits of weave had been scraped off – this did in fact look like a coat someone had been run over in!!) was a marvellous Kookai type coat that despite muck and holes and possible tragic history we thought good enough to sell. In fact we both tried it on! I think someone will buy it at a cheapish price thinking it was worth risking it: dry cleaning and dyeing may sort it out. (KB: Shop B)

So stuff is fairly brutally sorted out, but the quality of the stuff is markedly better than the crusted, flea ridden offerings I am continually fishing out of Shop A sacks . . . As Bernie says, here they have a "crotch control". No crusty crotches!! . . . Stuff here [is] all fragrant and folded and everything. (KB: Shop C)

---

2. Elsewhere we discuss the ways in which the charity shop connects with the lived experience of the body and how this in turn relates to normative constructions of the feminine body in first-cycle spaces of exchange.

As the above extracts suggest, when working as volunteers in charity shops the importance of the bodily in relation to second-hand clothing is never far away. Spatially, for example, charity shops exemplify Goffman's 'front' and 'back' zones, with their distinctively different bodily associations (Goffman 1959). So, whilst some of the work of the volunteer is that of the shop sales assistant (working on the till, restocking and tidying display areas etc.), much, much more occurs in the back shop zone, a space characterised for us by the distinctive smell of collections of second-hand clothing; a crusty, musty, fuggy, distinctive bodily aroma. And it is here, to the back shop zone, that bags of 'donations' come in, to be stacked up in the sorting area. Typically, they are black binliners, of the type usually reserved for household rubbish and refuse tips. And, for us, just as for those volunteers we worked with, there was a never failing hesitancy about opening them up. For one, there is the all-pervasive smell on opening. Then there is the visual: just what is going to be inside this? What unsavoury nightmares might there be lurking inside? Where are the rubber gloves? Fear; the unknown Other; discarded matter; dirt; the need to protect ones own bodily surfaces; all these thoughts, emotions and narratives run through the head. And then there is sorting. What amongst these mountains of discarded clothing is acceptable and what is unacceptable? What, with washing and/or a spot of ironing/steaming is retrievable? What is just 'raggable', altogether too threadbare, holey, 'bobbly', tired, smelly, stained? Here it is the degree of presence of previous owner/s, their traces in the clothing and their in/eradicability which matters. Volunteering in charity shops then, particularly the hours spent sorting through bags of donated goods, is fundamentally about discourses of the body and their negotiation. It requires, for example, one to cope with the associations which surround other people's discarded clothing; notably the tacit knowledge that frequently the clothes donated to charity shops are not just 'chuck-outs' but the discarded effects of the dead. Goods which are no longer needed by their owners and no longer wanted by those who donate them. Symbolic of loss, sadness, bereavement, unwanted memories, these garments enter the charity shop, whereupon one chapter of their biography closes and another (potentially) opens up. Yet it is the volunteer who makes these critical decisions, who decides just which of these effects are still usable, wearable, re-enchantable, and which are not. Who negotiates in short the taboo of dead people's clothing. And then there is a range of issues about bodily dirt. Sorting through discarded clothing forces one to acknowledge the constructedness of one's own body boundaries and surfaces, as well as one's own personal hygiene/bodily dirt thresholds and their day-to-day variability, compared with those one works with and those who donate. It also emphasises the importance of the absence of previous bodily traces – visible and olfactory – in selling second-hand clothing, for what is all the subsequent steaming and cleaning about but the erasure of bodily presences – stains, smells, fluids.

And for those whose task is currently to reconstitute the charity shop, to recast its image through the discourses of retail capital, the bodily is critical too. Here, for example is one charity shop manager talking about the passage of goods from donation to the shop floor:

Sue: . . . generally we get all sorts – absolute rubbish which is no good to anyone.

Nicky: So do you have quite stringent criteria on what actually goes out?

Sue: Yes, I'm quite strict about what goes out; I have full control [laughter] – when I have a day off, I get one day off and it's generally Monday, so on Tuesday the first thing I do is get in that room and look at what they've lined up and I don't want some of it, so it's "I'm not putting out that". So if it's not sort of black bag-able – real rubbish – then I put it in a green bag for another shop – I'm not putting it out but they might. So I do that. I don't want old fashioned stuff or stuff with a hole in.

Nicky: So it's got to be clean and tidy?

Sue: Yes, stuff that we can wash and dry – we have that – but it's got to be worth washing and drying – we can't wash everything. Most of the stuff that comes in, a lot of it is alright; it's fine – and we have a steamer that gets all the creases out which is fine – and some of the stuff which comes in it's all crumpled, but that steamer gets all of that out, it's fantastic.

Nicky: So absolutely everything that's on the shop floor has passed your quality control?

Sue: Yes! Having experienced things before [in another shop where she worked as a volunteer]. It depends how much control you have up here. I suppose if I was doing something else then it would get put down, but then it's up to me to keep an eye on what's going on in the shop. I try to stop it before it goes down.

Washing and ironing then, those classic cleansing, purifying rituals, are a key component in the biography of the clothes which pass through this space. Much of this, given the over-riding importance of 'professionalisation' within the charity shop sector at present, is about presenting second-hand clothing as if it is new. And presenting it thus, repackaging it, requires the elimination of all traces of previous ownership. Hence the washing, ironing and steaming. Likewise, for this charity shop as for all charity shops, weekly sales targets are of primary importance and, whilst washing and ironing represent an increase in fixed costs, their effect – a greater likelihood of sale – is considered to outweigh this. Washing, ironing and steaming then add value to second-hand clothing. And yet there is more to what is going on here than just value and sales. As Sue says, she has her standards; she exercises an extreme form of quality control, surveillance and discipline in the constitution of this space. One gets a strong sense from this extract then that it is her own personal negotiations of the discourses of bodily dirt which are at work here, shaping the geographies of these goods. And that the shop floor itself, symbolically downstairs away from the sorting zones, is somewhere to be protected from potential pollution, from the contamination threats of certain types of second-hand clothing and from clothing which fails to reach certain (visual and olfactory) standards of acceptability.

And that there are these potential contaminating, polluting categories of second-hand clothing for charity shops is signalled most clearly perhaps by the absence from the charity shop floor of certain types of clothing: notably underwear and night attire. Working as volunteers, both were categories which were left unsorted. Deemed unsuitable for regular sale, repositaries of unsavoury dirt, these were discarded immediately, and on the explicit instruction of shop management: "we don't sell underwear"; "we don't sell nightwear". The tacit implication being that these items are sordid, tainted and tainting through association; garments which are too personal and intimate, even if seemingly clean or new. They are then, garments which are considered counterproductive to the professional image currently being constructed by charity shops, dangerous goods for the more professional charity shop. And yet, until recently at least, Sheffield charity shops would temporarily subvert such sales restrictions, saving up 'back shop' all items of donated nightwear for release onto the shop floor in the week preceding Pyjama Jump, a student organised charity fund-raising event requiring the wearing of second-hand night attire, preferably bought from a charity shop. Although now banned the event speaks eloquently to the points we are making here – risky, tainted, taboo clothing (you can't wear your own); stored and stacked away from the charity shop floor, precisely because of its contaminating associations. By contrast, however, other categories of clothing carry a greater degree of ambivalence, uncertainty. Notable in this respect are those which get reworked through the discourse of fashion. Indeed, a classic instance of this would be the late 1990s reclamation of slips, to be worn either as an 'outer-wear' dress or, more frivolously, as fancy dress. So, for example, working in Shop B, we regularly had differences of opinion with other volunteers over their status, or for that matter over certain brands of trainers. Deemed by us to be fashion items, and therefore eminently saleable, for other (older) volunteers these forms of clothing clearly transgressed certain boundaries of acceptability. Worn either close to the body (slips) or associated with strong personalisation and/or disease (shoes), they constructed them as polluted and polluting; as unsuitable goods to place on the shop floor.[3]

We come back to explore this notion of the (re)constitution of body boundaries through specific categories of second-hand clothing later in relation to charity shoppers, but for the moment we wish to make a further point about the production

3. Although beyond the category of second-hand adult clothing with which we are concerned here, it is important to add that sheets, bedding and mattresses constitute another set of dangerous, risky second-hand goods. Excluded from the space of many charity shops, particularly from those which construct themselves as professional, we suggest that it is the inscription of such items with the bodily which work to construct them as dangerous, risky, contaminating items.

of charity shop space through narratives of the body. This concerns the importance of the olfactory. Specifically, the importance of the absence of noxious and/or unacceptable bodily smells from charity shop space. Here, for example, is one charity shop manager talking about precisely this issue:

> Carol: . . . if we were on X Street, where all Kookai and things like that are, then we'd get that sort of people in. But because this is sort of alternative, and people are into that kind of thing, we do get people who are into that kind of thing. Though there are some who go "oh this is nice; a charity shop that doesn't smell!!" – laughter . . .

Moreover, the overwhelming smells of frequently-squirted air fresheners, together with the heavily scented pot pourri, soaps, scented candles and incense which feature strongly amongst the new goods sold by certain charities, seem to us to testify strongly to the critical import of smell. Indeed, we would argue that it is precisely because the goods sold by charity shops are second hand, and precisely because of the crusty smells which are conventionally associated with them, that it is important for those shops which construct themselves as professional to smell acceptable, fragrant, freshly perfumed even.

So, when we look at the production of charity shop space through the practices of charity shop managers and volunteers, the bodily is an ever-present trace. Inscribed in and defining of second-hand clothing, narratives of the body are used to assess, reject and accept donations; to repackage and sell them on. Too much bodily presence, be this conveyed through signs of leaky, messy bodies, just too much general wear or smell, spells rejection. By contrast, that which displays little trace of ownership, which looks as new or which can be rejuvenated through cleansing, purifying, freshening rituals, is to be valued; a garment which can realise further value precisely because of what it lacks. Turning now to charity shoppers, we find much the same set of bodily narratives and practices at work in the purchase and consumption of second-hand clothing.

Purchasing and Consuming the Body: Second Hand Clothing and Shopping with the Unknown Other

In the course of a year spent researching charity shopping we encountered little if any variation on the ideas articulated in this section. For those who engage in charity shopping, just as much as for those who do not, it is narratives of the body and the inscription of the body within second-hand clothing which provide some of the central discourses to be negotiated in the act of charity shopping. So, whereas for some the associations of second-hand clothing with unknown other, possibly dead, bodies is sufficient to deter them from even entering the space of the charity shop, let alone making any such purchases, for others, as we see here, these same associations continue to shape both purchasing decisions and the activities of second-hand clothing consumption.

Negotiating bodily dirt and reconstructing body boundaries: practices of erasure and re-incorporation

As with most research projects, getting people to talk about why they don't do something – in this case charity shopping – as opposed to why they do proved a difficult exercise, and one which we abandoned at a relatively early juncture of the research (and see too Barker and Brooks 1998). Requiring high levels of self-reflexivity as well as suggestive of charity shopping as a normative practice, such attempted discussions often floundered around at the level of "I don't know why I don't but I don't", whereas others talked about their construction of the practice of charity shopping (difficult, time-consuming, rummaging) as compared with the perceived ease, accessibility and ready-packaged nature of first-cycle shopping. Nevertheless, buried within a number of our interview transcripts, particularly those of young(er) charity shoppers, are numerous suggestive comments regarding the prohibitions on charity shopping – a fair few of which connect with the bodily, but which also reflect the mediations of the body with discourses of class. The following extract exemplifies what is at stake here. This is Sharon, a twenty-something student, discussing the difficulties which charity shopping had posed for her during her teenage years.

Sharon: Like when I was 14 or so and I used to charity shop, and there were these girls that used to hate me. They walked past when I was in one, and you get stick about it, and from then on in I was just like looking to see who was going past. So at some points you do feel a bit more self conscious because of the associations with second hand clothes and the lack of money and not being able to afford new clothes . . . Like I got a really nice shirt and I remember I got it for 79pence. And like it was a Marks and Spencers shirt. And one of my friends said it was really nice, "How much?" "79p!" "What!!" "From a charity shop!!" And that would get mixed reactions. Some would say, "Oh that's a really good bargain" sort of thing, and others would be going, "Oh what a skeg!"
Nicky: What's a skeg?
Sharon: Just sort of urmmmm – I dunno – laughs
Nicky: What's it mean?
Sharon: Just sort of urm, not caring what you're wearing sort of thing. Like not quite a smellie. Like a smellie is living out of a bag, and then you've got skeggies. So I got called a skeg occasionally.

As we see here, second-hand adult/teenage clothing is something which many people find problematic, and what is problematic about it is precisely its associations with *unknown* other people's bodies. So, whilst it is perfectly acceptable to wear the "hand-me-downs" of known, if somewhat distant even, familial relatives, it most definitely is far more risky to engage with those of unknown others. As Sam, a twenty-something secretary said to us, "you don't know where it's been". Second-hand clothing then is inscribed with notions of risk and fear, and these risks are particularly acute for the working class. So, for young working-class girls such as Sharon, or indeed Sam, there is just too much at stake here; too much to risk (and see too Skeggs 1997). Risks which, as McRobbie (1989) has pointed out, are just not the same for their middle-class counterparts.[4] Second-hand clothing then is, in short, polluted and, as Sharon's comments make plain, potentially polluting for those who wear it. Its purchasing and consumption have the potential to make one "a skeg", "a smellie", dirt, matter out of place; to label one as dangerous, non-conforming; different. Such then are the meanings inscribed in it; meanings which locate this clothing within a set of bodily discourses which construct those who purchase such clothing as at best rebellious and/or different, at worst plain deviant; and which work to prevent or at least deter many from engaging in the activities of charity shopping, or at least from openly admitting to so doing. Others, however, clearly do engage in the risky practices of charity shopping, and some have no choice but to do so. But as we see now though, these same discourses of the bodily continue to be cited and negotiated in the practices of charity shop shopping, purchasing and consumption.

Shopping, for example, as the following extracts from our field diaries show, is mediated by many of the olfactory and visual boundaries discussed previously:

Round the corner to another "Oh MY God!!" one – this is XXXX, which we both can't bear the stink in. It reeks at the door of human vomit! And the smell doesn't really go off once you're in there. So we beat a hasty retreat. I wonder just how the people in there can stand it: don't they have any sense of smell? Once again, we've reached our boundaries of what we find acceptable in a shop – even a charity shop. (NG, fieldnotes)

We cross the road and the first thing we both say is "car boot sale", and yes it is, because stuff in this shop spews out onto the street in front of the shop . . . As we go in I'm passed by an older guy in a leather jacket (very old and very tired), grubby trousers,

---

4. It is also worth emphasising that charity shopping, at least as we observed this, is an overwhelmingly white activity, unlike shopping in second-hand shops, or participating in nearly new sales or car boot sales. Again, researching this construction is potentially problematic, but we feel the whiteness of charity shopping to be highly significant; notably in terms of what it says about charity and the production of charity shops through volunteer labour (overwhelmingly white, female, elderly and middle class), and in terms of the geographical location of charity shops within predominantly middle-class neighbourhoods and/or city centres.

who just reeks and who evidently hasn't washed in years. And then the smell in this shop hits us. This isn't just the bog standard moth balls; this is filthy and conjures up immediate associations for me with fleas and nits. The clothes look as if they're covered in layers of grime and even flicking through things is more than an effort. (NG, fieldnotes)

Critically, as both extracts make apparent, it is the smells of bodily leakage – specifically vomit and perspiration – which act as the boundary markers here; the presences which render certain charity shop spaces problematic, no-go areas. Equally, as the second extract makes clear, a preponderance of dirty, unkempt, stained, soiled clothing can have the same effect. To draw too hard conclusions from these points however would be overblown. As many high investor charity shoppers said to us during the course of this research, rummaging is seen to be an important part of the pleasures of charity shopping. There can then be too much order, too much regularity in charity shop spaces; an order and a discipline which destroys the critical differences between charity shops and first-cycle shops. Yet, as these extracts make plain, the body remains a necessary discipline; a presence which can push certain charity shops beyond being attractive spaces for a rummage to ones where few wish to rummage.

Likewise, the activities of purchasing are riven through with the bodily. One of the most significant intimations of the importance here is revealed in the following extract. Here Val, a fifty-something secretary, talks about the ways in which she assesses potential charity shop purchases:

Val: . . . a lot of the stuff that you get in charity shops has hardly been worn, although one thing that I do do is to look at the label because if things have been washed a lot of times then the label usually washes out, and it gives a good idea of how old things are.
Nicky: Would that influence you in whether to buy something, how many times it seems to have been washed?
Val: In a way yes.
Nicky: So what are you actually looking for?
Val: I'm looking for something that's not very old, which hasn't been worn very much . . .

Note here the importance of the absence of signs of wear and of her assessment of the amount of times a garment has been washed, and therefore – by implication – the amount it has been worn and the amount of wear left in it. This is as important as her evaluation of potential purchases for flaws, holes and so on and so forth. Val is in short evaluating potential purchases in terms of their bodily traces. And this performance is one which was both re-enacted many times in front of us during the course of our participant observation, as well as something which we, as charity shoppers ourselves, engaged in too. Once selected out as potentially purchasable on the basis of style, size, colour etc. garments are subjected to the scrutiny of critique, and this scrutiny is as much about the presence/absence of the bodily as it is about price.

Beyond this though, and again as our research never failed to suggest, charity shoppers have clear distinct limits, boundaries, which they constitute through the purchase of second-hand clothing. They have categories of second-hand clothing which they just will not engage with, as well as categories which they will. So, in answer to the question "is there anything which you'd never look at in a charity shop?" we were consistently and without hesitation told "underwear" by everyone we interviewed. Moreover, the majority went on to add nightwear, shoes and bedding to their list:

I've never bought socks, I've never bought underwear, I've never bought shoes" (Simon, twenty- something student).

Kate B: So is there anything, would you ever buy shoes or underwear, that kind of thing?
Kate C: No I don't think I would. I've never seen, I mean I look at shoes in resale places, but you can always tell if someone's been wearing it, there's always something a bit odd about them.
Kate: So why wouldn't you, why won't you wear them then?
Kate: Just a feeling, shoes often look a bit scuffed, or dated, or they're a funny colour or an odd size usually.
Kate: And underwear, similar?
Kate: Oh certainly underwear. (Kate C, late 20s, university lecturer)

Kate: Would you buy things like shoes in charity shops?
Lydia: I'd be less happy about shoes to be honest cos of that whole foot infection number. I've had um some bizarre slipper things which came from a retro shop, but they, I think they were actually brand new. I think if it was hiking boots, sort of Doc Marten ones, I'd probably buy them, but then if they were wear next to your skin ones, or sort of court shoes I would think twice about that. But having said that I'd have a pair of shoes off somebody I knew.
Kate: Cos you know their infections!
Lydia: Well exactly. But also if you wear other people's shoes they're worn different, aren't they, cos it's very personal, how you wear your shoes down.
Kate: So it would be the fact that they were worn and also . . .
Lydia: Hygiene
Kate: Hygiene. What about underwear?
Lydia: Well as a rule, most charity shops, well you can't buy sort of, tight fitting knickers, as a rule. I mean, I'd buy a second-hand bra, cos a bra is only . . . I think it's all to do with what bits you're exposing. I mean I'd buy cami-knickers, probably, but they're not so tight. But they'd have to be clean. I'd have to wash them before I wore them . . . I wouldn't buy tight knickers . . .it's the gusset, it all comes down to gussets!! (Lydia, late 20s, technician)

This is clearly instructive, for as the above extracts all make abundantly clear, these excluded categories of clothing are the garments worn closest to the skin and/or items inscribed with strong normative narratives of personal hygiene. Clothing which practices instilled in childhood establish as necessary to be changed daily, to always be clean and which is constructed as highly personal, unique to the person. Which, on the basis of this evidence at least, has sufficient taboos surrounding it to render it non-transferable between persons and which make it consequently problematic within the second-hand arena.

There are, however, rather more subtle distinctions at work here too, which reveal the complex ways in which class might mediate decisions about which commodities are taboo. This is suggested strongly by the following extract involving a discussion with Rupert, a twenty-something graphic designer:

Louise: Is there anything you wouldn't buy at a charity shop?
Rupert: underwear, shoes.
Louise: What, even if you saw a fantastic pair of Paul Smith pants?
Rupert: Well, then I might have to reconsider because, by definition if they're Paul Smith boxers it's more likely that a young trendy person has worn them as opposed to an 80 year old grandad that hasn't washed.
Louise: So you don't mind the bodily odours of a young person?
Rupert: Well I do mind. It would have to be an exceptional pair. I'd be more likely to buy a pair of designer pants because a young person's worn them. I'd imagine they had a better body hygiene. And the fact that they're buying designer suggests that they're trying to pull, so they'd be especially careful about washing. They'd be washing hard.

Here Rupert reveals the potential for the disruption of the taboos surrounding certain categories of clothing. Whilst, in general, he makes it clear that he wouldn't consider purchasing underwear in a charity shop, he might – possibly – make an exception in exceptional circumstances. And this, as we see here, depends fundamentally on his construction of the type of body which he associates with Paul Smith underwear; a youthful, potentially sexual, scrupulously clean body, which he can identify with and which holds less fears for him than certain imagined others.

Beyond these problematic categories of clothing however lie others, ones which suggest that charity shop purchasing is riven through with notions of layering, layers which themselves are constructed in terms of risk and closeness to the body. As Tom (late 30s, graduate student) expressed it:

one of the things about the people in the glass factory that I used to work with, they all had a big thing about cleanliness, and urm for me, I think, I dunno, erhh. I think about how close they're going to be worn to me; how close they're going to be, like t-shirts and stuff like that, and trousers and socks. Though actually I haven't bought socks at a charity shop – maybe that's the reason why – reconstructing the body! – laughter.

So, whereas for some of our more casual charity shoppers, the extent of charity shop purchasing begins and ends at 'outer-wear' – coats and jackets – for others, typically those we have labelled 'high investors', it extends to encompass items worn increasingly closer to the skin – jumpers, tops, trousers. Abie, twenty-something and a student, is a classic example of the first tendency; an intermittent browser whose list of purchases runs to a couple of jackets. By contrast, Judy – fifty-something and a grandmother to a young baby – is a high investor, a woman who began her charity shopping "career" by buying the sorts of items currently being purchased by Abie – in her case a Windsmoor winter coat for £1.50. Later however, and as her skills and knowledges have developed, she has expanded her purchasing to include more tops, trousers, and the occasional pair of barely worn/unworn shoes/boots. This we can see from Box 1 which itemises her purchases over the year during which this research was being conducted.

Box 1: Charity shop purchases by clothing category (Judy)

Outer Wear (coats, jackets etc.): camel coat – £6; tweed jacket – 50p; green jacket – £2.99

Jumpers: grey wool – 50p; V-neck – £2.50; waistcoat (Principles); Monsoon jumper; M&S cardigan

Tops: mauve cotton polo – £2.50; white linen shirt (M&S) – £1.50; Laura Ashley top – £1.50; blue check shirt – £1; green top – £1; t-shirt – £1

Trousers: blue denim – £2; navy (Hammells) – £6; Navy – £4; 'jazzy' pair – £3.75; M&S leggings – £1.99; navy cotton – £1.99; black (Top Shop) – £3.50; Navy (M&S) – £1

Shoes: navy suede court – M&S – £3

Children's: cream dress – £1.50; dungarees – 60p; dungarees – £2.50; dress – 50p; trousers – 20p; top – 20p; sleepsuit – 9p; sleepsuit – £1.75; t-shirt – 89p; jacket, dungarees and vest – £2; sleepsuit; anorak

---

This pattern is one which we find interesting, one which we interpret as indicative of a progressive negotiation of the pollution taboos inscribed in various forms of second-hand clothing. So, the safest, least risky second-hand garments we maintain are those worn furthest away from bodily surfaces – coats, jackets, jumpers. Although worn by others, their inscription with the body of the unknown other, their pollution by this body, is less than that with other clothing categories. Small wonder then that these are the purchases which beginning charity shoppers frequently start off by making. By contrast, tops, dresses and trousers are riskier; clothes worn closer-in. Some of them come into close contact with intimate body zones; others have the potential to have absorbed various body fluids, notably perspiration, and – notwithstanding washing – often continue to display traces of these fluids. Purchasing such items then requires one to negotiate these pollution threats head-on, to place on one's own bodily surfaces clothing which has been similarly placed on and permeated by an unknown someone else. And as the following extracts make clear, there are various stages in this negotiation, steps which we suggest amount to a process of erasure and re-incorporation.

Barbara: . . . if it's got a mark on it and I don't know whether I'll be able to get it out then I will ask if I can have a bit off it, if it's something I really want, urm, but I had an unfortunate experience the other day. I don't want to put you off your tea! There was this rather nice little t-shirt, you know, it was a kind of rusty colour which I wanted. New Look. And I tried it on and it fitted very well, and I thought – "oh the smell". It was like somebody had thrown up on it. But there was no mark on it or anything, and I did say to the person, well it fits OK but it smells a bit. And she said, "well would you like it for 50p?" And I said, "no thanks, I don't want it for anything" – laughter
Kate: You weren't even tempted to take it home and wash it a few times?
Barbara: No, no. That's something I really draw the line at. I myself, if that happened to me I wouldn't even consider giving it to a charity shop. I'd throw it out . . . but on that same day there was a rather nice blue top, now that was a Debenhams, . . . and it had a little mark which could be white paint, so it might come off, or it could be bleach, and actually I don't think it has come off, but she did knock a pound off it, so I thought that's fair enough (Barbara, mid-50s, unemployed)

Lily: . . . I mean I don't buy underwear or anything like that, but I think that once something has been washed and pressed or dry cleaned and repaired, it's like nobody ever wore it before, and – there have been occasions where I've dry cleaned something twice!
Kate: What was that?
Lily: The suit I was talking about before, the pink and yellow suit. It was so lovely but it wasn't quite clean and I just really wanted it to go through again, I really, really did (Lily, mid-20s, fashion student and part-time model)

Lynne: . . . and there's a thing, I like a bag to be like new when I put all my things in it. I don't know why but, I suppose with the clothes you can wash them before you put them on, but with a bag it's harder to do.
Nicky: You mentioned something there that's really interesting, what sort of things do you do to clothes when you buy them at charity shops?
Lynne: I would say for the first time ever actually, a friend gave me a dress which she'd got from a charity shop and I wore it without washing it, and I was aware all day that it

didn't smell smell, but I was just aware that I wished I'd washed it before I wore it. But I always do wash everything before I wear them.

Nicky: And what's that about?

Lynne: I suppose because I'm never convinced that, although they say that they wash them and iron them and everything, I'm never convinced that they have. So I suppose that it makes it more mine if I wash it and iron it. It makes it sort of clean.(Lynne, early 40s, mature student)

What we find with all these items of closer-in clothing then is an initial pre-purchasing evaluation – "is this item stained?"; "what is this stain – bodily, non bodily?"; "does it smell?" Followed by further assessment grounded in a know-ingness around dirt, its removal and the distinctive differences between different forms of dirt: "can I remove this stain/smell?"; "Is this stain/smell unacceptable?"[5] Then, regardless of the visible and/or olfactory presence/absence of previous ownership, purchases of closer-in clothing are usually taken home and washed, a practice which we regard as highly symbolic.[6] This, in short, is the means by which the bodily presence of the unknown previous owner/s is erased; the means through which the taboos of wearing other people's clothes are countered; and – simult-aneously and critically – a means of personalising, of using one's own washing rituals to make a garment smell as if it belongs. The rituals of washing closer-in purchases then are practices of erasure and re-incorporation. They work to counter the polluting, contaminating threat of this previous unknown body and to recon-stitute clothing through the bodily associations of the self. Moreover, and unlike practices with outer-wear, which for the most part is worn without being subjected to further cleaning rituals,[7] such practices are clearly regarded as necessary acts prior to the wearing of closer-in second-hand garments. Cleansing, purifying and personalising, they work to protect the body's own protective surface, the skin; to reconstitute it, reconstruct it as a critical boundary, the imagined container of the self.

5. Indicative here of charity shoppers knowledgeability around different types of dirt is Barbara's distinctions between paint and bleach on the one hand (presences which she may have a go at eliminating) and human vomit (which she will not).

6. Just a few of our respondents – interestingly all men – admitted to occasionally not bothering about washing purchases. However, all acknowledged washing to be what ought to occur; they saw washing then as the normative practice. Rather than see their actions then as openly transgressive, we would interpret such lapses as 'permissable slips' (for men) to make, and 'permissable slips' to admit to us as women.

7. A number of our charity shop interviews made the point about not buying outer-wear which would clearly require dry cleaning, except in exceptional circumstances. Much of this is to do with the way in which paying for dry cleaning is seen to add to the cost of the garment, and therefore as negating any sense of capturing the saving through the bargain (and see too Gregson and Crewe 1997a).

Negotiating the death taboo: illness, disease and dead people's clothing

Whilst the pollution/contamination threats of bodily dirt constitute one set of bodily narratives to be negotiated by charity shoppers, the other is that of the association between charity shop clothing and the material effects of the recently deceased. An instance: one of the first charity shop purchases made by one of us (NG) years ago now, was of a man's tweed overcoat. Big, baggy, with raglan sleeves, it was bought entirely for its aesthetic qualities. Yet the response of my father to this purchase was immediate, and negative: "what do you want with a dead man's coat?!!" The same taboos are clearly at work in the following testimony:

Emma: I've got this little tale . . . My friend Kate works at this nursing home and an old lady died, and this old lady had some really nice clothes. Now I don't know what your view on this is! But these clothes, and a hat, went to some charity shops in Wythington, and I took the afternoon off work to go and try and find these clothes. Now everybody at work took the piss out of me chronic, saying it was really horrible and I was disgusting going to find dead women's clothes, but my point of view was, that woman's clothes were gonna go to somebody who would have loved them. I mean, OK it's really sad that this old lady died, you know, but she had like 'Penny round' shirts and 60s leather caps, and I would have loved and treasured those clothes.
Kate: Why couldn't you have had them before they gave them to a charity shop?
Emma: Well Kate was off work when she died! [laughter]
Martin: It's bloody body hunting!
Emma: They all thought I was really sick at work, and now they tell this, they relay this tale to everybody at the hostel: 'Emma's disgusting, she wears dead women's hats! She took half a day off work to go and look for a dead woman's hat!' Which I didn't even find I hasten to add! (Emma and Martin, twenty-something, Levenshulme Mods)

Similarly, in the following extract, Tom – a thirty-something graduate student – wrestles with some of the same associations:

Tom: . . . I have quite a lot of clothes for Sam from people that I know; things that their children have grown out of, which is really nice.
Nicky: Does that make a difference?
Tom: Yes, definitely.
Nicky: In what ways?
Tom: Because I guess that I know the stories behind the clothes, and how they were worn and who wore them, and whatever, and in some way, urm, getting stuff from charity shops has an added excitement to it, but what if you know this is from a dead child? What if this is from a dead child and they were wearing it when they died?

That Tom can come up with nothing by way of coherent reasons for why it might matter that these are the clothes someone might have died in is itself instructive.

Probably, he is right – there are no logical reasons why it should matter, but in articulating these ideas Tom suggests that somehow, in some imprecise, unspecified way which is impossible to pin down, it does. And what we think is going on here is the subconscious re-enactment, the re-articulation, of historical narratives which entwine the clothes of the recently dead with narratives of illness and disease. So, for my father, as he later told me, the fear of the dead man's overcoat is about a fear of the killer diseases which narratives absorbed in childhood identified as lingering on in clothing; specifically tuberculosis and scarlet fever. And similarly, as the following discussion amongst others of the same generation indicates, certain possession rituals enacted around coats would seem to have more than a little to do with oral and/or popular traditions concerning disease eradication procedures:

Kate: You don't mind wearing things that other people have worn?
Phil: Oh I usually like things I can wash, and if I don't wash them I put them in a plastic bag in the freezer and leave it for a few days.
Kate: Oh right!
Phil: Yes I read in a Good Housekeeping or something, because they're good as, then they're germ free you see.
Judy: There's a tip.
Kate: So what would you put in the freezer then, coats and things?
Phil: I shall put that dress actually, the one I paid out, although it's new I fancy it's got the smell of a charity shop.
Judy: Actually knitwear would be quite good.
Kate: Yes, you don't dry clean things then; you'd rather put them in the freezer?
Phil: If I can't put them in the washing machine. They're so expensive, cleaners!
Kate: Well you might as well, you spend about £2 on a coat . . .
Judy: Like that bear [fur] coat that I bought, it cost me £7 and to clean it would have cost £16! So I just hung it outside! It still smells like someone died in it though. I can't help it, I'm not paying that!
Phil: No I don't blame you, hang it outside in the fresh air on a frosty night, preferably.

So, notwithstanding various advances in understanding the processes of disease and virus transmission, and the power of discourses of scientific rationalism, these associations and connections remain, persisting within the popular imagination. Charity shop clothing, particularly adults' clothing, continues to be inscribed with death and disease, however 'irrational' this might be. And consuming these clothes, consequently, remains construed as a risky practice. All the washing, laundering, cleaning and so on then conducted in relation to second-hand charity shop clothing needs to be seen not just as about erasure and re-incorporation but as about discourses of health and disease too.

Conclusions

More broadly, there are two sets of conclusions which we would wish to draw from this discussion. The first concerns the complex ways in which value is inscribed in second-hand adult clothing and its intimate connections with the bodily. As we have seen, in the space of the charity shop both second-hand exchange value and use values rest on the absence and/or erasure of previous traces of ownership and consumption. Clothes which look 'as new', which have been barely worn, and/or which don't betray traces of wearing, command a higher price in charity shops than those which do, and it is these very same qualities which charity shoppers look for in assessing the exchange value and use value of garments. Moreover, wearing these clothes, opening them up to re-enchantment through consumption, accessing their second-hand use value, is frequently achieved through the cleansing, purifying rituals of washing. Although, as we have noted, even these practices fail to re-enchant certain categories of clothing, notably underwear and night attire. So, the value of second-hand adult clothing exchanged within charity shops can be said to vary; some categories are valueless, others have greater value, but seemingly this value is in all cases mediated through bodily presences/absences, rather than, as with first-cycle clothing, simply production costs.

And yet, as our research on both retro and vintage shops and our earlier discussion of slips as fashion suggests, this isn't quite all there is to second-hand adult clothing. Garments such as Victorian underwear, nightshirts and so on, the very categories of closest-in clothing which cause problems in the charity shop setting, become prized, sought after, relatively high value goods in the space of the retro or vintage shop. And practices of washing, laundering and certainly dry cleaning in relation to such clothing might be considered to be potentially damaging. This we find intriguing, and highly suggestive. It is as if distance, history and the authenticity encoded in such purchases over-ride the potential contamin- ation of the body here; as if the bodily loses its potential to contaminate with temporal distance. Whereas, with charity shop purchases no such mediations exist. Instead, by comparison, the majority of goods sold therein are of a relatively recent vintage, mass produced, closely entwined with the presence of their previous owner/ s – and therefore requiring of acts of symbolic release. So we would suggest that space, in this case the space of exchange, matters to the ways in which the bodily gets entwined within second-hand clothing. And – unlike retro and vintage shops – charity shops we maintain are constructed negatively in relation to the body. Bodily dirt, contamination, pollution are ever constant threats within, to and for charity shops. Associations which they continually have to negotiate and counter, which permeate and threaten to contaminate the goods they sell and which consequently loom large in the purchasing and consumption practices of charity shoppers themselves. All of which, of course, begs the question why? Why should it be that the adult clothing sold through charity shops be riven through with such associations?

The answers which we offer here are, of course, speculative rather than definitive, but they combine many of the points made during the course of the development of our argument. For one, and unlike the second-hand clothes exchanged between mothers at nearly new sales, or for that matter those exchanged at car boot sales, charity shop goods are cloaked in anonymity. We just do not know who has donated these items of clothing, what biographies lie within them, what histories and geographies they have. Rather there is only the unknown, the imagined. And this emphasis on the unknown Other we suggest is further compounded by the lack of temporal distance between the unknown charity shop donor and the purchaser. So, unlike the goods sold in retro and vintage shops, these goods are not ones which have acquired the safety of distance. Instead, and more riskily, they have for the most part been worn recently. And it is this combination of recent wearing with the unknown Other which we feel makes charity shop clothing particularly vulnerable to discourses of the bodily. In short this combination is one which we maintain places an emphasis on practices of containment and metaphorical layers; which reconstitutes the body as a surface capable of infiltration, porous, and consequently requiring of protection, protection from the lingering traces of the bodily presences of the unknown Other caught between the weft and the weave.

Ultimately then, as we have shown in this chapter, charity shop clothing, inscribed as it is through the bodily, is itself used to cite and recite the classic discourse of the Western, masculine body – sealed, contained and bounded, yet continually threatened by and needing protection from the polluting excesses of the leakiness of the feminised Other. Yet importantly this is a leakiness which is about more than just the body; a leakiness which goes beyond body boundaries and body fluids, which is imparted from the material body to the clothing which has covered it, and which remains within this clothing as a vestigial trace, the mark of possession. Clothing then is not just about fashion and adornment, body shape, disguise and aesthetics, or even functionality, but an extension of our own corporeality. It becomes us; we personalise it and possess it through our own leakiness. And this corporeal presence matters. It is why we wear the clothing of the specific significant Other; the lover's jumper for instance. Through the act of wearing we signify our closeness to, intimacy with, another and simultaneously smell the presence of this other body. Equally, yet very differently, it is why the recent discards of the unknown Other are so troublesome. Corporeal presence then, the personalisation and possession which remains trapped in the cloth, is critical to the exchange and consumption of second-hand clothing. Indeed, it is what makes second-hand adult clothing a unique category of second-hand good.

Nicky Gregson, Kate Brooks and Louise Crewe

Acknowledgements

This research was conducted with financial assistance from ESRC (R000222182). We would like to thank participants at the ESRC funded seminar at UCL, May 1998 for the stimulating discussion of an earlier draft of this chapter.

References

Barker, M. and Brooks, K. (1998), *Knowing Audiences: Judge Dredd, its friends, fans and foes*, Luton: University of Luton Press.

Blomley, N. (1996), 'I'd like to dress her all over: masculinity, power and retail space', in N. Wrigley and M. Lowe (eds), *Retail, Capital and Consumption*, Harlow: Longman, pp. 238–56.

Bowlby, R. (1985), *Just Looking: Consumer Culture in Driesler, Gissing and Zola*, London: Macmillan.

Chaney, D. (1990), 'Subtopia in Gateshead: the MetroCentre as a cultural form', *Theory, Culture and Society*, 7: 49–68.

Clarke, A. (1998), 'Window shopping at home: classified, catalogues and new consumer skills', in D. Miller (ed.), *Material Cultures*, London: UCL Press, pp. 73–99.

Crewe, L. and Gregson, N. (1998), 'Tales of the unexpected: exploring car boot sales as marginal spaces of consumption', *Transactions Institute of British Geographers*, 23: 39–53.

Domosh, M. (1996), 'The feminised retail landscape: gender, ideology and consumer culture in nineteenth century New York City', in N. Wrigley and M. Lowe (eds), *Retail, Capital and Consumption*, Harlow: Longman, pp. 257–70.

Dowling, R. (1993), 'Femininity, place and commodities: a retail case study', *Antipode*, 25: 295–310.

Douglas, M. (1966), *Purity and Danger*, London: Routledge and Kegan Paul.

Foucault, M. (1977), *Discipline and Punish: the Birth of the Prison*, London: Allen and Lane.

Goffman, E. (1959), *The Presentation of Self in Everyday Life*, New York: Doubleday.

Goss, J. (1993), 'The magic of the mall: an analysis of form, function and meaning in the contemporary retail built environment', *Annals of the Association of American Geographers*, 83: 18–47.

Gregson, N. and Crewe, L. (1997a), 'The bargain, the knowledge and the spectacle: making sense of consumption in the space of the car boot sale', *Environment and Planning D: Society and Space*, 15: 87–112.

Gregson, N. and Crewe, L. (1997b), Performance and possession: rethinking the act of purchase in the light of the car boot sale', *Journal of Material Culture*, 2: 241–63.

Gregson, N., Crewe, L. and Longstaff, B. (1997), 'Excluded spaces of regulation: car boot sales as an enterprise culture out of control', *Environment and Planning A*, 29: 1717–37.

Gregson, N. and Crewe, L. (1998), 'Dusting down *Second Hand Rose*: gendered identities and the world of second hand goods in the space of the car boot sale'. *Gender, Place and Culture*, 5, 1: 77–100.

Gregson, N. and Rose, G. (2000), 'Taking Butler elsewhere: performativities, spatialities and subjectivities', *Environment and Planning D: Society and Space*, 18, pp. 433–52.

Grosz, E. (1994), *Volatile Bodies: Toward a Corporeal Feminism*, Bloomington: Indiana University Press.

Hopkins, J. (1991), 'West Edmonton Mall: landscapes of myths and elsewhereness', *Canadian Geographer*, 35: 2–17.

Jackson, P. (1993), 'Towards a cultural politics of consumption', in J. Bird et al., *Mapping the Futures*, London: Routledge, pp. 207–28.

Jackson, P. and Thrift, N. (1995), 'Geographies of consumption', in D. Miller (ed.), *Acknowledging Consumption*, London: Routledge, pp. 204–37.

Kopytoff, I. (1986), 'The cultural biography of things: commoditisation as process', in A. Appadurai (ed.), *The Social Life of Things*, Cambridge: Cambridge University Press, pp. 64–91.

Lancaster, W. (1995), *The Department Store: a Social History*, London: Pinter.

McRobbie, A. (ed.) (1989), *Zoot Suits and Second Hand Dresses: an Anthology of Fashion and Music*, London: Macmillan.

Miller, P. and Rose, N. (1997), 'Mobilising the consumer: assembling the subject of consumption', *Theory Culture and Society*, 14: 67–88.

Morris, M. (1991), 'Things to do with shopping centres', in S. Sheridan (ed.), *Grafts: Feminist Cultural Criticism*, London: Verso, pp. 193–225.

Nava, M. (1995), 'Modernity's disavowal: women the city and the department store', in M. Nava and A. O'Shea (eds), *Modern Times: Reflections on a Century of English Modernity*, London: Routledge, pp. 38–76.

Porter-Benson, S. (1986), *Counter Cultures: Saleswomen, Managers and Customers in American Department Stores, 1890–1940*, Urbana, Illinois: University of Illinois Press.

Reekie, G. (1993), *Temptations: Sex, Selling and the Department Store*, Sydney: George Allen and Unwin.

Shildrick, M. (1997), *Leaky Bodies and Boundaries*, London: Routledge.

Skeggs, B. (1997), *Formations of Class and Gender: Becoming Respectable*, London: Sage.

6

Consumption Without Scarcity: Exchange and Normativity in an Internet Setting

Don Slater

'Getting something for nothing' – the limit case of the market imperative to 'buy cheap and sell dear' – is apparently the aim of optimising self-interested action. This paper argues that while this aim may be dear to capitalist modernity, its realisation can be experienced as socially disastrous and personally scary. More precisely, we will be dealing with a social space whose inhabitants could get *everything* for nothing – a space that we will characterise as a 'post-scarcity pornotopia' – and yet they go to considerable lengths to produce structures of valorisation, boundaries and forms of normative regulation as a prerequisite for social order and personal identity. The setting is one constituted within computer-mediated communications: Internet Relay Chat is a very popular system for 'chatting' via typed lines of text that are exchanged in real time; IRC also allows people to transfer any kind of digital file, hence scanned photos and drawings, video clips, sound bites and music. This has developed into a large and complex scene for exchanging sexually explicit material, usually referred to locally as 'sexpics'. In the scene that was studied, this material was hardcore, but nothing that would not be legally available off-line, at least in the United States.

The burden of the exposition will be the ultimately Durkheimian contention that what is at stake in the normative regulation of the sexpics scene is the desire for an ethical social order itself and not (only) a utilitarian effort to secure pragmatic conditions for the rational pursuit of individual self-interests. Specifically, value – including quasi-economic exchange rates – is one means by which social order is accomplished rather than social order being a cost-efficient means to maximise utilities. Underlying these issues are questions about the nature of material culture and the objects of consumption, questions which are intensified by (but not unique to) virtual environments: in the IRC sexpics trade – as in many other social spaces both on-line and off – the problem with the notion of 'something for nothing' are the great question marks hanging over both the terms 'something' and 'nothing'.

We need to examine the processes of objectification whereby things come to have both substance and value, to exist and to have worth, whether that existence be virtual, symbolic or material and whether the value be denominated in prices, good taste, ethical stature or whatever. Exchange in cyberspace is interesting because both the materiality and the value of things are deemed by participants to be intrinsically unreliable: 'sexpics' are merely digital packets that are infinitely reproducible and manipulable. What becomes apparent fairly quickly is that participants are concerned not merely to determine the values of already existent things, but that they also use value systems and judgments to make things real or existentially reliable. In a monumental inversion of the positivist assumptions underlying liberal consumerism, the existence and the value of an on-line thing are fundamentally interdependent: it is partly through judgments of worth that on-line things are given shape as existent objects of consumption. Moreover – and this is largely the crux – this applies not only to the 'objects of consumption' but also to the equally unreliable social relationships in which they are exchanged.

IRC Sexpics Trading

My discussion is based on ethnographic research covering about eighteen months in various sexpics venues, plus associated research into sexually explicit web sites, email lists and newsgroups. Internet Relay Chat (IRC) is a medium for 'chatting' in real time with other people who are connected to an IRC network. People first connect to the Internet, as they would for email or WWW. Instead of loading an email program or browser onto their local computer, they connect to an IRC network by loading 'client' software and are then able to interact with any other client connected to their network, either individually or in collective spaces known as channels. Users may choose amongst an ever-growing number of IRC networks. The network used for this ethnography usually had about 20,000 clients simult-aneously connected at peak time (evening in North America).

Participants can find and chat with each other in two basic ways. First, they can talk directly and privately with one other person. They make a connection which opens a window on each participant's screen; if one person types a line of text, it will appear on both screens. Conversation takes the form of a flow of text lines. Second, one-to-one chats – the private sphere of IRC – generally cluster around channels, the public spheres, in which any number of participants may commun-icate communally. Channels have names and topics which reflect their content. At the time of research both the largest channels and the largest number of channels tended to be sex related, though this seems to have changed on at least some networks. These can be divided into those more oriented to trading sexpics and those more oriented to meeting others for cybersex or flirting or innocuous partying and hanging out, but there is huge overlap of both participants and activities between these spaces.

If you can transmit lines of text over IRC, you can transmit anything that is digitised, hence any kind of representation: photos, drawings, video clips, sound files, streamed (i.e. real-time) sound or video, software program files. Hence the sexpics trade: 'sexpics' – the local term used in preference to porn or erotica or other possible terms – usually refers to any kind of sexually explicit material circulated within this scene. People meet up or advertise their wares in and around designated channels, chatting either publicly in the channel or privately. In addition to channel-centred trading, more experienced participants usually have networks of friends and contacts whom they meet independently of channels. Alongside the chat, they can send files to each other (technically, this is done by a facility called DCC, direct computer to computer communication).

However, participants can also use a facility called 'fserve' (file server): someone offering an fserve allows others (usually by way of a 'trigger' word that can be typed in a channel window) to peruse directly the hard disk of their local computer, looking through subdirectories and lists of files, and then to select and download the files they want, usually up to a limit (either time, number of files, or number of kilobytes downloaded). As discussed below, people can also set exchange ratios (you will be allowed to download x bytes for every y bytes you upload).

As against the enormous amount of generalising about cyberspace and virtuality in recent days, we need to focus on the specific, unique and indeed extreme character of this particular setting. IRC is an extraordinarily disembodied and dematerialised social setting because it combines two features: textuality and 'dynamism'. It is their combination that is so very specific. By 'textuality' I mean that everything that circulates on IRC – both images and interactions – takes the form of a file of information, a collection of bits. This means, firstly – as current cyber-literature never tires of emphasising – that cyber-identities are apparently or potentially freed from their anchorage in off-line bodies and identities, capable of being seen as performatively or discursively constructed (typical discussions include Bassett 1997; Featherstone and Burrows 1995; Heim 1991; Ito 1997; Kiesler 1996; Plant 1997; Porter 1997; Shields 1996; Springer 1996; Stone 1996; Turkle 1995; Wiley 1995). However, contrary to the claims of this literature, IRC sexpics participants are extremely concerned about the authenticity of their and other's identities and the fact that no on-line presence or identity claim can ever be properly verified (Rival, Slater and Miller 1998; and Slater 1998). Participants' objectifications of both the images and the social order is arguably done with the aim of stabilizing their own identity, and particularly in order to avoid dissolving their own identities into the stream of representations they exchange.

Secondly, and more importantly for this article, the textuality of all 'things' on IRC means that *both* the presence of participants and the material that they are trading take the form of visual and verbal texts: there is a kind of Baudrillardian implosion in which subject and object, reader and text, consumer and object of consumption, are all (potentially) flattened onto one field of circulating information files. The result is a kind of merging of the chatters with the pornography they trade, an ability to enter the stream of pornography. At a basic level, there is a powerful temptation on the one hand to see the pornographic images as being of real people, and on the other hand an ever-present possibility of treating everything said by the other as pornography, of objectifying the other in an erotic framework. Hence there is always the possibility – driven by all kinds of desires – of objectifying an interactive subject (consuming them as an object of desire) or of subjectifying an object (seeing the image as indexing the presence of a desiring subject).

However in addition to the textuality of IRC (which it largely shares with other on-line media), it is also characterised by existing 'dynamically', in real time. IRC happens in the present tense and entirely depends on the presence of the other. If I receive a message or pic or any other information it is because it emanated from a live person who is on the network *just now*. The texts that comprise my IRC experience are perceived as live (inter)actions. By dynamism I mean not only that all IRC events happen in real time in the present, but that they *only* have a present tense: IRC has no past, memory or transmittable material culture, no archive that is held collectively (though participants may of course store images and even logs of conversations on their own hard disks). Two examples of this dominate life on IRC: Firstly, channels are dynamic: I can call a channel into being simply by typing a command: /j #Slater. I am then 'in' channel '#Slater' and can invite others into it. However when the last person leaves #Slater that channel vanishes without a trace – it leaves no record, no sign that it existed. A channel exists only by virtue of someone's presence in it. There is no way of leaving things behind in it and when I join a channel that has been ongoing before me there is no record of the conversation that took place before I entered it.

Similarly, when on-line, I am identified by a 'nick' or name which I choose on signing on, which can change at any moment and which cannot be traced to my real identity. Moreover, I don't own my nick: if someone chooses it before me, it is theirs until they sign off, at which point I can claim it again. And if someone else changes theirs, then I may not be able to find them again. IRC is characterised by a paradoxical relationship to the identity of both self and other: it can involve huge investment in an Other whose identity cannot be confirmed and may evaporate at any moment into the void. This affects emotional attachments (which can be simultaneously intense and yet provisional, full of constant doubt and suspicion), 'work' relationships (e.g. maintaining a channel may require an enormous amount of teamwork with others whose presence and reliability is always provisional), ethical regulation (where the enforcement of rules and punishment or exclusion of offenders is always compromised by an inability to bring to account a unique ethico-legal subject – an identity – anchored in a unique and locatable place – a body with an address).

Social spaces and identities, then, are evanescent, unstable, precarious. They do not endure over time through the kind of material culture (spaces, buildings, rituals, objects and documents) on which real-world communities depend to make themselves appear to endure beyond the presence of particular participants. Even its *agora* – the channel window – vanishes when the last citizen goes home. This is exacerbated by its ever-changing population: there is no continuity of participants, while experienced members are constantly being flooded by culturally untrained 'newbies'. As against the cyberutopian myth that the mere temporal coincidence of a lot of people technically capable of communicating with each other is sufficient to create and sustain complex social relations – let alone 'communities' – IRC demonstrates practically that sociality requires intersubjective or objectified memory. IRC channels and social relationships are both tragic and irritating because they are constantly forgetting who they are and how they do things.

It is worth noting that IRC is therefore hugely different from the MUDs (multi-user domains) and virtual worlds on which much of the cyber-literature is based, following the lead of Turkle (1995). Turkle's kind of setting (MUDs) allows participants to leave behind descriptions of self and setting that constitute the players' on-line biography. This allows for complex identity play and warrants investment in identity over time. Turn your back on IRC and it – and you – vanish.

Pornotopia

The conjuncture of textuality and dynamism – hence the extreme 'demateriality' of IRC – may pose both awesome possibilities and problems. Anything may happen (whatever you type will be, exist) but the status and value of everything is always unreliable. This is reflected in a paradox that is more specific to the sexpics scene: on the one hand, the sexpics scene is a 'pornotopia', a place of limitless access to inexhaustible (sexual) goods; on the other hand, participants devote great efforts to limiting these goods and their exchange, to establishing forms of exchange that constrain the sexpics scene around stable and artificially limited objects.

We might characterise the IRC sexpics scene as a post-scarcity 'pornotopia' on several counts. Firstly, and most straightforwardly, there is an ever-renewed volume of explicit material in circulation, covering all media and genres, that dwarfs any participant's ability to see, let alone collect, all of it. Average participants' hard disks can contain thousands of files, measured in gigabytes. Fserve subdirectories can each contain several hundred images, with twenty to thirty subdirectories per fserve. The participants' experience is of an infinity of images.

Secondly, the seemingly endless sea of porn seems inexhaustible because it is fed by numerous streams. There is a flow of images that have been collected from other on-line sources: web-sites, newsgroups, email lists, bulletin boards, each of which itself represents the circulation of many thousands of images. These include both non-pay sources and commercial sites from which material has been downloaded and can now be circulated and reproduced freely. Additionally, pictures are brought on-line (either firstly into commercial sites or directly into free circulation) by people scanning in images from a vast range of off-line sources (magazines, frame capture from video, private, amateur or semi-professional pictures either taken for web-based circulation or somehow finding their way there). Finally, new net software and hardware technologies themselves produce more and more of the available imagery (e.g. Cuseeme events are saved as stills and circulated separately), and the vast on-line porn business now produces material specifically for net distribution.

Thirdly, and probably the most obvious point, the sexpics ocean is inexhaustible because the imagery can be infinitely reproduced and infinitely circulated. It can be everywhere at once without any limits set by an original. Moreover it can do so without any apparent costs of reproduction, transportation or storage. In fact, the belief that these dematerialised commodities are 'free' or 'costless' is mistaken, or rather depends on a slippage between conventional economic calculations and those required in informational contexts. For example, there are clear hidden transaction and opportunity costs involved – the time taken to copy a file and send it to someone, albeit marginal, needs to be reckoned in terms of phone and ISP bills for on-line time, the time taken to organise and send files, investment in storage capacity and faster modems, time taken to master the numerous software and hardware technologies required for a simple file transfer, etc. These costs are rarely perceived in the single transaction. The feeling of pornotopia – of inexhaustible free sexual representation – arises in the slippage between the 'costless' individual transaction and the investment incurred over the course of involvement in IRC.

Fourthly, the material exchanged is indeed 'free' in the sense that there is no monetary value or payment involved: just dip into the sea and take what you want. There is also no effective property right: web sites pay lip service to copyright, but IRC circulates everything indiscriminately without reference to any ownership or authorial origins. It is a Sherwood Forest in its notion of the moral economy (Thompson 1971). The sexpics scene employs a version of freedom located in an anti-commercial anarchism of the 'property is theft' variety. This establishes it as politically libertarian in relation to the governmental and commercial agencies which are increasingly regulating the circulation of pornography and other net goods as well as the forms of exchange within the net (Slater 2000). The irony, as we shall see, is that sexpics traders often regulate themselves through the use of very similar mechanisms, including notions of property right. Nonetheless, it is intrinsic to the sense of 'pornotopia' that where goods are both non-material and hyper-abundant, money and value are inappropriate notions. A clear example: participants will constantly say that they never look at their huge collections, indeed will sometimes lose everything through a hard disk crash or simply throwing it all out because they need the space. No problem: just go out and get some more.

Fifthly, earlier I characterised the textuality of IRC sexpics in terms of an implosion of subject and object, of traders and the sexpics they trade. This means that not only the images, but the interchanges and actions of participants around the images may be treated as sexual. Although much of the sexpics trading can be technocratic and impersonal, trading scenes are embedded in chatting and cybersex scenes. The ones studied were organised – like all the pornography traded – according to an unchallenged norm of male heterosexuality and female bisexuality (male homosexuality and gay porn is quite rigorously split off into other channels and scenes; is policed through homophobia; and is sublimated or subverted through men taking on female personae). Relations between men tend to be comradely or techno-oriented (making the scene or the exchanges or the technologies work, trading information on pics and collections (see below: one could say that the relationship is hobbyist). On the other hand, according to these norms, anything said by a female presence on-line can be interpreted as sexual. There are extremely abrupt movements from seeing the interactive Other as an active subject to reading all their communications as if they were pornographic stimuli. People do not simply exchange porn, they *pornographise*: it takes a transitive verb to understand how presences come into being as objects of a sexual intentionality. Sexual objectif-ication is not just a matter of consuming images, but an act of will, a will to objectify the other as an erotic stimulus. All of this again renders the potential flow of sexual objectification infinite in both principle and in people's experience of the setting: *everything* can be freely sexualised.

Finally, sexpics trading on IRC (and even IRC itself) is very close to the world depicted in the pornography that participants trade. Both porn and IRC are alike, or at least homologous, in ways that we normally use to characterise very utopian notions of consumption (as, e.g., in some of the post-modern literature on shopping). Above all, IRC sexpics (even IRC more generally) and pornography are constituted as fantasy dreamscapes, both out of space and out of time, insulated from the mundane and the material and their constraints. Participants make constant references to being lost in a dream place, in which one loses all sense of time (until one looks away from the screen to find that hours have passed), in which ego boundaries, the lines between inside and outside 'one's head' are confused or blurred (participants invariably describe the eroticism of cybersex as 'being inside a pornographic novel' or film) and in which there is no physical risk or consequence.

We are dealing here with moments of pure consumption: porn pics are like manna from heaven and have no origin or producer. Direct questions about the actual models (for example, about the visibly unprotected sex they engaged in for the camera) are met with total incomprehension. If anything, the moment of production is itself eroticised and assimilated to or within the consumption of porn: for example, high quality pics are treated as acts of homage or worship of the sex goddesses; amateur pictures and 'personal' pictures (putatively pictures of the person who has sent them) are highly prized because the moment of production (a 'real' woman was photographed by a guy like you or me) was an erotic one rather than a commercial one. This is a world beyond scarcity partly because the moment of production is itself mythically transfigured into one element of orgy. Moreover, there is no failure of supply: desire is insatiable and ever-ready.

In sum, then, throwing the term 'pornotopia' at the IRC sexpics trading scene implies many things: Most literally an inexhaustible and (economically and legally) free source of a particular consumer good: pornographic material; the porn circulates within a highly sexualised sphere in which participants themselves enter the flow of pornography, pornographise self and other in a world of inexhaustible and free desire. Beyond the immediately sexual, IRC in general can be taken as a consumerist paradise: pornotopia at this level represents a kind of triumph of the pleasure principle in a space which allows – because of its virtual character – a fantasy of infinite yet always satiable desire. Something for nothing: total freedom of choice, free from labour, price and danger.

'Leeching'

The strange paradox of IRC sexpics trading is that this world without scarcity is completely obsessed with property rights, with rules of exchange and with exchange ratios. The most compelling example of this is the obsession with 'leeching' and 'leechers'. 'Leeching' means literally getting something for nothing: it happens in direct trade when someone accepts pictures without returning a just measure; or in fserving when someone carries on downloading without sending any back. Hence, 'draining someone dry like a leech': though the metaphor is of course inaccurate since one can never actually take away a file, but only a copy, and therefore cannot ever deplete the source. Nonetheless, leeches are the lowest of the low on IRC, and leeching is probably the greatest insult to IRC as such: although there is very heavy policing against various taboo representations (children, animals, violence), often based on great outrage, this regulation is closely tied to off-line moral agendas and is sometimes seen as a kind of pre-emptive self-censorship. Leeching, on the other hand, is obviously a crime specific to this setting. It is constantly castigated through channel messages and rules; leechers are publicly exposed in channel windows ('Don't trade with X!'); if leeching is even suspected – for example, when someone is slow in returning the just measure – people are quick to anger and self-righteousness ('So where are the pics? What's going on?'). An irate victim may hound a leecher from channel to channel in hot vigilante-style pursuit.

Most direct one-to-one trading feels its way towards some sense of reciprocity: it carries on so long as each party feels the stream of images is satisfactory in both quantity and quality, with constant negotiation of categories desired, particular pictures sought, and reasons given for the rate of return (technical problems, insufficient supply of the requested genre, being busy with too many simultaneous trades and chats). The moments of exchange and of consumption are in any case usually simultaneous: the picture comes up on the recipient's screen once it downloads. This represents a constant interpersonal negotiation of norms, ever renewed and relearned and always subject to the handicap that IRC lacks tradition and memory (negotiating with newbies is proverbially a pain to everyone). However, IRC participants solved this problem in a technocratic manner by hardwiring their normative expectations into the software of IRC itself, effectively producing a material culture: fserves, described above, can be automated through programming and in such a way that the server's client can routinely regulate all aspects of exchange. During the course of fieldwork, sexpics scenes were rapidly overwhelmed by the recently introduced 'Hawkee's Leech-Proof Fserver', an add-on to the most popular IRC client program (mIRC), and since then followed by many more complex equivalents. Hawkee's main feature was the ability to set exchange ratios, measured in kilobytes: a 10:1 ratio means that one could download 100k worth of picture, sound, text, video file for every 10k one uploaded. Ratios could be set at any level, including 'leech rights' granting unlimited access to the server's hard disk. Hawkee could regulate many other normative aspects of exchange: keeping accounts for every client that connected (ensuring equity between serves and ensuring that one could not cheat by connecting under alternate nicks); checking uploaded file names against the directories to ensure that duplicates were not accepted; weeding out files beginning with particular characters (like '!') which indicated old and common pictures.

Ratios – whether set by fserves or private barter – are not prices or terms of trade in any literal sense. They are set arbitrarily and there is not a glimmer of quantitative equivalency between a ratio and any notion like cost (in time or money) or labour. Nor is there any mechanism by which an fserve with a 2:1 ratio might reflect different community evaluations or market demand than one offering 10:1. At best it could be said that the former is probably more choosy or jaded and the latter either indiscriminate or a beginner needing images. The issue is whether they are particularly concerned to get more pics, or would rather not wade through megabytes of dross. Indeed the most common basis on which people justified ratios was as recompense for managing the monstrous volume of material: handling, ordering, sifting and making available. The least people could do is send a few back . . . Moreover, all that handling is frequently presented as a public service to the community ('send some back and help build up this collection') rather than a private enterprise oriented to self-interested accumulation.

One can also compare those who set ratios with the survival of some traders or channels who are concerned that trading reciprocity be based on an unforced or honour system, in keeping with the free spirit of IRC and indeed the Internet. Many of these argue that charging is something they may be pushed into as a last resort: if I am forced to charge, it will be the fault of you anti-social or lazy leechers. The very idea of a *quid pro quo* is used as a threat designed to enforce normativity rather than actually to realise a price or gain recompense. Conversely, the compulsion ('I'll have to charge if you don't reciprocate') is symbolic rather than economic (no bankruptcy would result, nor even an opportunity cost in lost pictures). Rather, the real loss is an ethical one, a sense of injury and of having been used. What is interesting is that the ethical issue is translated into an economic and quantitative idiom and then enforced through quasi-prices: ethical value is rendered pragmatic by mutating into economic value; personal obligations are rendered into impersonal steering media, to borrow terms from Habermas, and as in Habermas a sense of irrevocable yet inevitable loss is expressed by participants facing the fact that co-ordination of an increasingly complex social structure necessitates a colonisation of the lifeworld, rendering its previously tacit under-standings visible in the form of objectified modes of regulation and strategic action, or – in this case – in the software itself.

In fact, and this is what IRC veterans lament, the imposition of fserves with ratios is very much bound up with a deeper impersonalisation: the automation of IRC. Not only are fserves automated, but so too are the activities of channel 'ops' – participants with the role and software rights of enforcing normative regulation through warnings, bans and kicks – who now use software that automatically checks for various infringements and takes appropriate action. These days, most sexpic channel windows have little or no conversation, simply a running scroll of auto-mated channel advertisements for fserves, punctuated by people typing in triggers or being regulated – automatically – by ops. To reiterate, IRC relies increasingly on automation – building normativity into the software – to solve the problem of memory and dynamism, the fact that the constant on-line presence of human participants is impossible or unreliable. However, this automation is double-edged, both establishing an ersatz material culture which embodies, transmits and even enforces a normative social order and yet – as an extreme and legalistic form of objectification – rendering that order impersonal and implacable. Indeed, this kind of cyberspace seems to be more apt as a metaphor for disciplinary modernity than for the decentred postmodern that so much of the literature apparently finds in it.

However just as bizarre as the castigation of leechers and the measures taken to prevent 'free riding' in a situation of obscene overabundance are the lengths to which people will indeed go to leech on others, to get that free ride. People will gleefully 'steal' the whole shop. The public discourse – reflected in interviews – is about ethics and reciprocity; the private experience seems to be more in tune with the notion of pornotopia: that the situation *should* be one of pure consumption, of post-scarcity, of limitlessness; and if anything stands in the way of this experience, then there is the sheer joy of literally hacking through barriers and regulations by dint of theft, banditry and cunning.

Having established the seeming paradox of IRC sexpics – an obsession with submitting inexhaustible goods to a rule of value in exchange – let me hazard three guesses at the underlying issues: Firstly, *reciprocity*: stable exchange and circulation of goods requires normative community, while normative communities require equable exchange of goods. However, how can reciprocity have any *meaning* until one has sorted out the ontological status of the things exchanged – a difficult issue where all that is exchanged, both pics and communications, take the form of dematerialised (unstable, infinitely reproducible, inexhaustible, priceless) digital packets. The war against leeching – setting ratios and automating their enforcement – normatively stabilises these digital goods in the familiar form of property and commodity, rendering them as things that can be assessed and regulated in respect of reciprocity. Leechers may point to the absurdity of this, but nonetheless come to measure their own success by the same standards: how many *things* did you get for nothing.

Secondly, *objectification*: because of the implosion of porn and chat discussed above, there is both a desire to merge with the representations traded (the will to pornographise self and other) and at the same time a need to separate self from traded representations. This is accomplished by objectifying the pictures in the form of property, distancing them as mere commodities, and de-eroticising the exchange through impersonal steering mechanisms and automated interactions (particularly important in exchange between heterosexual men). This objectification of the consumable and exchangeable goods seems to preserve a notion of individual ego boundaries in a social space that ever threatens a double-dissolution of the ego: into sexuality and into the dynamic textuality of IRC itself. Leeching fails to honour the structures of value and property that keep the pics separate from self. And yet leechers – like all hackers – tend to have low cathexis with the things stolen: they are more concerned with the technical problems of 'liberating' them. The important relationship is a distanced one between self and an objective order one is trying to conquer.

Thirdly, *ordering*: any sense of labour and production meriting recompense on IRC seems bound up with the work that goes into producing order under conditions of boundlessness: ordering the inexhaustible sexpics or ordering the channel society which has no memory or past. In many respects, the activity of ordering is an end in itself, a condition we can label the 'nerdish' or technocratic orientation to social life. The complex directory structures of an fserve, endless labour of cataloguing pictures into genres, weeding out dross, making collections available, the fetish-isation of file sizes, exchange rates, tracking down leechers, the obsession with rules and with automating them – all this is about a desire for order itself, about contending with the limitless and unbounded character of the setting by containing it within stable normative and nomological frameworks. For example, fserve directory structures organise thousands of pics in terms of categories such as types of actions, numbers of participants, types of models and so on. It is an effort to tame the infinite and ever renewable sea of images by applying to it a standard accepted sexual cosmology (and this cosmology is indeed very standard and conventional). Each collection evokes the vastness of the pornotopia without falling into its formlessness; each collection aims to seem inexhaustible, but in human terms. While the nerdish obsession with ordering things positively requires that every thing and act be valued and placed within a framework, leeching (here cast as a simple anarchism) is about breaching order so as to evade all laws of value. And yet leeching itself is often a hugely nerdish endeavour – like hacking – in which any will to disorder is sublimated into a simple desire to penetrate machine systems by virtuoso application of technocratic knowledge.

Realising and Valorising

In the case of leeching and ratios, issues of identity, community and order are dealt with by turning 'free' things into property with value and ensuring that no one can get something for nothing. We can make a stronger argument, however, that these issues of identity, community and order are at some level *more* important, are more *the* issue, than the things traded. The aim of maintaining exchange is inseparable from the aim of maintaining the normative order itself; even the content of the exchange – pornography and sexual communications – may be merely an opportune idiom through which to deal other kinds of social relationship. In this respect, let us look at three extremely common social frameworks in which sexpic trading is often embedded. In each case, the way the exchanged sexpics are understood – their ontological status – is determined by socially legitimated frameworks of value, by notions of the good. We need to look at the way in which different normative frameworks, different grounds for investing in objects, cause them to be objectified in quite different ways.

Socialising

One of the most common claims made by informants is that they rarely look at their pictures and are actually only on-line in order to chat and be sociable. This is often narrativised as a progression from being new to porn and the net, fascinated by cybersex and taboo imagery, to being jaded, blasé about the sex stuff and now comfortably engrossed in chatting in an enjoyable social world. In the words of a long term op by the nick of Bronze:

[23:44] <Bronze> Me, personally . . . I lost my pics once (all of them) and decided it wasn't worth it to replace them so I stopped trading . . . I was bored with them all already . . . I kept coming back though because I had met and developed friendships with many people in there and liked to talk to them.

<Lash> so, for you it is now all about . . .? friends . . .?

<Lash> or watching the flow fo human life and sexuality?

[23:59] <Bronze> For me it's about not sitting at work for 8 hours and having nothing to think about but work . . . It's about going somewhere in the instant of thought and being in a roomfull of people and knowing for certain their aims and goals, and certainly the cynical side of me likes to watch the people gather for tidbits of things they should be trying to find in RL ['real life'].

He also argues, not unusually for participants, that a lot of traders and ops are lonely people, finding on IRC sexpics a sociality – indeed a sexuality – that is compensatory. Bronze talks about 'long-time users who are women, married, and all seem about to get a divorce'.

[23:26] <Bronze> Most female ops you see will have the same story . . . Either they are recently divorced, divorcing, or want one but too afraid to ask.

<Lash> we go from sex to blues at a speed of knots

<Lash> yeah . . . I think a lot of the latter, huh? unhappy but can't get out of the relationship

[23:27] <Bronze> Yep . . . And for the most part they are quite content just gabbing away for hours about anything.. That's why I said IRC is a form of escape.

In another example the web site associated with an IRC channel with the fairly explicit name #!0fuckmywife describes itself in the following terms:

Well . . . How do i explain what #0!fuckmywife channel is about . . .:) It is a Chat channel . . . People come in that are looking for others who live in

there towns or cities etc . . . And to make IRC friends around the world . . .
We have alot of fun chatting in the main channel and in private chat . . .:Þ

Come in and chat with the Reg's and the ops . . . Make some IRC and Real
Life Friends . . .:)

followed by descriptions of all the ops: for example:

Jan|s—> Well . . . She is our friendliest OP we have yet . . . She alway says
hello back to anyone who says Hi in the channel . . . Even when she is busy
in Cyber (and/or) Real life. :)

This is down-home American neighbourliness, without a single mention of sex or
the fact that the channel is oriented around fantasies of sub men watching their
partners having sex with dominant (usually well-endowed black) studs, a fantasy
carried on at the centre of a relatively long-standing friendship network which
extends from IRC to email, phone communications and web sites. Similarly,
#askfemanything was a somewhat bizarre network constructed around a game in
which the women (or female denominated presences) would answer any sexual
questions the men asked them. The group lasted at least several years, even
surviving a mass migration from AOL to IRC when the former changed its pricing
structure out of their reach. Though the sexual character of the game was important,
it was no more than one form of exchange through which a more important sociality
was pursued. Along the same lines, channels with flamboyantly outrageous or
knowingly disgusting names – e.g. #dogsex – may turn out to contain the truly
perverse or the simply sociable or an unholy alliance of the two.

Similarly, in more long-standing relationships, the exchange of pics may be a
kind of drone in the background, behind a chat about other things, eventually
petering out or else renewed when coming across something the other might like.
Frequently, the exchange of sexpics in the context of general chat substantialises
the relationship by indicating knowledge of the other. Informed exchange embodies
that familiarity and intimacy by which we treat a relationship as real in its pragmatic
and non-reflective everydayness: my ability to find and send you just the kind of
sexpic you like (and not send what you don't) gives substance to intimacy, proves
that we really know each other, and allows for gestures of affection and empathy.
The informed exchange of dirty pics plays a more strategic role under conditions
of virtuality where other cues of embodied presence are lacking, and takes its
place alongside similar familiarities such as enjoyment of the other's textual style
and timing in IRC chat. If, *pace* Bourdieu, 'taste classifies the classifier', we need
to understand that displaying knowledge of the other's taste may constitute intimate
rather than competitive moves.

We can see then that both the objects exchanged and the structure of exchange itself are understood and valorised in relation to the sociality desired, from being a mere occasion for general sociablity (where the sexual content of the images is irrelevant to the extent that the exchangers do not even look at them) to being tokens of a real intimacy (where the appropriate choice of image is evidence of a wider relationship).

'Real Women'

Contrary to much discussion of cyberspace, lack of immediate physical presence does not seem to make issues of identity and authenticity irrelevant. In fact, participants seem to oscillate between a complete cynicism (refusal to believe any on-line identity claims) and a powerful desire to authenticate the other, to find ever more secure grounds on which to believe in the other as an ethical subject. A pervasive strategy for authenticating the other involves 'progressive embodiment': locating the other's identity in a body or something like a body by fixing them at an address, brings more of their body into view (through mail, phone calls, meetings) and so on (Slater 1998). This places into the centre of IRC experiences the issue of the *realism* of representations: as I read the texts through which an Other presents itself, do I treat their emerging textual presence as true or false, as realistic rather than real (authentic, true, sincere), as an enjoyable facsimile (they are real/true enough for all practical purposes in the matter at hand) or the presence of an ethically constant and responsible Other.

In the IRC context of extreme disembodiment, then, it is not surprising that much on-line valorisation of representations hinges on a very literal understanding of realism: pictures of 'real women' are the most prized. There is a desire that representations have an indexical relationship to the subject they depict, almost literally to stand in for them. In the first instance, 'real women' pics are those that are taken or circulated initially within symbolic rather than commercial exchange: these can be either 'personal' pics (those claiming to be of the woman who has sent them), 'pics of my wife/girlfriend', pics that seem to be of *someone's* real wife/girlfriend; or 'amateur pics' (that is to say, pics taken of women who are not professional models and preferably taken by non-professionals in a non-commercial/erotic context). The reality that is desired and valued is a certainty that the woman is a truly desiring sexual subject rather than one paid to depict desire – i.e. that the picture is *authentic* rather than *realistic* – usually based on a belief that the making of the image was itself sexual rather than economic, requiring that the moment of production of the image be eroticised (e.g. the idea that the model is a sexy housewife making money on the side). Commercial operations may go to great lengths to depict themselves as the web site of an exhibitionist amateur showing pics taken by her boyfriend. There has been a great vogue for long pictorial series in which a single model is depicted in sufficiently 'real' locations in grainy realism to conjure up a sense of the amateur.

The photograph is valorised in relation to a tremendous desire that it be *true* in its most banal truth claim: that a real woman willingly presented herself to view. The photograph is valuable to the extent that it authenticates the existence of a certain kind of relationship between the depicted woman (seen as a *real* woman) and the viewer who is placed in a state of great immediacy to her. Sexuality and sexual representation is important but perhaps mainly because it plays such a central social role in establishing the truth of the person: the personal sexpic is as much the medium through which the reality of the other is produced as it is a means of pursuing sex as an end in itself.

The fiction is that a 'real woman' pic exists in the context of a symbolic exchange rather than a commercial one: the paradigm is a private exchange of intimate pictures of oneself and the Other. However the same fantasy is extrapolated to collecting pics as part of a fan relationship with public women: pictures of *named* models (famous *Playboy*, porn-stars or 'glamour' models); pics of 'legitimate' models, above all supermodels; pics of celebrities, above all naked or sexually compromising ones (paparazzi, naked pics from early in their career, captured 'mishaps' such as accidental flashing, and fake pics – often known to be fake, but funny or very rude). Again, the conjuncture of sexuality, (fictions of) non-commercial production and photographic realism is largely valued not because such pics are simply 'sexy', but because they deliver the most valued prize of all: her truth, a sense of her real (as opposed to textually realistic) existence. The fixation on real woman pics, then, is about substantialising relationships.

Collecting

The idea of authenticity seems evidently inappropriate to the digital files exchanged on IRC, given that they are infinitely reproducible and completely manipulable using the simplest software. Paradoxically, although one can alter any picture down to the level of the pixel, during research I encountered *no* examples of images that have been openly *worked upon* with the exception of one genre (faked nudes of celebrities). The extreme point of this refusal to touch the image takes the form of 'scan collecting'. This hobby originated around the work of 'Scanmaster', apparently a Spanish photographic technician who produced scans – digitised versions – of *Playboy* pictorials. Scanning is a complex craft, involving good equipment, great technical knowledge and experience combined with trained aesthetic judgment. Scanmaster was recognised as a master, as the producer of 'the best' scanned images. They were 'the best' in the sense of being most true to their originals – technically perfect on-screen reproductions of the *Playboy* originals; and they were best in embodying the aesthetic of high-quality glamour photography (particularly a fetishisation of formal perfection almost to the exclusion of any interest in sexual content, in contrast to the grainy sexpics elsewhere which simply show the body or the act with no consideration of formal qualities). In fact, Scanmaster had constant copyright problems, and was rumoured to be endlessly pursued by *Playboy* legal representatives. Scanmaster and his fans were unhappy about this not only on the basis of their generally libertarian, anti-property perspective (a paradox given their own fetishisation of this property) but most articulately on the basis that Scanmaster's work was not so much a theft of *Playboy* property as an act of homage: it was a work of dedication and appreciation of the aesthetic embodied in *Playboy* and its women.

Scanmaster scans were valorised by collectors as both true to an original (*Playboy*) and true to themselves (the highest technical standards of scanning). To be a true collector of Scanmasters meant to preserve this authenticity. This took two overall forms: firstly, it was anathema to alter either the name of a Scanmaster file or to change its file size by reducing either picture size or resolution (it was inconceivable that anyone would want to muck about with its perfect colour balance or contrast, and therefore this didn't need to be stated). Secondly, the aim of collecting was not to pick and choose the best Scanmasters but rather to collect all of them: Scanmaster collecting – like collecting stamps or football stickers – was about amassing, owning and ordering the intact corpus.

Scan collecting is pure hobbyism. The obsessive concern is with the management of objects. The hobby features web sites that publish authoritative lists of Scan series, with scholarly notes on various errata, mislabelling of pictures, correct original sizes; there is fairly sophisticated bespoke software which will automatically compare one's own directory listing of pictures against an authoritative listing of the series and generate a list of errata and missing images; there is a wide range of networked media (web sites, newsgroups, email lists, IRC) to inform people of which pics are wanted/offered and to match up traders; there are interviews and other communications with Scanmaster and other scanners along the lines of a fan club.

What is most striking here is the coincidence with hobbyism: hobbies are objectified structures of activity which arise when activities and objects which are often previously without value (or valorised within purely utilitarian frameworks) are relabelled as desirable. One can collect anything (stamps, phone cards, matchbooks, etc.) for it is the hobbyist frame of reference which establishes worth through the 'fetishism of small differences' (eg., a particular stamp with an error) or through defining a complete set or series, a universe of valued objects which can ultimately be completed. Hobbyism and collecting reconstruct the ontology of the object on the basis of normative evaluations, on the basis of judgments of worth that are internal to the collectors' world. As Benjamin put it rather more poetically: the collector redeems objects and endows them with an intrinsic worth, for 'the most important fate of a copy is its encounter with him, with his own collection . . . the acquisition of an old book is its rebirth'. The collector renews objects but since this 'has no public significance whatsoever but results in a strictly private hobby, everything "that is said from the angle of the true collector" is bound to appear "whimsical"' (Arendt citing Benjamin in Benjamin 1977: 43).

Scanmaster collectors, then, do not collect Scanmasters because they are valuable: given that they are no more than digital files with no material stability or 'reality', they can be barely said to exist as objects, let alone valuable ones. To the contrary, they exist as collectible objects precisely because the normative social order of the hobbyist fixes them as objects with more or less of various desired qualities (technical perfection, authenticity in relation to *Playboy* and Scanmaster himself, completeness/integrity of the collection as a whole). The social networks of exchange – of pics, information, software, etc. – do not simply facilitate the collector's quest. They *constitute* it and its objects in the first place. In a weird sense, it is the market that creates the objects exchanged within it.

A hobbyist orientation is also evident in the aesthetic embodied in the pics and the scans, indeed they are precisely those aimed at in male amateur 'glamour' photography: techno fetishism combined with formal stylisation and kitsch content/ treatment. As in glamour photography, the fetish of technical perfection completely desexualises both the image and the woman in it: to mangle John Berger's (1972) famous distinction, these models do not even appear to be naked because they are so utterly nude; their skin is a kind of dress. This simply reiterates the overall theme: although the idiom of the Scanmaster trading scene is erotic/sexual, the real issue appears to be order, control, the moulding of something infinite – sexuality, the mystery of the feminine (cf. Williams 1990), the infinite universe of sexual representation, relations of exchange within a collecting community – into discrete, measurable, accumulable forms; the taming or domestication of the sacred. Given the hobbyist form it takes we might equally sum all this up as the 'nerdification of the erotic', an attempt to contain wildness within nomological orders, transforming excess into scarcity (where by definition there can be no scarcity), arduously constructing taboos so that any underlying sense of transgression (these *are* dirty pics after all, one tries hard to remember) is lost (Rival, Slater and Miller 1998).

Conclusions

Socialising, 'real women' and Scanmaster collecting, all demonstrate that in some respects the very last thing that is going on in the sexpics scene is sexual. Though flooded with sexual objectifications, the main issue is the objectification rather than the sexuality. In all three cases the valorising of things in the idiom of sexuality turns out to be equally about the existence and stabilisation of normative relationships with both things and people, about objectifying, substantialising, constituting a world.

Although I have wanted to be ethnographically attentive to the specificity of my setting, I certainly do not want to treat IRC sexpics, or more generally Internet sociality, as exceptional, bizarre or futuristic. In fact, the interest is in extending fairly old-fashioned economic sociology or anthropology into new terrain (see Slater and Tonkiss 2000): in what ways can we connect sexpic trading on IRC with various kinds of shopping, or with exchange of services in an informal local economy, or with the interplay of virtuality and objectification in the exchange of ideas (intellectual property) between academics. In any of these cases we need to know about how particular forms of exchange arise from the interplay between processes of social valorisation and objectification, between ethics, ontology and social order. Any social order comprises a huge variety of types of exchange, each of which is deemed appropriate to, and constitutive of, some social relations and not others. As Davies (1992) points out, concluding an impressive enumeration of nearly a hundred types of everyday Western exchanges ranging from theft to credit card payments, a person's involvement in the full 'repertoire' of exchange types can also tell us something about what it means to have a 'full life' or be a 'whole person' in a particular society.

No less on IRC: despite the absence of any economic pressure to structure exchange – or perhaps precisely because of the hyperabundance which seems to render economy redundant – various social value frameworks are deployed to structure objects, exchange and social relations into stable and normative forms. Indeed, in contrast with the liberal-utilitarian focus on exchange as ideally constituted through free individual choice it is an interest in social order that seems to determine the way in which exchange relations and consumption goods are structured and objectified. Although sexpics traders could have everything for nothing, they might may well experience this as the worst possible outcome.

References

Bassett, C. (1997), 'Virtually gendered: life in an on-line world', in K. Gelder and S. Thornton (eds), *The Subcultures Reader*, London: Routledge.

Benjamin, W. (1977), *Illuminations*, London: Fontana.

Berger, J. (1972), *Ways of Seeing*, Harmondworth: Penguin.

Davis, J. (1992), *Exchange*, Buckingham: Open University Press.

Featherstone, M. and Burrows, R. (eds) (1995), *Cyberspace, Cyberbodies, Cyberpunk: Cultures of Technological Embodiment*, London: Routledge.

Heim, M. (1991), 'The erotic ontology of cyberspace', in M. Benedikt (ed.), *Cyberspace: First Steps*, Cambridge, MA: MIT Press.

Ito, M. (1997), 'Virtually embodied: the reality of fantasy in a multi-user dungeon', in D. Porter (ed.), *Internet Culture*, London: Routledge.

Kiesler, S. (ed.) (1996), *Culture of the Internet*, Erlbaum.

Plant, S. (1997), *Zeros and Ones: Digital Women and the New Technoculture*, London: Fourth Estate.

Porter, D. (ed.) (1997), *Internet Culture*, London: Routledge.

Rival, L., Slater, D. and Miller, D. (1998), 'Sex and sociality: comparative ethnography of sexual objectification', *Theory, Culture and Society*.

Shields, R. (ed.) (1996), *Cultures of Internet: Virtual Spaces, Real Histories, Living Bodies*, London: Sage.

Slater, D.R. (1998), 'Trading sexpics on IRC: embodiment and authenticity on the internet', *Body and Society* 4 (4)

—— (2000), 'Political discourse and the politics of need: discourses on the good life in cyberspace', in L. Bennett and R. Entman (eds), *Mediated Politics*, Cambridge: Cambridge University Press.

Slater, D. and Tonkiss, F. (2000), *Market Society: Markets and Modern Social Thought*, Cambridge: Polity Press.

Springer, C. (1996), *Electronic Eros: Bodies and Desire in the Postindustrial Age*, Austin, Texas: University of Texas Press.

Stone, A.R. (1996), *The War of Desire and Technology at the close of the Mechanical Age*, Cambridge MA: MIT Press.

Thompson, E.P. (1971), 'The moral economy of the English crowd in the eighteenth century', *Past and Present*, 50: 78–98.

Turkle, S. (1995), *Life on the Screen: Identity in the Age of the Internet*, New York: Simon and Schuster.

Wiley, J. (1995), 'NoBODY is "Doing It": Cybersexuality as a Postmodern Narrative', *Body & Society*, 1 (1): 145–62.

Williams, L. (1990), *Hard Core: Power, Pleasure and the "Frenzy of the Visible"*, London: Pandora.

Part III

Introduction:
Consumption, Audiences and Commercial Culture

Peter Jackson

The chapters in this third section, like those elsewhere in the book, have the common aim of encouraging a dialogue between 'cultural studies' and 'political-economy' through an inter-disciplinary approach (drawing in this case on anthropological, sociological and geographical perspectives). Each of the chapters is empirically-grounded, addressing theoretical issues through historically- and geographically-specific examples concerning food marketing in Norway (Lien), the retail book trade in Britain (Stallard), and the readership of men's 'lifestyle' magazines in various parts of the UK (Stevenson et al.).

An organising framework for reading the chapters is provided by a reappraisal of Richard Johnson's (1986) 'circuit of culture' concept. The idea of the circuit is to break with conventional linear readings of the links between production and consumption. Rather than following such a linear path (from production to consumption), the circuit emphasises the flows and connections that exist between specific contexts of production, the commodity form assumed by particular goods (and representations of those goods in advertising and marketing) and the different contexts of consumption (where the same good can have quite different meanings for different consumers according to their lived cultures, social relations and personal identities). The chapters in this section could be read as moving around the circuit in a fairly conventional manner, from production and marketing (Lien) to retailing (Stallard) and consumption (Stevenson et al.). Here, however, we wish to problematise this kind of linear logic, showing the linkages and leakages that occur at various stages in the 'circuit'. Lien's chapter, for example, demonstrates how market research is designed to anticipate the (culturally-specific) reactions of consumers in particular national contexts, while the chapters by Stallard and Stevenson et al. both show how consumers are capable of reading particular products (books or magazines) 'against the grain' of the meanings that may have been intended by their producers.

The three chapters in this section have different degrees of involvement with the consumers of commercial culture. In Lien's study of the Norwegian food industry, consumers are approached indirectly through the protocols of professional market research. In Stallard's analysis of a national chain of bookstores, reader-centred marketing strategies have become increasingly popular (approached here through interviews with various levels of management), while in the chapter by Stevenson, Jackson and Brooks the consumers of men's lifestyle magazines are approached directly through a series of focus groups with readers and non-readers.

The argument of all three chapters can also be seen to reflect recent changes in 'audience studies' (Ang 1992, 1996; Morley 1992). As studies have moved away from a preoccupation with the text towards greater involvement with actual audiences and readers 'on the ground', consumers have been credited with an increasingly active role in the creation of meaning. Morley provides the following caricature of this intellectual trajectory in relation to his own research on television audiences:

> In the bad old days television audiences were considered as passive consumers, to whom things happened as television's miraculous powers affected them. According to choice, these (always other) people were turned into zombies, transfixed by bourgeois ideology or filled with consumerist desires. Happily, so the story goes, it was then discovered that this was an inaccurate picture, because in fact these people were out there, in front of the set, being active in all kinds of ways – making critical/oppositional readings of dominant cultural forms, perceiving ideological messages selectively/subversively etc., etc. (1992: 18)

Several strands of this argument are worth examining in greater detail. Prior to the development of reader-response theory (Tompkins 1980), literary studies tended to assume that a finite number of readings was already coded into the text, seriously circumscribing the agency of 'ordinary readers' in relation to the authority of the text. If meanings tended to be assumed rather than explored empirically in this literary tradition, a cultural studies approach to television and other forms of popular culture led to the development of more ethnographic work with audiences. Simultaneously, the site of such studies moved from the literary space of the text into the domestic space of the living room, while linear models of 'encoding-decoding' gradually gave way to more complex models of cultural circuits and multiple meanings. This, in turn, gave rise to a new emphasis on readers' discourses and reading practices, and a need to explore the social relations that embed all such readings within specific cultural contexts. More recently, the 'circuit of culture' idea has been extended to include questions of regulation, representation and identity (Mackay 1997) as studies of consumption have explored other models with varying degrees of linearity (such as commodity chain analysis).

The chapters in this section are all aware of the dangers as well as the appeal of a 'cultural circuits' approach. While the approach signals a welcome move from texts to social relations, a concerted effort is still needed to connect the *discourses* of marketing, retailing and consumption to the *practices* which shape the range of meanings available to various socially-situated actors. Without making this effort, an emphasis on the active construction of meaning by ordinary consumers risks romanticising their agency, exaggerating the scope for oppositional readings of various kinds. As Morley (1992: 31) reminds us, 'active' should not be equated with 'powerful'.

Each of the chapters in this section strives to avoid such a slippage, exploring the construction and negotiation of meaning empirically rather than assuming it a priori, emphasising ambiguity and ambivalence rather than championing consumer 'resistance' in an uncritical fashion. This involves (in Lien's case) opening up of the 'black box' of production and marketing to explore the institutionalised practices through which products are ascribed with meaning. In Stallard's case it involves approaching the retail book trade as a 'collaborative manufacture', among management, book-sellers and customers, while in the case of Stevenson et al. it involves an exploration of the way in which preferred or dominant readings are contested through various strategies of 'reading against the grain' (as well as through a range of more ambivalent responses that are harder to theorise in such directly oppositional terms). In different ways, each chapter tries to balance the agency of 'ordinary consumers' with an understanding of the degree to which their cultural competencies are socially structured and materially determined.

In adopting a 'cultural circuits' approach, we would also emphasise the dangers of drawing the boundaries of such systems too tightly. The circuits of culture described in these chapters might best be thought of as very leaky systems that permit all kinds of interconnections and blurred edges. Thus, for example, in Stallard's chapter on book retailing, individual booksellers (who have developed a close understanding of their particular customers) have considerable scope to implement, adapt and subvert senior management's more abstract marketing strategies. Likewise, in the research of Stevenson et al., the focus groups show how readers collude with (and sometimes contest) the editors' self-presentation of effortless success, in contrast with their understanding of the more manipulative character of other areas of the publishing industry. While the 'circuit of culture' idea is used to structure the following chapters, it is the flows and inter-connections between different parts of the circuit that should be emphasised rather than assuming it to be a tightly-drawn, all-encompassing circle.

Turning now to each chapter in turn, Marianne Lien's account of 'imagined cuisines' builds on her previously-published ethnography of the fictitiously-named 'Viking Foods' (Lien 1997). Here, she examines the manipulation of consumer taste for convenience food through a case study of the marketing of frozen pizza in Norway, showing how the marketing department at Viking Foods use constructions of national difference in an attempt to create new markets for different brands of pizza without 'cannibalising' their existing markets. Lien shows how market research in Norway conventionally recognises four consumer segments, each of which is approached through different culturally-encoded marketing strategies (via metaphors of Americanness, Italianness and, most interestingly, Norwegianness). Lien's chapter provides an important qualification to the general argument that in contemporary commodity culture "difference *sells*" (Rutherford 1990: 11) since the successful marketing of frozen pizza in Norway rests on simultaneous appeals to sameness and difference. The marketing industry's emphasis on constructions of 'ethnic' difference reflects back on dominant national constructions of what is regarded as 'typically Norwegian'. Lien also casts her argument in terms of recent debates on globalisation, showing that the use of symbols of ethnic and national difference may have specific meanings for different local audiences. From this perspective, the marketing of frozen pizza in Norway is shown to be simultaneously global *and* local.

There is no implication in Lien's analysis that Norwegian consumers are fooled into thinking that Viking Foods' pizzas are genuinely Italian or American. Questions of 'authenticity' are beside the point. What is of interest, however, is why these particular national symbols have such specific connotations for contemporary Norwegian consumers, enabling them to be used as an effective marketing strategy representing in highly condensed form, the difference between three relatively similar products. In the mutual recognition of national difference there is an apparent complicity between the buyers and sellers of frozen pizza that might be defined in terms of 'constructed authenticity'. In this process, the coding of Pizza Superiora as the people's pizza is particularly telling, relying on the coding of what Lien describes as a 'non-ethnic national identity' against which the 'ethnic Otherness' of American and Italian pizzas can be opposed. While the commercial appeal of *folkepizzaen* rests on its apparent ability to transcend ethnicity, its differentiation from other (ethnically marked) products such as (American) Pan Pizza and (Italian) Pizza Romano shows, paradoxically, that it is still firmly rooted in a logic of ethnically-defined national difference.

While Lien's chapter successfully unpacks the 'black box' of production and marketing, she does not probe the way that consumers actually 'read' the brand images with which they are presented. Such an understanding would require a different style of ethnographic work, moving closer to the lives of actual consumers. Such a move is begun in the following chapter where Paul Stallard presents an analysis of the British retail book industry and its increasing advocacy of a reader-centred approach to book-selling. Stallard shows how the managers of one particular chain of booksellers (referred to here as 'Haversham's') have drawn on the academic tradition of reader-response theory in an attempt to gain a better understanding of their customers' growing reflexivity. While Haversham's commercial strategy is avowedly reader-centred, 'readers' are usually understood as an abstraction rather than in terms of actual readers and their specific reading practices. Stallard's research employs the methods of participant observation (at one bookstore within this national chain) as well as more formal interviewing of senior staff and managers at Haversham's head office, together with focus groups and interviews with the store's customers. He draws on the language of actor-network theory and material culture studies to try to close the gap between readers, books and the retail industry.

The blurring of boundaries is also evident in Haversham's approach to book-selling which seeks to emphasise the knowledgeability of its staff and the relative autonomy of individual managers within the chain. While Haversham's is commercially a highly successful and entrepreneurial business, its self-presentation is more open and democratic, stressing how it differs from its competitors by being more egalitarian and informal. Besides the relative empowerment and autonomy of individual managers and booksellers, the purely commercial aspects of book-selling are down-played. Haversham's like to declare their "passion for books", involving themselves in various public-minded initiatives (links with national charities, collaboration with public libraries and involvement in high-profile literary prizes). All these activities contribute to the aura of "a shop that's not a shop" where purely commercial imperatives are downplayed in favour of an apparently disinterested "celebration of literature". In turn, 'booksellers' at Haversham's (never referred to as 'shop assistants') distinguish themselves from retail workers in other stores. In this respect, Haverham's staff embody many of the characteristics discussed by Frank Mort (1996) in terms of the professionalising discourses of contemporary consumer cultures. Their customers likewise appear to share this disdain for the purely commercial aspects of buying and selling books, characteristically disliking shopping for other goods besides books.

While, from a purely commercial perspective, books are merely a commodity, booksellers such as Haversham's are profoundly aware of the cultural significance that attaches to reading as a social process and of the positive associations attached to the owning (and giving) of books. Haversham's has turned this cultural understanding to commercial advantage, identifying a group of people among their customer-base for whom the readership of certain kinds of books is a key component of their cultural capital and self-identity. Significantly, Stallard contends that Haversham's appeal to their readers involves a specifically *gendered address*, contrasting reading as a social process with an academic knowledge of literary theory or the kind of critical analysis displayed in media book reviews (both of which are coded as 'masculinist'). This is certainly consistent with Haversham's emphasis (in common with many North American bookstores) on a range of book-related social events, from the provision of coffee and armchairs to author signings and book readings. Through strategies such as these, Haversham's are not simply capitalising on the increased reflexivity of their customers, they are actively cultivating it.

The gendered nature of reading as a social process is also pursued in the final chapter in this section by Nick Stevenson, Peter Jackson and Kate Brooks. In this chapter, Stevenson et al. explore the phenomenal growth of the men's magazine market as a vehicle for understanding contemporary masculinities and associated changes in commercial culture. The chapter draws on focus group research with a variety of readers and non-readers to explore the range of ways in which consumers 'make sense' of the magazines. In contrast to dominant media representations of an increasingly homogeneous culture of 'laddishness', Stevenson et al. reveal a wide range of readings including some that are supportive of the magazines' core values, some that are more ambivalent and others that are downright hostile. Having identified a series of 'discursive repertoires' that readers draw on in making sense of the magazines, Stevenson et al. map out the 'discursive dispositions' that different individuals and groups of men adopt towards these repertoires. Rather than insisting that reading these magazines is evidence of a fundamentally conservative or incipiently oppositional stance (cf. Radway 1987), the chapter explores the significance of a range of more ambivalent orientations, concluding by relating these ambivalent readings to the current instabilities of gender relations and identities.

As in the previous chapters, Stevenson et al. attempt to focus on the connections between cultural formations of gender and sexuality and specific commercial regimes associated, in this case, with the magazine publishing industry. The chapter illustrates the 'leakiness' of consumption circuits and commodity chains, where, for example, focus group participants relate the commercial success of men's lifestyle magazines to wider cultural transformations including the emergence of club culture, the blurring of distinctions between 'gay' and 'straight' commercial culture and the links between magazine publishing and other cultural forms such as popular television shows.

This last point raises questions about the limitations of different research strategies. Focus groups allow only limited access to the lived cultures in which public discourses are embedded. Likewise, editorial interviews take us only a limited way into the more expansive commercial networks in which a more rounded understanding of the culture of magazine publishing would need to be located. More generally, these chapters confirm the need for researchers to explore the links between personal narratives of identity, including the interiority of gendered and sexual subjectivities, and their public expression. Sociologists such as Beck and Giddens (drawn on by Stevenson et al.) provide only a broad-brush under-standing of such processes. More detailed understanding would require a more nuanced understanding of the psychology of personhood and its linguistic representations, exploring the orchestration of the self through consumer practices and related activities, as well as further research on the institutional dimensions of commercial culture.

References

Ang, I. (1992), *Desperately Seeking the Audience*, London: Routledge.

Ang, I. (1996), *Living Room Wars: Rethinking Media Audiences for a Post-modern World*, London: Routledge.

Johnson, R. (1986), 'The story so far: and further transformations?' in D. Punter (ed.), *Introduction to Contemporary Cultural Studies*, London: Longman, 277–313.

Lien, M.E. (1997), *Marketing and Modernity*, Oxford: Berg.

Mackay, H. (ed.) (1997), *Consumption and Everyday Life*, London: Sage.

Morley, D. (1992), *Television, Audiences and Cultural Studies*, London: Routledge.

Mort, F. (1996), *Cultures of Consumption*, London: Routledge.

Radway, J. (1987), *Reading the Romance*, London: Verso.

Rutherford, J. (1990), 'A place called home: identity and the cultural politics of difference', in J. Rutherford (ed.), *Identity: Community, Culture, Difference*, London: Lawrence and Wishart, pp. 9–27.

Tompkins, J.P. (ed.) (1980), *Reader-response Criticism: from Formalism to Post-structuralism*, Baltimore and London: Johns Hopkins University Press.

7

Imagined Cuisines: 'Nation' and 'Market' as Organising Structures in Norwegian Food Marketing

Marianne Lien

Introduction

Many authors have drawn attention to the interdependencies between commodification in late capitalism and globalisation, both in general (e.g. Friedman 1995; Featherstone 1990) and concerning food in particular (e.g. Fine and Leopold 1993; Cook & Crang 1996). This chapter discusses the commodification of difference as it is expressed in the brand marketing of frozen pizza. Drawing on ethnographic material from Norwegian food manufacture, the chapter explores how the differentiation of three remarkably similar products is achieved through the construction of complementary images of 'us' and 'the others'. It is argued that the outcome reflects considerations which are informed by both global idioms (of 'market', 'ethnic foods' and 'nation'), material conditions of food manufacture, and local interpretations of what it means to be typically Norwegian. The empirical account is based upon fieldwork in the marketing department of a major Norwegian food manufacturer referred to here as 'Viking Foods'.[1]

Commodification of Culinary Diversity

During the last couple of decades, the idea of local origin has emerged as an important idiom through which culinary distinctions are emphasised and expressed. This is apparent at large-scale global events such as international food exhibitions (Lien 1997b), in food legislation, and in small-scale marketing, as for instance in grocery stores and gourmet restaurants. Culinary differences are often expressed

---

1. The material described in this chapter draws upon an ethnographic analysis of a series of events and cases that took place while I conducted fieldwork in Viking Foods in the early 1990s. For a more thorough description of context and related events, see Lien (1997a).

and reproduced through reference to 'ethnic cuisines', a concept which through its connotations to something unfamiliar and exotic implicitly evokes (and even reinforces) a complementary image of the more familiar 'non-ethnic' national cuisine. The distinctions thus emphasised tend to reinforce the idea of a nation (or ethnically distinct region) as a homogeneous cultural entity with negligible internal variation, while simultaneously underestimating both intra-national variation and international similarities.

The commodification of culture through the construction of such 'imagined cuisines'[2] represents a possibility for considerable diversity in the market, and thus also in the diets of local consumers.[3] Although the extent of culinary diversity varies a great deal, we may observe an enhanced emphasis on diversity in general, and the value of being able to experience 'the world on a plate' seems to remain uncontested (Cook and Crang 1996).

Diversity in consumer goods is often interpreted as a reflection of the ways modern consumers embody multiple identities. Due to the centrality of food in the expression of identity, a diverse food market may increase the possibility for expression – and experience – of multiple identities (Lupton 1996). As such, diversity in consumer goods (and foods) may simply be seen as a sign of post- or late-modernity (Giddens 1991). This chapter pursues a different argument. Seeking to go beyond the simple observation that 'diversity sells', I wish to examine why it is marketed in the first place. I will argue that the emphasis on diversity in the food market may be explained by the ideological and material conditions characterising modern food manufacture and marketing, rather than simply reflecting consumer demand. More specifically, I will suggest that the use of ethnic and national imagery lends itself particularly well to the requirements of industrial mass production in capitalist societies where food is plentiful and market segmentation is a dominant ideology of product promotion. In spite of the fact that the commodification of culinary difference seems to take place practically everywhere, I contend that the specific construction of ethnic and national cuisines is indeed a local endeavour.

The commodification of culinary diversity may be analysed as an aspect of globalising processes. The idea of globalisation as a homogenising process has been strongly opposed by post-modernists and anthropologists alike, who have convincingly demonstrated that the global spread of commodities does not imply

---

2. The term 'imagined cuisines' derives from the notion of *imagined communities* (Anderson 1983). While Anderson applies this term primarily in relation to nations as they are imagined from within, the concept may easily be extended to images of a 'collective other', and to material representations of the other, as in the notion of imagined cuisines

3. This diversity does not necessarily imply a great deal of variation as far as raw foodstuffs or nutritional components are concerned. Often, the diversity relates primarily to methods of preparation and combination of a relatively narrow range of foodstuffs.

a corresponding spread in the meaning attributed to the same commodities (see, for example, Miller 1995; Das 1995). 'Homogenisation' has later been replaced with terms like *hybridisation, creolization* or even *glocalization* to indicate the mixed character of such new global forms, or to account for institutionalising processes which implies a global creation of locality (Pieterse 1995; Robertson 1995). On the other hand, going beyond the polarities of global hegemony and local appropriation, Richard Wilk argues that the global stage does not consist of a common content, but rather of a common set of structures that mediate between cultures (Wilk 1995: 111). Referring to international beauty contests, he brings attention to what he calls 'global structures of common difference'. Rather than suppressing local differences, he argues, global cultural systems may actually promote local differences. But the differences thus promoted are differences of a particular kind. Some kinds of diversities are celebrated, while others are necessarily suppressed.

In this chapter, I will take Wilk's position as a starting point for understanding the ways in which global structures inform product managers' efforts to promote frozen pizza in Norway. This perspective requires a brief description of two distinct concepts which serve as structures that help to 'put diversity in a common frame' (Wilk 1995: 111). One such concept is 'the market', a key concept both within the discipline of marketing and in day-to-day discourse. Another such concept is 'the nation', one of the most powerful models for organising modern society, and an idiom through which cultural differences are increasingly expressed.

Metaphors of the Market

The term marketing refers to at least two different entities that are analytically distinct, although empirically intertwined:

(i)   Marketing is a system of knowledge which marketing professionals will frequently consult when they make their decisions. In this sense, marketing is an applied branch of the discipline of economics. As a semi-economic discipline, marketing is basically a North American invention, but as it is disseminated and appropriated practically everywhere, marketing is indeed a global system of knowledge, and to some extent, a global hegemony. The global hegemony consists, I suggest, of some *authorised ways of attributing meaning* to local and global events, condensed by means of models, theoretical concepts and metaphors.

(ii)   Marketing is local practice. As a system of knowledge, marketing is only influential to the extent that it is taken into account by its practitioners in day-to-day decisions. While marketing as a system of knowledge exists on a global scale, marketing practice is necessarily localised in time and space. Marketing practice refers to whatever people in the marketing profession do. In this particular case, this implies the actions and struggles of a dozen men and women in their twenties and thirties, with a University MBA (Masters of Business Administration), who are employed in the Viking Foods marketing department.

Marketing consists of concepts and phrases that are applied by practitioners and in textbooks to make sense of significant features in their environment. Some understanding of these concepts, their applications and their implications is generally a minimum requirement for anyone who wishes to appear competent in the field of marketing. Analysing these concepts more closely, I discovered that they were loosely tied together in what I have elsewhere referred to as key metaphoric structures (Lien 1997a).

Metaphors are ways of understanding and experiencing one thing in terms of another (Lakoff and Johnson 1980: 5). Applied in the field of marketing, certain metaphors are particularly helpful in product managers' attempts at making sense of information which is often both massive and rather fragmented. As they are continuously reproduced in marketing textbooks and day-to-day discourse, such metaphors also become the key idioms for attributing meaning to local events. In this way, they inform and legitimise certain types of interpretations, and thus justify certain types of marketing practice. In other words: metaphors proliferate in the interface between marketing knowledge and marketing practice.

One of the most important terms in marketing discourse is the term 'the market' (in Norwegian: *markedet*). The market is a key point of reference in the marketing department, encompassing both knowledge and practice as it serves both as a *model of* the world as it is, and at the same time as a *model for* appropriate action (Fernandez 1974).

An examination of the application of the term 'market', reveals four metaphoric structures which all accentuate different aspects of the phenomenon.[4] One central metaphoric structure, frequently applied in the marketing department, draws attention to the 'market as territorial space'. Often visualised in figures (e.g. as a pie chart indicating various companies' market shares) this metaphor draws attention to the market as something finite and given, whose extension is defined a priori. External borders are emphasised, and the market thus appears as an entity that no one can acquire more of, except at the expense of someone else (Lien 1997a: 91). The image of the market as something finite thus supports the idea of competing products as potential threats, an image which is widely elaborated in what I have referred to as the 'market as battlefield' metaphor. Although the image of market as battlefield appears frequently in marketing textbooks, and in flashy promotions (e.g. of marketing consultancy), it appears to be less salient as a basis of day-to-day decision-making in the marketing department. Among Viking Foods' product managers, doubt and uncertainty were the most central traits as the market

---

4. For a more thorough account of the metaphors of the market, see Lien (1997a: 89–98).

was approached as something highly unpredictable. This approach leads us to the final two metaphoric structures, which I have referred to as 'market as an environment of natural selection', and 'market as a flux of transformation' (Lien 1997a).

The former evokes principles of natural selection in an environment in which products are referred to as entities with a certain 'life-span', facing the constant threat of 'death'. One elaboration of this metaphor is a diagram of products' anticipated life-cycle (see Figure 7.1). According to this model, each product has its natural life-cycle, and needs some promotion at regular intervals in order to 'stay alive', i.e. maintain its position in the market. In other words, the time it takes to reach the bottom line, depends, partly, on the level of marketing investment. This metaphoric structure is referred to both in order to gain support for marketing expenditure and in order to explain product failure. Another way of 'prolonging a product's life' is by careful adaptation to changing consumer demand. This idea is supported by the image of a highly fluctuating market (cf. the latter metaphor: market as flux of transformation). According to this metaphoric structure, adaptation is crucial, and must be achieved through careful interpretation of consumer demand (Lien 1997a: 95).

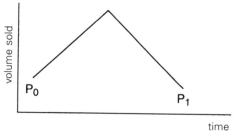

Figure 7.1   Product's anticipated life-cycle

In the following, I will argue that although metaphors of the market are subject to local interpretation, a general idea of the market serves as a common, global 'tool' which offers the possibility for structuring objects, resources and information, and for organising these along a limited number of dimensions. In this sense, the market concept and its potential for metaphoric elaborations represent what Wilk (1995) refers to as a global set of structures.

Notions of the Nation

Another example of an extremely powerful image is the concept of the nation (e.g. Friedman 1994). The most important observation for the present analysis is simply that the concept of the nation evokes an image which appears to be extremely 'good to think', not least in the field of marketing.

The notion of the nation state has a profound impact on the way we think about social process and cultural difference (e.g. Anderson 1983). The conceptual collapse of nation and people (*land* and *folk*), which implies an equation of national and cultural boundaries is central to the modern concept of the nation. Like the concept of the market, this idea of the nation places an emphasis on territoriality and on external borders. Furthermore, internal homogeneity is emphasised at the expense of local variation.

However, this collapse does not exclude the possibility of a certain distance. According to Harvey (1996), the modern world is apprehended through a central dualism which is made possible by a *distinction between representation and reality*, as may be witnessed for instance at museums and universal exhibitions. I suggest that it is precisely the awareness of this distinction that makes possible the commodification of cultural differences in the food market. Foreign cuisines are rarely commodified in a crude form. Rather, certain products are carefully selected to *represent* a particular cuisine, and from this moment they are generally modified and refined in order to appeal to common demand and expectation of future consumers. Such transformations do not, however, preclude considerable elaboration of claims to authenticity, for instance in marketing (Lien 1995, 1997a). The fact that a vast number of such 'hybrid', yet allegedly authentic, constructs are continuously marketed and consumed may be interpreted as an indication of a silent acceptance among the majority of consumers that such products do not have to be identical to what they purport to represent. In other words, a distinction between representation and reality is an accepted part of the buyer-seller-product triad.

Product Differentiation: the Case of Frozen Pizza

Let us now turn our attention to Viking Foods, and the promotion of their range of frozen pizza products that took place in the early 1990s. The main character in this account is Kristoffer; a young and ambitious product manager who has recently been granted the responsibility for Viking Foods pizza products. This is an occasion for Kristoffer to feel both pride and excitement. He is proud because pizza is an extremely profitable product for the manufacturer and his recent appointment is thus interpreted as an indication of trust and honour. He is also excited, because pizza is one of the most interesting products to work with, from a professional point of view. More precisely: it is about the only product category within Viking Foods' product range which allows for the use of consumer segmentation strategies. According to product managers at Viking Foods, one of the problems of working on the Norwegian market is that it is '*too small*' to allow promotion of differentiated products to distinct consumer segments. In this situation, pizza represents a rare exception. According to professionals in the marketing department: 'Pizza is the only market which is large enough for us to enter with consumer segmentation ... without cannibalising.' Cannibalising – in this context – is when the growth of one product takes place at the expense of another product by the same manufacturer. Kristoffer is therefore excited to be selected as the one who gets to do what he conceives that practically every product manager in his department would want to do: launch a promotion of three distinct brands of pizza products.

Pizza is a very successful product in Norway. Since it was introduced in the early 1970s by an American-inspired restaurant called Peppe's, its popularity has been overwhelming. The popularity of fresh pizza is, however, only surpassed by the popularity of frozen pizza, for which consumption has increased steadily since the early 1980s . In 1992, the consumption of frozen pizza had reached a total of 14 million pizzas sold, giving Norway a rather curious world record with regard to per capita consumption of frozen pizza. In this market, Viking Foods is considered to be definitely in the lead, holding a market share of more than 60 per cent. This is mostly due to their famous Pizza Superiora, the market leader which holds a market share of 50 per cent. Pizza Superiora is the kind of product that will be available at practically every supermarket in Norway. Most people will know it, and although most will admit to buying it now and then, few people claim to like it very much with the exception of children for whom it seems to be an all-time favourite. In the popular press, it is often referred to as a symbol of how Norwegian eating habits are deteriorating, exemplifying a low-quality, pre-prepared meal (Lien 1999).

As pizza has been appropriated in the Norwegian diet, it has simultaneously undergone a material and symbolic transformation which makes it rather different from both its Italian and American counterparts. The frozen pizza which is promoted by Viking Foods ought therefore to be conceived of as a local (Norwegian) product, rather than an example of authentic ethnic food.[5] According to the basic grammar of Norwegian popular cuisine, a pizza consists of a circular piece of dough, with tomato sauce and grated cheese on top. Additional filling may include some kind of meat, some kind of vegetable, and a variable amount of herbs and spices – but usually not very much. Within this basic format, one may

---

5. The focus of the present discussion is not on whether claims of Italianness are more or less authentically achieved, but rather on the concept of Italian and American as it is applied in the Norwegian context. This approach has much in common with Cook and Crang's concept of 'working on the surfaces' that commodities have (1996: 147) or: 'paying less attention to deepening or thickening surfaces, and more to thinking about their productivities, what they are used for. The issue becomes not, then, the authenticity or accuracy of commodity surfaces, but rather the spatial settings and social itineraries that are established through their usage' (ibid.: 147).

substitute ham for beef or pepperoni, green pepper for mushrooms or red pepper (paprika) etc.

Kristoffer enters the project when several Viking Food pizza products, including the Superiora market leader, are already well established. Thus, he has to find the proper balance between the need to revitalise a product, on the one hand (cf. Figure 1), and the idea that you should never change a winning team, on the other. In order to achieve this balance between maintenance and change, Kristoffer decides to alter only the *symbolic properties* of the products, and leave their material properties unchanged.

The Virtue of Consumer Segmentation

Viking Foods manufactures three major frozen pizza products: Pizza Superiora, the market leader; Pizza Romano, which is fairly similar but a bit more spicy; and Pan Pizza, a more recent invention which has a deeper crust. All products are firmly based upon the Norwegian pizza format, within which they appear as slight variations upon a similar theme. Kristoffer's main challenge is therefore to alter the symbolic properties of the products so that each sells more than before, but not at the expense of the others. Or, as my informants put it: how do you promote one product without *cannibalising* another? The solution, according to contemporary marketing theory, is *brand differentiation*. The only way one may promote three products without 'cannibalising' is by ensuring that each product is distinct. Even if their physical properties are not that different, their symbolic properties must be. The question thus becomes: how do you make three similar pizzas symbolically distinct? The clue – again according to marketing theory and marketing textbooks – is *consumer segmentation*.

To promote a product by means of *consumer segmentation* means that products are classified and differentiated in a way that corresponds directly to perceived differences between the consumer target groups of the respective products. In other words, one strives to create similarities between the product and its consumer, while at the same time emphasising differences between related products. Ideally, the product differences thus achieved reflect differences between consumer target groups. Elsewhere, I have discussed this simultaneous emphasis on sameness and difference as totemic classification (Lien 1997a; see also Sahlins 1976; and Moeran 1996). The idea is illustrated in Figure 7.2.

The notion of product differentiation rests upon the assumption that consumers are different and that they are different in a rather systematic manner. This assumption is strongly confirmed by market research institutes, which have enormous influence on decisions made in product development, marketing and advertising in Norway (Lien 1993). The market research institutes make a

P   #   P   #   P

|| || ||

C   #   C   #   C

Figure 7.2   *The principle of sameness and differentiation in consumer segmentation strategies*

considerable profit by providing detailed and updated descriptions of consumers, and of significant differences between what they portray as different consumer groups. For product managers, who conceptualise the market as a natural environment requiring constant adaptation, or as a flux of constant transformation, this kind of updated information about consumer segments and current trends is considered crucial.

The leading consumer segmentation survey in Norway in the early 1990s was called Norwegian Monitor (NM). Based on bi-annual surveys among Norwegian consumers, NM offers what is claimed to be a detailed description of current changes in the Norwegian population. The stated aim of Norwegian Monitor is to understand individual behavioural choices. The theoretical approach rests upon a causal model in which social characteristics shape values, which influence attitudes, which in turn have an impact on behaviour. Yet, the survey focuses almost exclusively on values, a choice which reflects cost-benefit considerations (Lien 1993: 156).

Survey results are subject to correspondence analysis and usually visualised graphically in a cross-diagram. In this diagram, the vertical axis has been labelled the *modern-traditional dimension*, while the horizontal axis has been labelled the *materialist-idealist dimension*. These labels are clearly inspired by contemporary social theory and have been achieved as a result of an interpretation of the diagram as it appears after initial correspondence analysis (Lien 1993).

These axes provide four different combinations, referred to by product managers as *upper left* (modern and materialist), *upper right* (modern and idealist), *lower left* (traditional and materialist) and *lower right* (traditional and idealist), each reflecting categories of consumers who are considered significantly different in terms of values, attitudes and lifestyle. Depending on the level of detail required, the presentation of the diagram may be altered to produce different numbers of consumer segments (e.g. 4, 6, 9 or 16).

Subscribers of NM (including Viking Foods) paid (in 1992) the equivalent of more than £20,000 for an update of the NM consumer segmentation survey. In order to plan the promotion of certain products, they may pay an extra £3–5,000

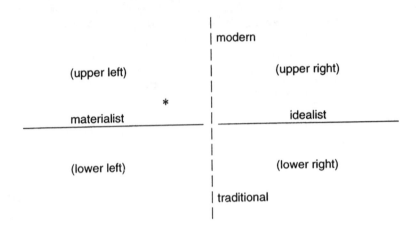

Figure 7.3   The dimensions of The Norwegian Monitor sociograph

to receive a target group analysis of the products in question. This analysis *locates* the users of the product within the diagram (as indicated in Figure 7.3).

Based on attitudes and values on various matters, each person will have a specific location on this map. Similarly, a category of persons may be indicated by locating the point of gravity for this particular group (see also Lien 1993). The consumers of Pizza Superiora are located in the upper left. According to local terminology in the marketing department, "Pizza Superiora would be located in the upper left". In other words there is a marked tendency to describe the product in terms of its consumers (and vice versa) thus blurring the conceptual distinction between product and consumer.

What Should a 'Modern Materialist' Pizza Look Like?

According to target group analyses, consumers of frozen pizza tend to be located in the upper-left quadrant. They belong to a segment sometimes referred to as 'live-for-the present', and are characterised as modern, materialistic, young and orientated towards status and consumption. Unfortunately, as Kristoffer looks more closely at the target groups for the three different Viking Foods pizza products respectively, he discovers that these consumer target groups reveal no significant differences at all. All located in the same area, they appear to be fairly similar with respect to values, lifestyle etc. According to Kristoffer, this implies that the three pizza products compete heavily with each other, thus running a constant risk of being 'cannibalised'. In other words, he may have discovered more or less the same people eating Superiora one day, and Romano the next.

For Kristoffer, this is bad news. In order to sort out this problem, he consults the market research institute requesting a detailed description of the pizza market and a suggested solution. After many discussions with his superior, Kristoffer settles on a market strategy, which in fact relies heavily on the analysis provided by the market research institute. The marketing strategy consists of three central elements:

(i)   Fortify the position of Pizza Superiora, the market leader (for a detailed analysis, see below: 'the emergence of *folkepizzaen*');

(ii)   Expand the target group in the upper left segment (the modern materialist segment) where the heavy-users are located. This may be achieved by an emphasis on convenience, modernity and American symbols which is likely to appeal to consumers located in the upper left. In the report from the market research institute, this consumer segment is described as being orientated towards American ideals and lifestyle. Furthermore:

> If we relate this to frozen pizza, it implies that symbols emphasising convenience and modernity will have appeal. Examples are names like 'King Size' and the use of 'square American letters' with 'stars and stripes' elements, contra varieties like 'Pizza Italiano' and a focus on Parisian baguettes[6] and red wine. (Target group analysis, my translation)[7]

This strategy of 'Americanisation' is pursued through the promotion of the American Pan Pizza, a product which corresponds closely with the recommendations regarding 'King Size' and 'stars and stripes'. On the package, which is decorated with stars and stripes, we find the silhouette of the Statue of Liberty, surrounded by the text: "Real American[8] Pan-Pizza". On the back, there are drawings of a cowboy on a bucking bronco, two jazz musicians and an American football player, all common symbols of the US in Norwegian popular culture.

(iii)   Reach the upper right (the modern-idealist segment) which is a consumer segment in which the so-called heavy-users of frozen pizza are few and far between. Earlier, Viking Foods tried unsuccessfully to reach this group by promoting a vegetarian frozen pizza. Apparently, this is a rather critical group of consumers. According to a target group analysis:

6. This dichotomy between North American culture on the one hand and European or Mediterranean culture on the other is commonly made in Norway. The close association which is made here between Parisian baguettes and Italian pizza, which may appear rather peculiar from a French perspective, makes sense if we consider the fact that from a Norwegian perspective, both represent something European.

7. This and subsequent citations are based upon Norwegian Monitor target group analyses of pizza products available during fieldwork, and are also cited in Lien (1997a).

8. In Norwegian, the term 'American' is often used to denote the US, rather than the American continent. Reference to other parts of the American continent than the US are usually specified, by terms such as 'South America', 'Latin America', Mexico or Canada.

The cosmopolitan persons who are interested in food and cooking have increasingly reduced their use of frozen pizza. They are in favour of French cuisine, and frequently read about gastronomy and the art of cooking . . . They are interested in culture and often seek background information for what they are doing, including cooking. Because of this machine produced factory-pizzas with soy meat fall right through. (Target group analysis, my translation)

In order to reach the segment in the upper right, Kristoffer decided upon a strategy which emphasises authenticity and Italian symbols. An existing variety, Pizza Romano, appears to be a promising candidate for emphasising 'Italianness' in the pizza product range. But, according to the target group analysis, it needs a more distinct profile:

Romano is a variety which was supposedly 'more Italian'/stronger taste more 'fein-schmecker'[9] directed than Superiora. However, it does not seem to be perceived this way. These two (Superiora and Romano) compete heavily right in the middle of the pizza market. The reason is probably that Romano has not managed to attain a distinct profile. It has become very similar to all other manufactured pizza.

Consequently, a much more distinct emphasis on Italianness is called for.

In the marketing department, this three-fold strategy is described by making a simple drawing of the upper-left quadrant of the diagram, in which frozen pizza target groups are located (see Figure 7.4). In this figure, the two asterisks pointing up and to the left represent Pizza Romano and Pan Pizza respectively, while the third asterisk pointing towards the right represents Pizza Superiora, the market leader.

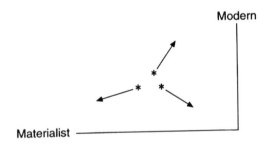

Figure 7.4   Marketing strategies for three leading pizza products

9. '*Feinschmecker*' is a German word commonly used in Norwegian which indicates a sense of 'fine taste' or 'gourmet' quality.

To summarise: it is by the simultaneous *elaboration of difference* that Viking Foods tries to expand their position and sell even more pizzas. Differentiation is achieved through a strategic effort to match the symbolic image of each pizza product to the assumed lifestyle and values of its future consumer segment. In this process of linking product and consumer segment (or pizza and person), idioms of nationality play a central role. By postulating diverging preferences between different consumer segments for various national idioms (America and Italy respectively), the market research institute provides a link which may align product and person. This is possible because certain national idioms, like 'Italy' and 'America' are condensed symbols in Norway, in the sense that they carry the potential of attributing meaning both to food products and to a certain type of persons and lifestyle.

The role of national idioms in linking product and consumers may be illustrated as in Figure 7.5. In other words, the idea of nationality represents a necessary link between the differentiation that has to do with the material and edible aspects of the product, that which has to do with text and visual design, and finally the assumed differences of values and lifestyles between consumers.

$$
\begin{array}{ccccc}
P & \# & P & \# & P \\
\| & & \| & & \| \\
N & \# & N & \# & N \\
\| & & \| & & \| \\
C & \# & C & \# & C
\end{array}
$$

Figure 7.5 *The role of national idioms in reproducing sameness and differentiation in consumer segmentation strategies.*

Imagined Cuisines

National symbols are locally defined, referring to stereotyped idioms which are influenced not only by the countries they claim to describe, but also by the cultural position and cultural preconceptions of the countries in which they are applied. Many authors have argued that food provides a particularly suitable medium for representing 'the other', making ethnic cuisine an excellent paradigm, or metaphor, for ethnicity itself (see, for instance, van den Berghe 1984; Appadurai 1988;

Levenstein 1985).[10] This implies that each national stereotype may be analysed as part of local imagery, or local images of the other. As commodities move from the sphere of production to the sphere of consumption, the imagery may take several forms. According to Cook and Crang, 'the geographical knowledges associated with foods can potentially be produced at a variety of sites within the "worlds" of those products by a variety of actors involved in their provision and consumption' (Cook and Crang 1996: 141). The exact configuration of each 'imagined cuisine' is thus not an authoritarian expert view, but rather images of the other as they are supposed to be shared by most Norwegians, as part of a conceptual cultural scheme.

It should be clear that claims of foreign origin do *not* require a careful matching of the products' material properties and the foreign culinary tradition. Rather the link is achieved metonymically, by adding something (material or in visual design) which captures the essence of what – according to local interpretations – constitutes a particular culinary tradition. Pizza Romano serves as a case in point. Pepperoni sausage and green pepper are the only elements which make the 'Italian' pizza distinct from its 'American' pan pizza counterpart. As green pepper is not conceived of as particularly Italian in Norway, we are left with pepperoni as the only signifying feature, an element which according to Norwegian interpretations could easily pass as Italian. Furthermore, pepperoni gave Pizza Romano a stronger taste, a feature which was also associated with Mediterranean cuisine. Thus, literally 'baked into the pizza product' is not only an image of its future consumer, but also assumptions about these consumers' image of Italian cuisine (Hennion and Méadel 1989).

A foreign cuisine of which few consumers have first-hand knowledge will lend itself easily to the technical requirements of mass manufacture, and easily pass as an acceptable product. I have suggested elsewhere that *it is precisely the "imagined-ness" of foreign cuisines which makes them suitable to industrial production* (for a more thorough analysis, see Lien 1997a). In the light of tourism, travelling and other globalising processes which imply cross-cultural encounters, one might expect that the possibilities for manufacturing 'imagined cuisines' will narrow down. As first-hand knowledge of foreign cuisines becomes more widely shared, the manufacturers' inventions may simply appear as too 'inauthentic'. Considering the Norwegian food market throughout the 1990s, this seems, however, not to be the case. In spite of a significant increase in foreign travel, especially to non-

---

10. In his account of the American response to Italian food from the 1880s to the 1930s, Levenstein (1985) demonstrates that the gradual transformation of American consumers' attitudes towards Italian food from unacceptable to highly accepted may be partly explained by the political situation of the United States, and especially the role of the US as Italy's ally during World War I.

European destinations[11] and a proliferation of ethnic and gourmet restaurants in Oslo, neither of these experiences seems to have curbed the popularity of frozen pizza. In fact, from 1991 to 1996 consumption both of frozen pizza in general, and of Pizza Superiora in particular, has increased steadily.[12] This development runs parallel to a heavy emphasis on authenticity, both in food advertising and in the niche-marketing of gourmet foods.

The Norwegian case suggests that an increased awareness of local origin and a preference for authentic, exotic cuisine may, in fact, run parallel to an increasing acceptance of products that, in spite of their 'Italian' claims are heavily modified and transformed to suit a local market.[13] This massive consumption of a fairly simple and highly 'Norwegianized' product, in spite of increased emphasis on local origins and authenticity in the food market, may appear as a paradox. However, if we accept, as Harvey (1996) suggests, the distinction between representation and reality as one distinctive trait of the modern gaze, the seeming contradiction disappears. Following Harvey, we may assume that Norwegian consumers simply accept artificiality and authenticity as two different representations, neither of which are particularly 'real'. The preference for one or the other might then depend on a consideration of the social occasion (frozen pizza would hardly be appropriate for a party among adults), how much money one wants to spend, and on personal taste and appetite. From this perspective, an effort to recreate an original Italian meal may be a preferred pastime on Saturday afternoon, while Pizza Superiora serves as supper with the children on Wednesday night.

The case of frozen pizza could be interpreted as another example of the superficiality involved when ' ethnicity becomes spice' through processes of commodification. hooks refers to this as a situation of 'consumer cannibalism that not only displaces the Other but denies the significance of that Other's history through a process of de-contextualization' (hooks 1992: 31, cited in Cook and Crang 1996: 145). I contend, however, that such a denial is only relevant when it is assumed that the consumer good is a 'true' representation of another culinary

---

11. According to national statistics, the total number of tour charters increased by more than 50 per cent from 1993 to 1997 (from 492,658 in 1993 to 752,527). In the same period, there was a considerable increase in charter tours to the Caribbean, Egypt and East Asia (Official Statistics of Norway, 1997).

12. According to the Norwegian Monitor, in 1991, 17 per cent of Norwegian adults consumed frozen pizza at least twice a month. In 1996 the comparable figure was 26 per cent. In the same period, the proportion of the population using Pizza Superiora at the same interval increased from 13 per cent to 17 per cent, while the comparable proportion for Pizza Romano increased from 4 per cent to 8 per cent. In all cases, a significant increase took place in all age categories, but were far more significant among women than among men (Market and Media Institute, Spisefakta 1996).

13. Market analyses indicate that the consumers of frozen pizza are not very different with regard to values and lifestyle, than those who regularly consume more 'gourmet'-style alternatives such as chilled, home-made or home-delivery pizzas (Market and Media Institute, 1996).

tradition. When, on the other hand, a distinction between representation and reality is integrated as part of the 'consumer's gaze', neither a denial nor a verification takes place. Instead, a multitude of interpretations and responses may occur. A similar situation is described by Harvey, in her study of the universal exhibition (Expo 1992). Visitors to the Expo, she argues, did not 'require either the exhibits or their responses to them to express a rationalising coherence'. Rather, in their interpretations of the purposes of the displays she found three distinctive responses: 'nations show things as they are, they show the best that they have to offer, they show an image that does not conform to any particular reality' (Harvey 1996: 142).

From this perspective, the massive consumption of frozen pizza represents an example of a thorough and radical recontextualisation of a dish in which process the dish's origin is less important than the particular purpose it may serve in the homes of contemporary Norwegian consumers. Among these purposes, convenience and the emphasis of children's preferences are particularly important, possibly at the expense of authenticity and culinary distinction.[14]

The Emergence of "Folkepizzaen"

The process of appropriation of pizza in the Norwegian culinary context is most clearly illustrated in the case of Pizza Superiora. While a move towards the 'upper left' (modern-materialist) was achieved through an emphasis on Americanness, and a move towards the 'upper right' (modern-idealist) was achieved through an emphasis on Italianness, a 'fortification' of the position of Pizza Superiora (the market leader) should be achieved by a move towards the centre of the Norwegian Monitor diagram (cf. Figure 7.4). But how is this achieved?

Technically, the centre of the diagram is the point of gravity of the entire Norwegian population, the hypothetical location of a target group which is not differentiated in any way at all. At the same time, each piece of promotion needs to play upon something distinct. Kristoffer wants to sell more Pizza Superiora, but not at the expense of the other pizza products. Thus, he needs to come up with a catchy phrase which emphasises the symbolic distinctiveness of the product, yet this distinctive property can neither be Italian, nor American. Furthermore, it must appeal to the average Norwegian consumer. According to Kristoffer it should appeal to everybody while not offending anybody. After a few weeks, Kristoffer comes up with the solution. He formulates a Pizza Superiora brand strategy in which he describes the product as follows:

---

14. A more detailed analysis on the context of consumption is provided in Lien (1999).

Superiora is the pizza for pizza lovers . . . it is to be positioned as Norway's clearly most popular [Norwegian: "mest solgte"] pizza. This is the pizza that everybody likes, regardless of age, sex and other demographic data. Superiora is *the people's pizza in Norway* [Norwegian. "*Folkepizzaen i Norge*"] (my emphasis).

Recodifying Pizza Superiora as *folkepizzaen i Norge* ("the people's pizza in Norway"), Kristoffer plays upon the idea of sameness between product position and the product target group. More than any other pizza product at Viking Foods, Superiora is consumed by "nearly everybody", and Superiora is given its distinct characteristic precisely through the image of being the Norwegian people's pizza.

This distinct characteristic is simultaneously the result of a deliberate effort to construct difference. The conceptualisation of Pizza Superiora as the Norwegian people's pizza makes explicit the notion of a "non-ethnic national identity to which the 'ethnic' Others are opposed" [in this case: Romano and Pan Pizza] (Cook and Crang 1996: 145). In this way, Kristoffer recontextualises this particular pizza as something very Norwegian. Kristoffer's achievement is simply that he applies the notion of a non-ethnic national identity to describe a product which has earlier been interpreted as a foreign import. Through this example of re-codification, the appropriation of pizzas in Norway has, in some sense, become complete.

In addition, the concept *folkepizzaen i Norge* introduces a second dimension that is not immediately apparent through English translation. The prefix *folke-* connotes egalitarian values that are deeply rooted in Norwegian society. In her description of central themes in Norwegian culture, Marianne Gullestad emphasises what she considers to be the typically Norwegian notion of *equality defined as sameness*. Highly apparent in Norwegian discourse, she argues, the egalitarian tradition involves "not necessarily actual sameness, but ways of under-commun-icating differences during social encounters" (Gullestad 1989: 85). This theme is reflected in a wide number of ways, including social institutions whose primary purpose is to ensure equal access to various resources, such as, for example, the social security system (*folketrygden*), or the public educational system (*folkeskolen*). In Norwegian, quite a number of such institutions are referred to by applying the prefix *folke-*.

Consequently, when he conceptualises Pizza Superiora as *folkepizzaen i Norge*, Kristoffer locates his product right at the heart of Norwegian notions of equality and social democracy. Most importantly, perhaps, he transmits a notion of a pizza that is non-pretentious in terms of social hierarchy. In Norwegian discourse, the term '*folke*' and notions of high culture, elite or upper class are almost contradictory. Something which is termed *folke-* is almost by definition *non-exclusive* in terms of social class.

In a more recent paper, Gullestad (1997) draws attention to the revitalisation of national identification as a response to both global (transnational) and regional (local) politics. Gullestad suggests, on the basis of studies of Norway, that traditional national themes are at present transformed by people with different and new experiences. In particular she draws attention to the metaphors of the nation which tend to be mirrored on the division between the home and the outside. Despite increased cultural pluralism, such metaphors tend to emphasise a sense of homogeneity among people with a shared, local past thus potentially legitimating an understanding of immigrants as not properly belonging to the nation in the present (Gullestad 1997: 53).

The prefix *folke-* appears to capture precisely this notion of a homogenous, non-ethnic, and inclusive us. Yet, underneath this seemingly tolerant (in the sense of being non-pretentious) inclusion of the average Norwegian, one may sense a fairly rigid and traditional understanding of who this average Norwegian might – and might not – be. I suggest that if the idea of *folkepizza* works, it is partly because those Norwegians who happen to share a local past are likely to recognise the multiple meanings implied, and thus to feel included. For others, who do not grasp the subtleties of the term, it might not make that much of a difference.

The fact that Kristoffer chooses the term *folkepizzaen* to describe his product, does not necessarily imply a deliberate effort to link the product to the values mentioned above. Drawing on a shared cultural repertoire of concepts and metaphors, he may simply have come across one that seemed to fit. He needed a concept that would cover the average Norwegian, not exclude anybody, and not evoke the notion of the traditional, nor the very modern. When Kristoffer comes up with the term *folkepizza* he describes a person for whom no describing characteristics apply, except for 'ordinariness' – being just the same as everybody else. This is exactly the notions that the term *folke-* conveys. Pizza Superiora thus appears as a 'non-ethnic' national product whose distinctiveness rests precisely on an assumed lack of distinction, both in the sense of class and in the sense of cultural differentiation.

Localising Global Diversity

According to Richard Wilk, globalisation implies a hegemony, not of content but of form. He writes:

> The globalizing hegemony is to be found in structures of common difference which celebrate particular kinds of diversity while submerging, deflating or suppressing others. The global system is a common code, but its purpose is not common identification; it is the expression of distinctions, boundaries and disjunctures. (Wilk 1995: 118)

Global structures may be of different kinds. Wilk mentions international beauty contests as an example, and we might also include other international events such as the Olympic Games, or the World Exhibition as examples of structures *within which cultural diversity may be organised*. However, the exact ways in which diversities are expressed are subject to local interpretations. Our focus of interest is therefore both the *implications of structures* for communicating differences, and also the ways in which *local interpretations of this particular structure* serve to accentuate differences of particular kinds.

I have drawn attention to two central structures which are applied to organise and express difference in food marketing in Norway. Marketing represents one such structure, particularly by providing a set of metaphors by means of which product managers are able to attribute meaning to their environment. Applying models of the market, product managers are able to discern differences that make a difference, and justify their strategies on the basis of these. In this way, marketing (as a system of knowledge) provides a set of models and metaphors within which certain differences may be expressed.

The idea of the nation as an overarching organising principle in modern thought represents another structure by which differences are organised and expressed. The empirical material reveals an underlying dichotomy of foreignness and familiarity. This dichotomy tends to be conceptualised through the idiom of nationality. In the case presented above, the notion of national origin constituted a key element by means of which product differences were expressed. In this way, the idea of nation provided a conceptual scheme for differentiating a product range in a way that corresponded to differences which were perceived as significant in an 'ever-changing market'.

To the extent that marketing is hegemonic, I suggest, in line with Wilk (1995), that it is a hegemony of form rather than content. This particular form draws attention to local differences which may be utilised in matching product and consumer. National idioms represent one type of difference that is frequently exploited in this manner. Capable of attributing meaning both to products and to distinct categories of persons (consumer segments), national idioms serve as differentiating features in the market place, and are accentuated as a result. However, it is important to note that in terms of content, this endeavour is highly local, substantiating what I have described as an 'imagined cuisine'. The persistence of such imagined constructs, exemplified here by three brands of frozen pizza, does not seem to be threatened by a simultaneous celebration of authenticity, which may be witnessed in the food market in general. I have suggested that the presence of these opposing tendencies may be interpreted as implying a modern 'consumer gaze' which neither expects nor requires a close continuity between representation and reality.

References

Anderson, B. (1983), *Imagined Communities*, London: Verso.

Appadurai, A. (1988), 'How to make a national cuisine: cookbooks in contemporary India', *Comparative Studies in Society and History*, 30: 3–24.

van den Berghe, P.L. (1984), 'Ethnic cuisine: culture in nature', *Ethnic and Racial Studies*, 7: 387–97.

Cook, I. and Crang, P. (1996), 'The world on a plate', *Journal of Material Culture*, 1: 131–53.

Das, V, (1995), 'On soap opera: what kind of anthropological object is it?', in D. Miller (ed.), *Worlds Apart. Modernity through the Prism of the Local*, London: Routledge, pp. 169–89.

Featherstone, M. (1990), *Global Culture*, London: Sage.

Fernandez, J. (1974), 'Persuasions and performances; of the beast in every body and the metaphors of Everyman', in C. Geertz (ed.), *Myth, Symbol and Culture*, New York: W.W. Norton, pp. 39–60.

Fine, B. and Leopold, E. (1993), *The World of Consumption*, London: Routledge.

Friedman, J. (1994), *Cultural Identity and Global Process*, London: Sage.

—— (1995), 'Global system, globalisation and the parameters of modernity', in M. Featherstone, S. Lash and R. Robertson (eds), *Global Modernities*, London: Sage, pp. 69–90.

Giddens, A. (1991), *Modernity and Self-Identity*, Cambridge: Polity Press.

Gullestad, M. (1989), 'Small facts and large issues: the anthropology of contemporary Scandinavian society', *Annual Review of Anthropology*, 18: 71–93.

—— (1997), 'Home, local community and nation: connections between everyday life practices and constructions of national identity', *Focaal*, 30/31: 39–60.

Harvey, P. (1996), *Hybrids of Modernity*, London: Routledge.

Hennion, A. and Méadel, C. (1989), 'The artisans of desire: the mediation of advertising between product and consumer', *Sociological Theory*, 7: 191–209.

Lakoff, G. and Johnson, M. (1980), *Metaphors We Live By*, Chicago: University of Chicago Press.

Levenstein, H. (1985), 'The American response to Italian food, 1880-1930', *Food and Foodways*, 1: 1–24.

Lien, M. (1993), 'From deprived to frustrated: consumer segmentation in food and nutrition', in U. Kjærnes et al. (eds), *Regulating Markets, Regulating People: On Food and Nutrition Policy*, Oslo: Novus Press, pp. 153–70.

—— (1995), 'Fuel for the body – nourishment for dreams: contradictory roles of food in contemporary Norwegian food advertising', *Journal of Consumer Policy*, 18: 1–30.

—— (1997a), *Marketing and Modernity*, Oxford: Berg.

—— (1997b), 'Nation, technology and nature: constructions of safe food in the market', *Social Construction of Safe Food; Health, Ethics and Safety in Late Modernity*, Report no. 5/97, Trondheim: Centre for Rural Research.

—— (1999), 'Djevelen spiser pizza', (The Devil eats pizza), *Samtiden*, 1: 82–8.

Lupton, D. (1996), *Food, the Body and the Self*, London: Sage.

Market and Media Institute (MMI) (1996), *Norsk Monitor 1996: Spisefakta* (Norwegian Monitor 1996: facts about eating), Oslo: Market and Media Institute (cited with permission).

Miller, D. (ed.) (1995), *Worlds Apart. Modernity through the Prism of the Local*, London: Routledge.

Moeran, B. (1996), *A Japanese Advertising Agency: an Anthropology of Media and Markets*, ConsumAsian Book Series, Richmond, Surrey: Curzon.

Official Statistics of Norway (1997), *Statistics on Travel (table 50)*, Oslo: Statistics Norway.

Pieterse, J.N. (1995), 'Globalisation as hybridisation', in M. Featherstone, S. Lash and R. Robertson (eds), *Global Modernities*, London: Sage, pp. 45–69.

Robertson, R. (1995), 'Globalisation: time-space and homogeneity-heterogeneity', in M. Featherstone, S. Lash and R. Robertson (eds), *Global Modernities*, London: Sage, pp. 25–45.

Sahlins, M. (1976), *Culture and Practical Reason*, Chicago: University of Chicago Press.

Wilk, R. (1995), 'Learning to be local in Belize: global systems of common difference', in D. Miller (ed.), *Worlds Apart: Modernity through the Prism of the Local*, London: Routledge, pp. 110–33.

8

Reflexivity, Reading and Gender in the Retail Book Industry

Paul Stallard

The following account derives from research undertaken on the retail book industry.[1] The wider research project from which the following arguments are drawn involves a consideration of the presence and effect of the book in a range of social practices. The project takes a theoretical position derived from Actor Network Theory (Latour 1993; Law 1986, 1994) and the material culture framework of Daniel Miller (Miller 1987) both of which problematise the subject-object dualism of much social theory, seeing subject and object as a relational conjunction rather than ontologically separate. I mobilise this theoretical agenda to explore forms of subjectivity which incorporate the book as a relational component. This is examined in two settings: firstly amongst readers for whom I show that the book plays a significant role in establishing and mediating broader practices of identity and sociality. And secondly amongst booksellers for whom the characteristics of the book play a major role in structuring their working practices. I use the arguments regarding subjectivity which ensue from the application of this theoretical agenda to my empirical study to critique the boundedness of the concepts employed in the commodity chains literature, arguing for the hybridity rather than the distinctiveness of production and consumption.

This wider project is drawn from empirical research involving long-term participant observation within and around a UK bookselling chain (referred to here fictitiously as 'Haversham's'); interviews with employees at all levels of the company's hierarchy; and a series of interviews and focus groups with readers/consumers. Participant observation was recorded via a research diary and all interviews were taped and transcribed. All research material was analysed using a thematic framework.

This chapter draws primarily on interviews with Haversham's personnel, as well as with a member of a peripheral organisation which operates as a consultant to both Haversham's and to the library service and other areas of the publishing

1. The research was funded by ESRC as part of my PhD at the University of Sheffield.

industry. I also draw on research material and experiences from interviews with readers. The chapter describes changes underway in the retail book industry during the period of research.[2] Changes which I argue reflect an ongoing restructuring of the industry in line with a particular view of the subjectivity of their customers. Specifically, I want to connect these changes to a heightened self-reflexivity amongst readers, customers and employees and argue that gender is implicated in these changes.

I employ the term self-reflexivity fairly broadly to encapsulate a general shift wherein "self formation, identity politics and risk taking come to centre stage in modern societies. [Consumption and identity] . . . are increasingly linked by the need to fashion a successfully communicated and communicative self and a clearly justified biography (of both self and others) (Glennie and Thrift 1996: 233). This encompasses both a cognitive reflexivity such as Giddens' (1991) and Beck's (1992) notion of the knowledgeable self, and an aesthetic self-reflexivity more like Lash and Urry's account derived from the 'mirroring' concept inherent to the romantic-aesthetic tradition (Lash 1993; Lash and Urry 1993). Both require a revived sociality for their operation, an emphasis on different identifications adapted to different social settings and the sites of sociality that promote this (Glennie and Thrift 1996: 234). This sociality "revolves around flexibility of social interaction and identity . . . a loosely bonded social group crystallising out of the mass" (Glennie and Thrift 1996: 226) akin to Maffesoli's (1996) tribes. Gender is both a dynamic and an outcome of this shift:

important because of the rise since the nineteenth century of discourses on sexuality which in combination with growing biographical pluralism have led to sex becoming the object of increasing cognitive and aesthetic reflexivity, blurring traditional constitutions of gender . . . Sexual identity ceases to be anatomical destiny and more and more becomes a lifestyle issue . . . Gender variety has become both a cause and effect of increasing reflexivity . . . [whilst] the crowd is first of all a place where new gender identities can actually be identified, tried out, explored . . . the throng and its inherent sociality are crucial elements of both consumption and gender in late modern, high modern or post-modern times. (Glennie and Thrift 1996: 232 and 236)

In this chapter I shall consider ways in which this notion of subjectivity, this "dynamic, narcissistic view of self as project, as object to be continually worked on and improved" (du Gay 1996: 113) is manifested in the retail book industry and the ways in which this reflects gender roles. One might point to various ways in which changes in this sector parallel and complement this reflexive shift. The

2. Participant observation was undertaken between 1995–1998. Most of the interviews and focus groups took place in between September 1996 and May 1997.

emergence and expansion of the Haversham's brand in the last fifteen years represents a national emergence of a particular style of bookselling.

The Haversham's Brand

Central to the Haversham's brand, for instance, is a (qualified) decentralisation of power away from the centre to the level of local shops and the shop floor employee. Thus individual shops have absolute responsibility for stock profiles and a certain proportion of marketing decisions, a decision-making exercised at the shop floor level partly via the autonomy of individual booksellers. The raison d'être for this is twofold. Firstly, this empowerment operates as a means of disciplining the retail worker into an 'enterprising' subject position as a means of "productivity through people, treating the rank and file as a source of quality and productivity gain" (Peters and Waterman 1992: 14) to allow and encourage provision of high levels of customer service:

> If it was a fantastic experience and you really had a nice time then that's surely what will drive you back in rather than being insulted at a till. You must have had it when you go into a shop and you think 'bastards, I'm never going in there again' just because of their indifference to you . . . I think we do manage it quite well and that's because our staff are empowered. They're not paid huge sums of money but they're given responsibility to use their brains and their initiative and they can therefore care about what they do. Everybody who works for Haversham's makes a difference to the way that the business runs and that has a huge effect on the overall impression I think. If you go into [name of another UK chain bookseller] and you ask for help they can be as polite as they like but if they don't have the skill or the nous to help you with what you want then it's frustrating all round. It's frustrating for the customer and it's frustrating for them. (Haversham's senior manager)[3]

Secondly, it acts as a means of heightened response to consumer reflexivity. Employees are seen as responsive to consumer demand because "they're the same people, they're customers as well", a similarity understood both cognitively, in

3. Whilst bookseller testimonies (and personal experience) suggest motivations for working which do not necessarily equate with this 'enterprising' subject position (such as lack of employment alternatives, the out-of-hours social life afforded by workplace colleagues, the comparatively undisciplined nature of work and subsequent opportunities for resistance by not working etc.) motivations for working commonly included factors such as the satisfaction obtained from the social encounters involved in customer service and particularly the opportunity to project and affirm personal identity by making use of knowledge and skills associated with the job and the employees' interest in books. This was often contrasted with emphasis upon the lack of motivation for working provided by the relatively low wages.

terms of employees' and customers' ability to "describe and define" each other, and aesthetically in the sense that "they mirror each other" (conversation with Haversham's marketing director, male). The significance of this understanding to the operation of the organisation is emphasised by an admission by two interviewees that a primary motivation in the implementation and pursuance of an equal opportunities policy was the recognition that a greater diversity of staff has a noticeable impact in breadth of customer profile (Haversham's manager; Haversham's director).

Similarly, the organisation consciously sets out to produce spaces in which the kind of sociality required for reflexivity can flourish. At the level of basic shop design space is designed to feel at least semi-public, encouraging time-rich browsing whilst operational practices lend an air of liberal tolerance of difference and behaviours not necessarily associated with the act of purchasing, at least in contrast to some other retail spaces. The (paradoxical) suggestion is of an only semi-commodified venture:

> [a] shop that's not a shop. We're a haven, that's a crucial part of why people come and shop in Haversham's. You're on the high street, you go and bash your way around the shops then you go and enjoy yourself in Haversham's. That's how we're perceived by our customers. (Haversham's Director)

More recent developments in shop design meanwhile revolve around the addition of features which represent a deliberate emphasis on establishing shops as 'leisure spaces' rather than merely retail spaces such as US-style coffee shops and theatre/presentation areas for author events etc.

It is some of these emergent trends within the company which are my primary focus in this chapter, and specifically the slight shift in discourse and rhetoric which underpins some of these and associated other practices. In brief this might be summarised as a shift in emphasis from a primary focus upon product – the book – to a shared emphasis on product and consumer – book and reader. Central to the Haversham's brand since its inception has been a 'passion about the product':

> The experience of Haversham's should be a celebration of literature. Customers should sense this, staff should embody it, everyone should feel this celebration of literature as a pulse beating through everything we do. (Haversham's undated: 3)

> In the personnel manual there's an outline for what you're looking for in staff . . . first and foremost it's a passion for books. (Haversham's manager)

As John Law suggests however, organisations driven by enterprise cannot remain static:

You've got all these balls up in the air and the art of management is to keep them all up in the air at the same time. And to do that you have to keep on moving. (Law 1994: 188)

Enterprise . . . tells of the way in which agents – heroes and organisations – are sensitive to shifting opportunities and demands. It tells of capitalising on those opportunities. (ibid.: 75)

There is a sense currently within Haversham's that movement and opportunity[4] might derive from an expansion of their founding rhetoric to incorporate 'the reader' as well as 'the book':

It's probably fair to say that the company has gone as far as it can in doing really good promotions which celebrate books and establish the company as an authority for books and there's room now to think about other areas where the company can develop without compromising what we already do, such as in the area of reading. (Haversham's senior manager)

There is therefore an emergent rhetoric surrounding readers and 'reader-centred promotion' partly deriving from the organisation's desire to "enrol" (Shapin and Shaffer 1985; Latour 1992) other organisations into the Haversham's network of influence as a means of both consolidating further the presence of Haversham's within the habitus (Bourdieu 1977) of its clientele and broadening that customer base. Typical organisations include:

charities and other organisations where there's a natural relationship or I hope there's a natural relationship, like The Tate Gallery, The Turner Prize and increasingly looking at visual arts and music as well as written text because I think the relationship should be just as strong. Our relationship with children's organisations and people like Index and International Pen – the issue of censorship is certainly very close to home. It's just generating support and understanding about the brand without necessarily being seen to mention professional activity. . . It's a club that they want to belong to. A lot of my work involved with charities and organisations is something they always want if they're looking for an AB1 literate audience because they're always exactly the same people. The people who give most to charity are likely to be Haversham's customers. The people who go to galleries or become Friends of the Tate are most likely to be Haversham's customers. It just goes on wherever you go . . . These are our tentacles spread everywhere [laughs]! (Haversham's senior manager)

---

4. This is currently regarded as more pressing as the company ensures it remains a market leader in the face of competition from US incomers and to justify itself more than ever before in terms of enterprise in preparation for its upcoming flotation on the stock market.

Networks of Meaning and Practice

One particular arena considered worthy of enrolment are the networks of meaning and practice associated with the library service. This liaison is articulated as a relationship in which Haversham's is dominant:

> using the fact that our literary counter space can be terribly useful for other people and not underestimating how useful that can be especially to a smaller organisation like the library association struggling still to get libraries out of the 'ladies in tweed skirts' image. They like the idea of being associated with Haversham's and I like it in reverse because it shows we're more generous. (Haversham's senior manager)

This veils a less often articulated valorisation of the spaces and practices of public libraries in their more recent, modernised, professionalised forms, (Greenhalgh 1991) in terms of their community building, sociality and the breadth of 'audience' they serve. Part of what Haversham's really wants to enrol is the inclusiveness of library spaces and practices as a means of broadening their customer base. A director at Haversham's concluded a conversation with me about the merits of incorporating a reader-centred approach into the Haversham's strategy with the comment that what really worried him was that the brand 'missed people' – that the brand was not sufficiently fine tuned to provide a 'mirror' or point of recognition for the maximum possible profile of people. Reader-centred promotion, imported as a set of discourses and practices from the library service, offers a means for fine tuning the brand, centred still upon the product to maximise this mirroring effect by making readers and customers themselves part of the mirror.

An important conduit channelling these discourses and practices into Haversham's network of ordering is, in John Law's terms an "heroic agent" (Law 1994: ch.3)[5] in the form of a consultancy which has pioneered 'reader-centred promotion' within the library sector and has now been contracted to introduce certain aspects of this approach to Haversham's. The philosophy of the consultancy derives from a number of sources. Its agents have backgrounds which include adult education, arts administration, community publishing, as well as their own graduate educations. Informing their approach in a general sense is a notion of 'critical literacy' akin to that found in a wide literature ranging from the critical

---

5. The agent in question appeared aware of the double-sided status of this heroism: "the danger now is for a while that voice became personalised and people talked about the [consultant's name] effect, having had [consultant's name] and it was like a conversion and people used my name as shorthand because there was a lack of vocabulary to talk about what we talk about . . . that was very dangerous because it implied that this thing depended on an individual and personal enthusiasm and did not depend on a set of ideals that could be learnt and transmitted and used" (Reading consultant, female).

pedagogy of Paulo Freire (1987, 1993; Taylor 1993) to the Reader Response Criticism of Wolfgang Iser (1978, 1989, 1995), Stanley Fish (1980) or Louise Rosenblatt (1970; Clifford 1991). Common to all of these is a focus on the act of reading or 'reception' and an insistence on the potentially emancipatory, improving or liberating character of the act either in terms of the individual self or wider society. Similarly, an explicit aim of the consultancy is to turn the notions of reading as the creative process in the chain that links author and reader espoused by structuralism and post-structuralism into praxis:

> the people who expounded a philosophy of reading best are the structuralists, the post-structuralists. So in an academic world the reader has been recognised and the reader writes the text. The reader has been recognised all along but in a language that is not acceptable to anybody. It happens in a sealed off area that has been separate from everything else. (Reading consultant)

The foundation of their ethos might best be summarised by de Certeau's claim for reading as poaching:

> The reader takes neither the position of the author nor an author's position. He invents in texts something different from what they 'intended.' He detaches them from their (lost or accessory) origin. He combines their fragments and creates something un-known in the space organised by their capacity for allowing an indefinite plurality of meanings. (de Certeau, 1984: 169)

> All writing depends on the generosity of the reader. (Manguel 1996: 179)

So the consultancy operates on the basis of privileging reading as the creative process over and above the creativity of the text, the author or the authorities attributing meaning to that text. They define themselves as "the start of a new wave which values the creative role of the reader as well as the artistic impulse of the writer" (Van Riel and Fowler 1996: 8). This leads to a shift in emphasis from design, promotion, practice and marketing based around product to the same based around the process of reading. In practice this leads to attempts to privilege reader-response over the response of authorities external to the reader and an emphasis on the experience of reading and the 'use' of books in relation to existing subjectivities rather than the ascription of meaning to texts in terms of their relation to other texts (literary canon).

In Haversham's the consultancy has been involved in training staff how to facilitate reading groups in ways which allow (shared) experiences of reading to come to the fore rather than abstractions about 'meaning'; in encouraging a form of recommendation that avoids recourse to 'literary authority' but instead refers again to experiences of readers; and in developing generic promotions which focus on reading rather than product. The example here being a joint promotion between Haversham's and the library services for National Libraries Week intended to develop a language about reading which contrasts with the alienating languages of literary criticism and media reviewing:

> an accessible language which enables us to discuss the complexity of the reading experience and the way this is shaped by the creative contribution of individual readers . . . to lighten up the whole debate about reading and involve more people in it. (Haversham's/National Library Week press release, October 1997)

This was promoted via a campaign encouraging readers, shoppers and borrowers to draw comparisons between reading and their narrative and relational identities (Giddens 1991; Somers 1994) in terms of another area of broad, shared experience, in this instance relationships in their love life – "Play Around with a Book!":

> This comparison [. . .] encourages readers to think about what they are prepared to put into the relationship from their side and what they expect to get back from it. Just as in a relationship you make with other people, you may want different things from a book at different times in your life or in different moods. Some readers start lots of relationships and pack them in easily without regret; others read every page of a book and refuse to give up even when things go wrong. There are readers who stick with the same author for life and others who lurch from one promising affair to the next. Some of us are serial monogamists while others are promiscuous with half a dozen books on the go at once. Everyone has their dream read, their bit on the side, an old flame they go back to. (Haversham's/National Library Week press release, October 1997)

What is being suggested here then is an enhancement of the responsiveness of a commercial sector to consumer subjectivities and reflexivity – the fine tuning of the mirroring capabilities of a commercial brand via greater incorporation of the subjectivities being mirrored into that brand. The extent to which this occurs should not be overplayed. The strategy is not one of complete emulation of the (potentially) heterotopic space of public libraries (Lees 1997), their privileging of reading experience and subsequent breadth of acceptable subjectivities. Rather, any appropriation of that model is mediated by an ongoing commitment to the existing brand which targets a very specific customer profile.[6] The intent is to achieve a

---

6. 76 per cent aged 24–55; 30 per cent AB1; 60 per cent female; 39 per cent resident in London or South-East; responsive to book reviews; loyal to particular authors; promiscuous brand affinity; dislike shopping for other goods (Haversham's strategic review 1995/96).

broadening of this profile in a manner which doesn't weaken the core of the brand's design (based in product) and its appeal to this group. A corollary of this nevertheless is the increased responsiveness of this sector to gendered subjectivities. I turn now to a discussion of the way in which changes in practices and discourses surrounding reading in this retail industry reflect a gendering of practices amongst readers.

Reading Practices

Reading consists of a collision of practices. In his account of the reading practices of science fiction readers James Kneale (1995: ch.7; cf. Manguel, 1996) shows how reading styles, practices and contracts intertwine during his respondents' reading. He identifies a range of reading styles ranging from reading for realism – plausibility, mimesis of social reality etc.; reading for the fantastic – escape, otherness, new ways of thinking; reading beyond the narrative – for say the interaction of characters rather than plot development in the manner of soap opera (Ang 1996; Radway 1984) and reading for affect – physical pleasure, the traces of which are visible in descriptions of goosebumps, spines tingling or languorous sensation. To this I might add from my own research reading for practical gain – learning how to do something/reading for self-improvement; as well as various other non-textual motivations influencing reading style such as reading for social encounter – sharing books amongst friends, reading for topics of conversation etc. (Morley 1986; 1992) and location – reading to fill time and alter space (Tacchi 1998).

The picture, then, is of a web of practices and styles, different readers drawing on different parts of the web in terms to constitute their own reading style and relation to canon and genre. And indeed individual readers drawing on different parts of the web at different times and places in their reading experience. This web is cross-cut by hierarchies of class and gender. So for example Kneale, drawing on Bourdieu's (1986: 66-74) notion of the connoisseur and the pedant points to the complex use of strategies and tactics derived from different areas of this terrain of practice in terms of their relation to an 'elite' view of science fiction:

> The place of these readers both within and outside the cultural elite creates a fascinating set of movements backward and forward across the line between 'high' and 'low' culture . . . By demonstrating their knowledge of the 'right' way to read, and mimicking the strategies of the elite, these discussants attempt to gain access to their store of cultural capital. (Kneale unpublished: 232)

My study reader's responses similarly suggest a complex gendering of this terrain. This is illustrated by the difficulty I had in getting male respondents to acknowledge their occupancy of certain parts of this web of practices and styles. This was particularly true in terms of ideas such as reading for affect and reading to be transported elsewhere. Whilst the subtexts of their comments and their allusions to their practice suggested that frequently this did form part of their motivation for reading there was nevertheless a tendency (rather than a rule) for this to be avoided or steered away from as an explanatory factor by male respondents. This is not necessarily to suggest a binary male vs female reading style along the lines of affect vs practicality, realism vs escapism, individual vs social, cognitive vs bodily as 'the way that men read' and 'the way that women read'. Both male and female respondents frequently occupied positions transcending such binaries.

It is perhaps to suggest such a model in terms of gender-based power relations. My explanation of these encounters where I had the sense of account not matching subtext is that the respondents were reflexively accounting for themselves in terms of where they felt they were or wanted to be placed in terms of their perception of the power relations affecting reading. This would hold in terms of the power relations of the interview setting and the respondent's dialogical encounter with a male interviewer potentially positionable within this (masculine) elite reading position.[7] Thus a male tendency to emphasise their own positioning within these masculinised discourses and practices by avoiding their discussion and a female tendency to draw from both masculine and feminine positions but to feel the need to apologise for some of the feminine ones as 'guilty' pleasures.

Commercial Response

I want to finish by returning to my argument about the commercial response to this reflexivity. Haversham's understands its customers in terms of a simplified version of the network of reading practices described above, defining them in terms of a 'psychographic' typology regarding whether they have an 'internal' or 'external' orientation towards books and reading. The former broadly encapsulates the masculinist side of the dualisms listed above referring to cognitive, individualist, practical notions of reading. The latter the feminised side of the power equation encompassing affective and social attributes (Haversham's director; Haversham's manager). Both of these have been incorporated into the design of the brand. The gradual emergence of 'the reader' as an object of consideration and brand retuning,

---

7. All respondents knew of my academic background; some knew of my involvement in bookselling; many assumed my background was in English Literature; most assumed they could talk about genres, canons, authors, titles or assumed meanings of texts without the need for explanation or contextualisation. I frequently attempted to perform other positions in this network of practices although these may well have been read as strategic rather than 'natural' performances.

however, occurs in the context of the sense that where internally orientated customers are served well by the brand, and the book industry generally, the externally orientated have been responded to less effectively. The developments associated with reader-centred promotion might be seen in terms of an incorporation of the feminised aspects of the network of reading practices into the commercial framework, and to an extent therefore a favourable shift in the power relations between these feminised and masculinised styles. Certainly, the tenets of reader-centred promotion are based around privileging the affective, emotional response to reading and the social networks of reading.

This (emergent) attitude partly owes its existence to power relations within the commodity chain. In common with other sectors of the retail economy (Bromley and Thomas 1993; du Gay 1996: ch.5) a case can be made to argue that the balance of power between manufacturer/supplier and retailer has shifted in the retailer's favour. There is certainly a sense within Haversham's that this is the case and that their innovation and taste setting has an impact on the rest of the industry. One discourse that emerged from interviews at head office level was that it had taken the company a while to wake up to the fact that it did have a power and an influence over other areas of the industry. The 'retuning' described in this chapter can be seen in the context of a new confidence within the company and a sense that their innovation and responsiveness to consumer reflexivity can act as a mark of differentiation and a means of authority against other areas of the industry. Some of this 'innovation' has indeed influenced other areas of the commodity chain. The organisation has, for instance, worked collaboratively with publishers to produce guides to their novels intended for use by reading groups as starting points for discussion.

In this context, however, 'the industry' includes both actual suppliers/ publishers and the wider institutions of 'taste setting', notably the literary media. The rhetoric within the company surrounding the forms of reader-based promotion discussed in this chapter was often contrasted with the distinct lack of reflexivity or responsiveness to readers of the literary media, deemed "up [their] own arse" (Haversham's senior manager, female). In part this can be seen in terms of an enterprising, female (in this instance) agent reflexively aligning themselves within the network of gendered power relations in the manner in which my reader-respondents positioned their own selves, in this case defining themselves (and their agency within the organisation) firmly against the masculinist hegemony perceived elsewhere in the industry.

Conclusion

My argument, then, is that, driven by a discourse of enterprise and by a conscious understanding of notions of consumer reflexivity, the 'retuning' of the Haversham's brand has led to a heightened sensitivity to the subjectivities of consumers and a subsequent shift in the gendering of the practices and discourses of reading the organisation promotes. To a limited extent the hegemonic position of the company within the book industry means that this influence extends into the commodity chain beyond the retail sector.

There is a danger that this conclusion leads to a cheerful celebration of the retail sector as a democratising influence via its responsiveness to consumer demand. It is possible, however, to read this in other ways. In a discussion about the "dangers inherent in the extension of reflexivity", for example, Scott Lash draws upon the later Foucault to argue that "what appears as the freedom of agency for the theory of reflexivity is just another means of control . . . as the direct operation of power on the body has been displaced by its mediated operation on the body through the soul" (Lash, 1993: 19–20). For John Law, however, this becomes more a question about the nature of the "modes of ordering" which condition this reflexivity:

> it is plausible to go out and look for fairly coherent and large scale ordering patterns in the networks of the social . . . orderings which (to the extent that they are performed) generate, define and interrelate elements in relatively coherent ways. And in particular it is plausible to look out for specific strategies of reflexivity and self reflexivity. (Law 1997: 107)

Haversham's attempts to fine tune its brand and organisation by enhancing its responsiveness to its customers via a focus on reading might be seen in terms of the development of just such a mode of ordering for practices of reading. This mode of ordering is relationally defined by the existing practices and discourses of ordering which make up the Haversham's organisation. These are multiple and varied and allow for a relatively free play of subjectivities defined outside the organisation, as the set of influences (critical literacy, post-structuralism, gendered resistance to dominant discourses) constituting the agents involved in the promotion of these reader-centred approaches suggest. Nevertheless, the hegemonic mode of ordering within the company remains one of enterprise and commercial vitality defined in terms of profitability, market leading and innovation.

References

Ang, I. (1996), *Living Room Wars: Rethinking Media Audiences for a Post-modern World*, London: Routledge.

Beck, U. (1992), *Risk Society: Towards a New Modernity,* London: Sage.

Bourdieu, P. (1977), *Outline of a Theory of Practice,* Cambridge: Cambridge University Press.

—— (1986), *Distinction: A Social Critique of the Judgement of Taste,* London: Routledge.

Bromley, R. and Thomas, C. (eds) (1993), *Retail Change,* London: UCL Press.

Clifford, J. (1991), *The Experience of Reading: Louise Rosenblatt and Reader Response Theory,* New Hampshire: Heinemann.

de Certeau, M. (1984), *The Practice of Everyday Life,* Berkeley: University of California Press.

du Gay, P. (1996), *Consumption and Identity at Work,* London: Sage.

Fish, S. (1980), *Is There a Text in this Class?* Cambridge, Mass: Harvard University Press.

Freire, P. (1987), *Literacy: Reading the Word and the World,* London: Routledge.

—— (1993), *Pedagogy of the Oppressed,* New York: Continuum.

Giddens, A. (1991), *Modernity and Self Identity,* Cambridge: Polity.

Glennie, P. and Thrift, N. (1996), 'Consumption, shopping and gender' in N. Wrigley and M. Lowe (eds), *Retailing, Consumption and Capital: Towards the New Retail Geography,* London: Longman, pp. 221–37.

Greenhalgh, L. (1991), 'The Public Library as a Place' in *Comedia Working Papers: The Future of Public Library Services,* London: Comedia.

Haversham's (undated), *The Haversham's Book of Design,* London: Haversham's internal manual co-produced with Newell and Sorrell.

Iser, W. (1978), *The Act of Reading: A Theory of Aesthetic Response,* Baltimore: Johns Hopkins University Press.

—— (1989), *Prospecting: From Reader Response to Literary Anthropology,* Baltimore: Johns Hopkins University Press.

—— (1995), 'Interaction between Text and Reader' in A. Bennett (ed.), *Readers and Reading,* London: Longman.

Kneale, J. (1995), *'Lost in Space: Readers' Constructions of Science Fiction Worlds',* UCL: unpublished PhD thesis.

Lash, S. (1993), 'Reflexive Modernisation: The Aesthetic Dimension', *Theory Culture and Society,* 10: 1–23.

Lash, S. and Urry, J. (1993), *Economies of Signs and Spaces: After Organised Capitalism,* London: Sage.

Latour, B. (1992), 'Where are the missing masses? Sociology of a few mundane artefacts' in W. Bijker and J. Law (eds), *Shaping Technology, Building Society: Studies in Sociotechnical Change,* Cambridge, Mass: MIT Press.

—— (1993), *We Have Never Been Modern,* London: Harvester Wheatsheaf.

Law, J. (ed.), (1986), *Power, Action, Belief,* London: Routledge & Kegan Paul.

—— (1994), *Organizing Modernity,* Oxford: Blackwell.

Lees, L. (1997), 'Ageographia, heterotopia and Vancouver's new public library', *Environment and Planning D: Society and Space,* 15: 321–47.

Maffesoli, M. (1996), *The Time of the Tribes: The Decline of Individualism in Mass Society,* London: Sage.

Manguel, A. (1996), *A History of Reading,* London: HarperCollins.

Miller, D. (1987), *Material Culture and Mass Consumption,* Oxford: Blackwell.

Morley, D. (1986), *Family Television: Cultural Power and Domestic Leisure,* London: Routledge.

—— (1992), *Television Audiences and Cultural Studies,* London: Routledge.

Peters, T. and Waterman, R. (1982), *In Search of Excellence*, New York: Harpers and Row.

Radway, J. (1984), *Reading the Romance: Women, Patriarchy and Popular Literature*, Chapel Hill: University of North Carolina Press.

Rosenblatt, L. (1970), *Literature as Exploration*, London: Heinemann.

Shapin, S. and Schaffer, S. (1985), *Leviathan and the Air Pump: Hobbes, Boyle and the experimental life*, Princeton: Princeton University Press.

Somers, M. (1994), 'The Narrative Constitution of Identity: A Relational and Network Approach', *Theory and Society*, 23: 605–49.

Tacchi, J. (1998), 'Radio Texture: Between Self and Others', in D. Miller (ed.), *Material Cultures: Why Some Things Matter*, London: UCL Press.

Taylor, P. (1993), *The Texts of Paulo Freire*, Buckingham: Open University Press.

Van Riel, R. and Fowler, O. (1996), *Opening the Book: Finding a Good Read*, Bradford: Bradford Libraries.

9

Ambivalence in Men's Lifestyle Magazines

Nick Stevenson, Peter Jackson and *Kate Brooks*

Introduction

This chapter focuses on the production, content and readership of the new generation of men's 'lifestyle' magazines which can be dated from the launch of *Arena* in 1986 and which reached its apotheosis in the mid- to late 1990s with the phenomenal success of magazines like *FHM* and *Loaded*. While there have been many studies of women's magazines, emphasising the complex and contradictory ways in which they are read, both affirming and challenging established notions of femininity (McRobbie 1978, 1991; Winship 1978, 1987; Ballaster et al. 1991; Hermes 1995), there have been relatively few studies of the commercial or sociological significance of men's 'general interest' or 'lifestyle' magazines. Among the exceptions, Sean Nixon's *Hard Looks* (1996) devotes three chapters to magazine culture and the rise of the 'new man'; Frank Mort's *Cultures of Consumption* (1996) includes a discussion of 'style magazines' (especially *The Face* and *Arena*); and Tim Edwards' *Men in the Mirror* (1997) has a chapter on the style and content of men's magazines. These studies all focus on new visual codings of masculinity, including issues of 'spectatorship' and the politics of the gaze (see also Nixon 1997), rather than on the ambivalent ways in which contemporary masculinities are experienced by men as consuming subjects – the focus of our research.[1]

The analysis presented in this chapter also differs from current media commentary on the magazines which projects an image of a homogeneous and unrelenting 'laddishness'. Referring to the recent 'dumbing down' of magazines such as *Arena, Esquire* and *GQ*, for example, the *Guardian* (13 July 1998) reaches the depressing conclusion that "We're all lads now". Earlier articles also noted a homogenisation of the men's magazine market: "*Loaded* is only one year old and already its chicks-and-footy ethos has spread to all corners of male magazinery" (*Guardian* 10 April 1995) or "A decade ago, we had such high hopes of men's

---

1. The research was funded by ESRC (grant number R000221838).

magazines. Instead, we've ended up with a babes 'n' breasts bonanza" (*Guardian* 1 December 1997). Our research suggests a more differentiated picture. Alongside the dramatic success of 'lad mags' like *Loaded, Maxim* and *FHM*, more serious and 'upmarket' titles like *Men's Health* are also doing extremely well with sales having almost doubled since the mid 1990s (see Figure 9.1). More significantly,

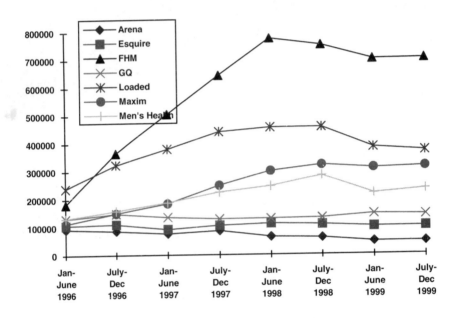

Source: Audit Bureau of Circulations

Figure 9.1   Circulation statistics (average monthly sales)

however, we wish to explore how readers 'make sense' of the magazines and their shifting representations of masculinity rather than taking those meanings as read (cf. Jackson et al. 1999). While we have found little evidence of directly 'opposit-ional' readings, actively resisting the 'laddish' ethos of the magazines, we have found considerable ambivalence in the way they are read, suggesting a pervasive disquiet with more hegemonic forms of masculinity (cf. Connell 1995). It is these ambivalences in contemporary masculinities that we wish to explore in more detail, defining ambivalence as a situation in which quite contradictory impulses and emotions co-exist, with positive and negative components remaining in opposition without easy resolution. As in Parker's (1995) work on maternal ambivalence, from which this definition is derived, ambivalence need not only be thought of as disabling but can also be creative.[2]

Method

This chapter draws on a series of focus group discussions with twenty groups of readers (and non-readers), most of whom described themselves as casual or uncommitted readers rather than regular readers, committed to one specific title. The groups (see Figure 9.2) were recruited through friends and friends-of-friends

Islington: public sector professionals, Asian/Jewish Londoners	**Derby women**: thirty-something, middle class, public sector
18 year olds: unskilled working class/unemployed Sheffielders	**Bristol students**: twenty-something media studies students
Gay men: forty-something Sheffielders	**Bristol lecturers**: middle-class academics
Pimlico: 25–35-year-old casual readers, London graduates	**Musicians and artists**: middle class, Bristol
Journalists: professionals and students, Londoners (one man, the rest women)	**Fashion shop assistants**, working-class Sheffielders
Turnpike Lane: 25–40-year-old London graduates	**Stoke Newington**: media professionals, London, upper middle class
Disabled men: working-class Sheffielders	**Unemployed men** (with care worker): London
Footballers: Sheffield postgraduates and professionals	**Manchester lecturers**: middle class
Art College students, London	**Bikers** (motorcyclists): working class, thirty-something, Taunton
Derby men: middle-class professionals	**Counsellors**, thirty-something, middle class, London

Figure 9.2   The focus groups

2. Katarina Weger suggests that sociologists have tended to regard ambivalence as a painful condition, characteristic of a wider 'flight from ambiguity' (Levine 1985) in contemporary social research. Instead, she suggests that ambivalence can be approached more constructively as indicative of two or more conflicting but intersecting moral vocabularies that reflect competing moral themes in the culture at large (1992: 89).

in Bristol, Derby, London, Manchester, Sheffield and Taunton and via advertisements in newsagents. Most of the groups were single sex (men only), though some were mixed and one was women-only. The groups were designed to encompass various dimensions of difference including men of varying age, class and ethnic backgrounds. Some groups were expected to have a relatively high investment in 'lifestyle' issues (such as those in the media and fashion industries). Others had relatively low levels of cultural and economic capital (such as the group of unemployed men). Some were anticipated to be enthusiastic about the magazines (including the various student groups), while others were expected to be more antithetical to them (including the Taunton bikers group and, from a different perspective, the London-based Counsellors group). In each case, discussion was loosely structured around a number of themes (awareness of the magazines, likes and dislikes, ideas about target audience etc.) with few direct questions from us as moderators. Each group met once for between one hour and an hour-and-a-half. The discussion was taped and transcribed in full. Analysis involved all three researchers listening to the tapes and reading the transcripts repeatedly, independently noting key phrases, ways of talking, patterns of response etc. leading to the identification of a number of *discursive repertoires* (see Figure 9.3).

harmless fun	laddishness
naturalness	trash (including 'disposability')
honesty	irony
openness (including 'visibility')	change (including 'backlash')
seriousness	women as Other

Figure 9.3   Discursive repertoires

As we have argued elsewhere (Jackson et al. 1999), these repertoires are used by different individuals and groups of men in order to 'make sense' of the magazines and the changing masculinities with which they are associated. In identifying these discursive repertoires, our approach was similar to Hermes' (1995) identification of the 'interpretive repertoires' through which women's magazines are made meaningful.[3] There are also parallels with Frazer's concept of 'discursive register': "an institutionally, situationally specific, culturally familiar, public, way

3. Hermes (1995) includes a number of descriptive repertoires such as 'easily put down' and 'relaxation' as well as interpretive repertoires such as 'practical knowledge', 'emotional learning' and 'connected knowing'. More analytical repertoires include those of 'vanguard', 'moral duty' and 'liberal-individualist'.

of talking" (1992: 195) which she used to suggest that teenage readers of *Jackie* engaged in frequent and dramatic shifts in register without these registers being necessarily contradictory.[4]

Limiting analysis to the identification of discursive repertoires risks obscuring readings that go 'against the grain' of dominant discourses, where a particular repertoire might be identified by a focus group participant ('harmless fun', 'laddishness' etc.) but where that individual may not personally have endorsed such a view (being critical or dismissive of it, for example). To address this problem, we have in this chapter attempted to identify a range of *discursive dispositions* that individuals took towards each of the repertoires, allowing for 'refusal' or 'rejection', for example, as well as dispositions that endorse a particular discourse, such as 'celebration' or 'compliance' (see Figure 9.4). While we found few examples

celebratory	vulnerable
compliant	distanced
hostile	refusing/rejecting
apologetic	analytical
deferential	dismissive
defensive	ironic

Figure 9.4   Discursive dispositions

of explicitly oppositional readings (implying an outright rejection of the magazines and a degree of 'resistance' to their discursive practices), we found many cases of ambivalence which we have attempted to distil and analyse in the remainder of this chapter.[5] Tactics, such as silence and humour, are also considered alongside more explicitly oppositional strategies (cf. de Certeau 1984). Some of these dispositions appear to be rooted in aesthetic or political attitudes that are more or less independent from the group context in which they were articulated. Others are clearly shaped by the context of interaction (with other members of the group and with ourselves as moderators). As such, we would agree with Pearce's remarks about the politics of reading when she argues that:

4. Many of these ideas can be traced back to Stanley Fish's (1980) work on the authority of 'interpretive communities' where he used the term 'repertoire' to describe a way of making sense of the world through systems of intelligibility shared by members of the same interpretive community.

5. The idea of 'resistance' implies a degree of coherence and intentionality, as well as a self-conscious ability to specify what is being resisted. Similarly, the identification of 'oppositional' readings would imply a singularity and coherence in the 'dominant' meanings attributed to the magazines for which there is little evidence in our focus groups.

why we end up approving or disapproving of a work will often depend on the (*interactive*) processes at work in the reading as well as on the ostensible frames of reference, aesthetic and political, to which we refer (1997: 217).[6]

Our approach is also informed by Janice Radway's pioneering study of romantic fiction where she argued that reading is "multiply determined and internally contradictory", with different readings "embedded in the social lives of their readers" (1987: 7–8). While there are multiple readings of any text, however, we share Radway's commitment to identifying a finite number of patterns or regularities on the basis that "similarly located readers learn a similar set of reading strategies and interpretive codes which they bring to bear upon the texts they encounter" (p. 8).[7] We also endorse Radway's emphasis on the ambiguity of reading, rather than making a definitive judgment about whether a reading is "fundamentally conservative or incipiently oppositional" (p. 209).

Discourses and Dispositions

At this point we want to make an analytical distinction between discourses and dispositions. Here, our approach comes close to Bourdieu (1990) in that the discourses and practices of culture (attending a football match, looking at a painting, reading a book) are clearly distinguished from our dispositions towards culture or what Bourdieu calls the *habitus*. The *habitus* is a class-specific set of dispositions whose content is determined by the dominant class relationships in a social field. It is a learnt bodily disposition which promotes feelings of in-group solidarity and primarily helps mark out distinctions and boundaries between different social groups. Following Bourdieu, we argue that an analysis of dispositions allows us to account for a link between culture and agency, which avoids more overtly structuralist concerns that have shown little regard for the creativity evident within everyday life (Giddens, 1984). However, where our analysis differs from Bourdieu is that by concentrating on group differences he obscures the reflexive capacity of individuals within groups to be able to adopt a range of dispositions during an

---

6. Pearce's own work concentrates on differences between groups of feminist readers who might initially be thought of as members of a single interpretive community. Looking at reading as a process where readers are 'implicated' (with the text and with other readers) she focuses on declared positions (where readers engage with or reject a text according to 'prepared grids') and on covert processes (involving notions of interpretive community, audience and text-reader interactions). Unlike our own work, however, Pearce focuses on readers' *written responses* rather than on transcripts of their conversations.

7. Although Radway does not refer to these as 'discourses' or 'dispositions' she does identify a number of such codes including fantasy, guilt, luxury, self-indulgence, 'reading for instruction' and reading as 'compensation'.

*Not Marxism
?*

on-going conversation. Whereas Bourdieu is primarily concerned with dispositions that are relatively durable within the domain of social class, we are concerned to map personally-held dispositions onto more public categories in a way that respects both macro and micro levels of analysis.

Discourses (or what we have termed 'discursive repertoires') are the public forms of talk that enable individuals and social groups to make the magazines meaningful. Dispositions, on the other hand, are more personal than repertoires and open the possibility of less ordered and more ambiguous spaces. To talk of dispositions in terms of our project enables us to break both with popular media perceptions of a homogenous and unrelenting laddishness and the language of outright refusal suggested by notions of resistance that were evident in earlier strains of cultural studies (e.g. Hall and Jefferson 1976; Hall 1980). The issue of ambivalence in this context raises the question of how far the dominant meanings and discourses of masculinity go in imprinting themselves upon the subjectivity of the 'audience'. It also points beyond a concern to be able to map the conversations held about the magazines onto more stable categories suggested by terms such as 'reader response'. Readers' dispositions towards the discursive repertoires which they hold are, then, a dialogic product of the relation between the wider social context and members of a particular group, the individual and publicly sanctioned discourses concerning the magazines, and the influence of the focus group moderator(s). Our analysis suggests that a notion of 'ambivalence' rather than ideological indoctrination or refusal will best help us to understand the ways that different dispositions are mobilised by different groups and individuals.

In the following section we identify a number of examples of such ambivalence, returning to one of the initial aims of our research – the possibility that the magazines might be read as opening up a discursive space for their readers, offering ways of 'doing masculinity' differently from its more hegemonic forms (cf. Connell 1995; Segal 1990). Despite the much-publicised 'dumbing down' of men's 'lifestyle' magazines, following the commercial success of the more 'downmarket' titles (such as *FHM* and *Loaded*), we wish to explore whether it is still possible to read the magazines against the grain of the more oppressively 'laddish' forms of masculinity that these magazines so resolutely promote. In the final section we attempt to identify whether these ambivalent readings correspond to any wider differences or distinctions (by class or education, for example).

Ambivalent Dispositions

The predominant tone in many of our focus groups was *celebratory*, championing the 'honesty' and 'lack of pretension' of magazines such as *Loaded* (hailed by a member of the Pimlico group as promoting "the unacceptable face of men").

195

According to the Bristol student group: *Loaded* "makes no qualms about it . . . they're not hypocritical". Or, as a member of the Stoke Newington group suggested: "there's a kind of freedom now to, you know, shout and be kind of loud and get pissed". Even for those with some personal reservations about the magazines, there was a general sense of *compliance*: "they don't feel the need to justify having women with very few clothes in them any more . . . it's shameless" (Manchester lecturers). Occasionally, however, our focus group participants expressed a different view, including several cases where readers were outrightly *hostile* towards the magazines: "I'm just amazed at the way they depict women . . . I'm deeply shocked" (Journalists), "I'm sorry but . . . it just gets a bit boring after a while, just treating people like sex objects" (Derby men). As these examples suggest, such views were often expressed in a (semi-)*apologetic* tone. In other cases, participants appeared to be monitoring their conduct for our benefit as researchers (particularly in groups that were moderated by Kate). To give a couple of examples: "I mean, you've got a pretty bird on the front [cover], er woman, sorry" (Unemployed men) and "No offence, but women are interested in things like that [relationships], aren't they" (Footballers). More commonly, participants would adopt a *deferential* tone towards one another, ensuring the (re)production of a group consensus as in this case where one participant is enumerating the stereotypical interests of *Loaded* readers, seeking approval from the rest of the group:

> They're talking about beer, football, women, clothes, music and films. I think that just about covers it, doesn't it? What else is there?

and later in the same group:

> Yeah, as I were saying, if you're into football, booze, women, films, what was the other one? (Footballers)

Likewise, among the Taunton motorcycle group, there was a general disdain for the readers of men's magazines, described contemptuously as 'muppets'. Though the group appeared to share this view of men "who haven't got a true bone in their body", it later became clear that one member of the group regularly bought *Men's Health*, while another spoke openly about his changing taste in clothes:

> *Hal*: You know how you can get stuck in your ways?
> *Billy*: I think so.
> *Hal*: Like, for instance I got a load of *Next* vouchers for Christmas so I went in there and I got a load of stuff and I waited a couple of months and then got a bit more. So, I'm thinking, why not?

Kate: Do they do biker things in Next?

Hal: No. I was nearly wearing the same tee shirt that I'd been wearing for the past five years. We were going out for a meal, you know, and wearing the same old tee shirt and jeans.

After some laughter from the rest of the group, he went on:

Hal: I do like to dress up now and again, smart and um . . .

Kate: So the magazines would help in that respect?

Hal: Um, yeah, maybe . . . just to see what was, what people are wearing and, um, I wouldn't look completely stupid when I went out.

In other cases, the conversation would open out into a hesitant critique of the magazines before being rapidly closed down again in a rather *defensive* manner, frequently through the use of humour or consensual references to sport:

John: But I think if you want to think about it, [the magazines] sort of legitimise laddishness, you know, whereas before, you'd be a bit quiet about that. You wouldn't be sort of upfront about talking about women like that . . . you know it's a bit of a group thing where you can have a bit of a chin-wag and a laugh, you know.

Nick: Right, and do you think that's a good thing or . . .

Larry: No I don't like it . . . it does offend me slightly.

Mick: It doesn't bother me one way or the other. It's a bit of fun really, isn't it.

and later:

Larry: I mean personally, I'm quite interested in men's health and problems, you know, and fitness and whatever, I think it's quite important. And it always niggled me that women were catered for in that area . . . you know sort of sexual problems or health problems that men tend not to talk about as much as women may and I think it's good that that sort of opens up as well . . .

John: There's an air of embarrassment, I suppose, you wouldn't discuss it openly and I certainly wouldn't, unless there was something seriously wrong with me, go to the doctors, you know just brush it under the door and hope it will go away . . . Men just kept those things to themselves. They don't generally talk to each other about them. You'd face ridicule from your friends down the pub if it was dragged up . . .

Larry: So I would say that's quite an important breakthrough [though] I could live without any of it, you know, I wouldn't miss any of it.

Nick. Right.

John: You know, to be honest with you, if I was going to buy any of these mags one subject it would be football . . . Health doesn't interest me very much . . . but football's my main thing. (Turnpike Lane)

The use of spatial metaphors in these extracts ('opening up', 'narrowing down', being 'upfront' etc.) is highly significant. It may be, as we have suggested elsewhere (Jackson et al. 1999) that the 'new' issues being covered in the magazines – a concern for health, relationships and bodily display – are not so new for individual men. What is new, however, is the sense of an emerging *public discourse* on men's health where a series of spaces have 'opened up' in which men can acquire the kind of practical and discursive competencies they may previously have lacked. While this may not be the case for some of the magazines which continue to treat health issues and sexual relationships in a jokingly 'ironic' way, it would certainly be true of *Men's Health* and one or two of the other magazines which try to provide serious advice in a non-judgmental and informative way.[8]

A similar kind of defensiveness is evident in discussions of sexuality, when, for example, the Bristol students attempt to defend the magazines' portrayal of women ("I don't think it's sexist at all . . . more of a celebration . . . they don't slag women off . . . they love women"). Some responses were less predictable, as when one participant spoke wistfully about the widening opportunities for men "to desire openly as a man" (Bristol lecturers), while another suggested that:

> the roles that men can adopt have widened [from] a very narrow definition of what was acceptable masculine role models. I think it's opened up . . . but now they're being narrowed in again (Counsellors).

This sense of a 'lost moment' recurred in other groups. One participant referred to men's roles "being expanded, then now being narrowed again" (Counsellors) while another suggested that:

> There was a moment there actually which I think was lost . . . There was a moment about the beginning of the 90s where *Iron John* [Robert Bly's best-seller on the men's movement] was published and there was suddenly, you know, there was a great concern, there was certainly a focal point for, you know, men who . . . for somebody to talk about masculinity, to talk about father and son relationships and what not, and it, I suppose, it was about the time maybe these things [men's magazines] were a twinkle in somebody's eye. (Stoke Newington)

But, he continued, things had then started to run in the opposite direction, towards a more rampant 'consumerism' and the moment had passed.

---

8. Compare the editor's claim that all the material in *FHM* should be sexy, funny or useful – and preferably all three (*The Guardian* 17 February 1997).

Many of our participants were suspicious of the power of the magazines and of the publishing industry generally: "it's like industry-driven, it's all manufactured, isn't it" (Footballers); "they suck you in" (Pimlico). In contrast to the magazines' image of an unapologetically laddish masculinity, several participants described men as *vulnerable* and needing reassurance: "a lot of times it's people aren't confident enough . . . to have their own personalities, people are a bit frightened to be individuals" (Disabled men). Men's insecurities were mentioned by several groups (Derby men, Stoke Newington), to be remedied by the purchase of appropriate products, including magazines which "legitimise a certain way of behaviour" (Musicians).

The blame for men's insecurities is, of course, often laid at the door of women, leading to some interesting reversals of conventional gender relations, as when feminism is described as having involved "a kicking for men" (Islington) or when the images of women in men's magazines are described as evidence of women's power over men:

Does she look like a fucking victim to you? She scares the shit out of me. You know what I mean? Going up to her in a bar and asking her for a date, you know, it would take a brave man . . . These are fucking strong, intelligent women . . . Fucking sexy women . . . powerful as well. (Islington)

A process of *distancing* was commonly used by other participants to avoid the charge of taking themselves or the magazines too seriously. Such a disposition was evident in men's description of their reading practices as 'browsing' or 'flicking through' with little or no sense of commitment to a particular title:

"I occasionally buy *Loaded* or *FHM* . . . found it quite amusing" (18 year olds).
"I guess I must have picked them up and browsed through other people's" (Journalists).
"I've never actually bought one myself", "I used to buy them but . . ." (Footballers).
"It's just the first one I happen to pick up . . ." (Bristol non-readers).
"I've actually not bought a men's magazine for maybe a couple of years now . . . I often browse on the shelf . . . I only ever read them in the dentist's" (Stoke Newington).
"I read them at work if I've got a bit of time to kill . . . or if you're going on a train journey" (Musicians).

Distancing sometimes hardens into outright *refusal*, as when a member of the Counsellors group spoke of "the funny mish-mash of things" that appear in the magazines which he couldn't actually imagine men reading, refusing the alleged coherence of the 'lifestyle' package that the magazines portray (cf. Chaney 1996). Likewise, many participants resented the idea that they needed a magazine to tell them what to do: "what's a magazine going to tell you that you don't already know?" (Bristol students).

Other men adopted a more *analytical* disposition (no doubt partly in response to their perception of our 'academic' interests), referring to processes of commercialisation and liberalisation:

> I don't think there's been a change in new man to new lad . . . they've always been there but [the magazines] have come about now . . . due to the massive commercialisation in like the dance music culture and the drug culture and the fact that you can get away with it . . . it's like a general liberalisation of society (Bristol students).

These themes are also present in one of the editor's reflections on the success of *Loaded*, symptomatically entitled "Getting away with it" (Southwell, 1998).

Other readers vehemently rejected such an analytical disposition, refusing to 'theorise' the magazines and entirely *dismissing* their political significance:

> *Derek*: Well, you could get all theoretical, couldn't you, and talk about postmodernism and all that kind of stuff and maybe that's it, maybe you know, now identities are a lot more complex . . . If you want to analyse it, *if* you want to analyse it . . .
> *Graham*: I think we're being far too theoretical about it.
> *Derek*: Yeah.
> *Graham*: I just don't think it's got anything to do with backlashes [to feminism] . . . I mean, buying *Loaded* is not a political act in any shape or form (Footballers).

Finally, several of our participants adopted an *ironic* disposition towards the magazines (as opposed to the ironic tone of the magazines themselves, epitomised in *Loaded*'s self-designation as "for men who should know better").[9] As is well known in literary theory, however, irony is double-edged (Hutcheon, 1994), as demonstrated by these remarks on the typical range of products ("toys for men") advertised in the magazines:

> you have to spend £2,000 on a Rolex and then you know, Oh a nice little Fiat Coupe. You know, buy a nice pair of Armani sunglasses for £400 etc. etc. . . . I mean £3,000 for a bike, you know, or a mobile phone . . . There's not you know 20 ways to spread your DSS [social security benefit]. (Unemployed men)

---

9. Significantly, however, *Loaded*'s editors repudiate the notion that the magazine is written or read in an ironic fashion: "Now what I've always thought about *Loaded* was there was no irony to it at all, everything was done from the heart . . . Half a million people are buying it . . . These people aren't reading it ironically and it's not being written ironically" (Southwell 1998: 254).

Members of this group were particularly critical of the magazines for pushing consumerism: "a catalogue of boys' dreams", "it's like the working-class people don't really matter, you know . . . a sort of upper class yob magazine". A member of another group also ironised the magazines' attempt to commodify men's current anxieties: "without a job/house etc.? . . . grab a magazine" (Pimlico). Another respondent claimed to have stopped reading the magazines because he felt their use of 'irony' was simply a cover up: "It was like, you were being implicated with them and you were sort of part of them . . . the irony was just a bit of a cover up . . . by the end I felt implicated in it . . . you're kind of buying into something . . . investing in it" (Manchester lecturers).

Finally, we identified various *silences and absences*, both in terms of the magazines' content and in terms of what men had to say about them. One glaring example was the almost total lack of discussion of parenting within the magazines and among our participants, whether in relation to men's personal experience as parents or their relationships with their own parents.[10] Among our respondents, there was almost no discussion of how their lives differed from their fathers or of what they had learned from them about 'being a man'. Other absences included issues of race (apparently 'invisible' to our predominantly white respondents) and domesticity (except as something to be avoided).

Differences and Distinctions

Much of the current literature on identity articulates a sense of the self that is caught between chaos and certitude. The breakdown of tradition, the globalization of culture and the refashioning of sexual identities have all been held to have had a marked impact upon the construction of the gendered self. While much post-modern discourse has pointed towards the fragmentation and commodification of modern identities, other currents have referred to the preservation of older social divisions that became associated with modernity (Giddens 1991; Lash and Friedman 1992). The modern self is seemingly caught between a more uncertain and reflexive disposition and more stable social markers. Taking the example of changing masculine identities, many of these features soon become apparent. Reviewing the sociological literature, Segal (1990) points towards the 'slow change' of masculine identity in respect of participation in child care, the declining importance of the role of the 'breadwinner' and adherence to heterosexual norms and practices. Yet it is undoubtedly the case that the commodification of masculine

---

10. Where such stories do appear, they are written in a predictably 'ironic' manner. See, for example, the discussion of parenting in *FHM* (September 1998) entitled "Know your enemy" which includes a section on calculating "the price of a baby". *Maxim* (June 1998) also included a short article with a series of bullet-points on "How to be a better dad".

anxieties, growth in awareness of health issues and a more reflexive disposition towards fashion and the body (all evident in the magazines) articulate more ambivalent frames.

Here we aim to take this dialectic further through a discussion of what Ulrich Beck has called 'constructed certitude'. For Beck, the construction of certitude represents a form of counter-modernity. If modernity has meant the increasing questioning of tradition, doubt, reflexivity and the unfreezing of gender relations, counter-modernity attempts to dismiss such issues. The attempt to replace questioning and doubt with more certain frames of reference can be related to a number of fundamentalist currents which talk in terms of certainty rather than risk. Beck writes:

> Certitude arises from and with the prevalence of a 'magic of feelings' (to use a modern term), an emotional praxis that sweeps away the trembling and hesitation of questioning and doubting with the instinctive and reflex-like security of becoming effective and making things effective in action. (1997: 65)

According to Beck, the construction of certitude offers a 'magical' solution to questions of identity, eradicating doubt and the need to orientate oneself in a world that is increasingly perceived as being fragile and uncertain. In terms of masculinity, the more 'certain' world of patriarchal relations is not only part of a wider nostalgia for a social order that protected men's material interests, but one that offered more straightforward codes in terms of what passed as 'acceptable' masculine behaviour. However, wider economic changes, the questioning of sexuality by lesbian and gay groups, the undermining of traditional notions of public and private, and the political role played by feminism more generally have all served to destabilise modern masculine identities. Hence, in a situation where certainties and tradition are being progressively undermined, they have (somewhat paradoxically) to be 'constructed'. The construction of certitude in cultural forms need not be read simply as a 'backlash' against feminism. Instead we suggest that while such formations have political implications, they may be understood as a more complex response to changing gender relations. Arguably the construction of 'certitude' gives both men and women a sense that the social world is more stable than it actually is. That is, images of phallic masculinity promote a culture of 'comfort zones' giving the self (however temporarily) a sense of fixity and psychic security. In this respect, many of the magazines carry 'how to' sections which usually involve the offering of advice in a semi-ironic tone so that readers can brush up on a variety of techniques from the monitoring of sexual performance to changing a car tyre. For example, *Maxim* (July 1997) carries a typical section called 'How to be better than her last lover'. In many respects the article reaffirms binary divisions between men and women: whereas she needs to feel relaxed, intimate and that she can trust her partner, he simply wants to have sex. However the article stops some way short of simply reaffirming old-style patriarchal relations as the reader is made aware that he is likely to be compared to his partner's former lovers and unless he 'proves himself' a good lover the relationship may founder. In this sense the magazines can be read as offering a space of both certitude and reflexivity. They can be seen simultaneously as a material force seeking to rework gender relations and a cultural fantasy with few if any practical implications. The magazines are politically important as such cultural practices continue to mark contemporary culture's 'distance' from modern feminism, while remaining pertinent as fantasies, allowing temporary forms of closure from men's current gender troubles.

In many respects, the magazines provide a meeting point between the new culture of reflexivity and a way of granting masculinity a more ontological definition. Many of the reflexive spaces first noticed within the magazines' content by earlier commentators such as Mort (1988) have been colonised by a culture of 'laddism'. On the other hand, we also contend that ambivalence can still be detected in terms of the magazines' content (spaces of anxiety, advice in terms of relationships etc.) but more importantly in terms of the ways in which the magazines are read and talked about.

We have already demonstrated how these ambivalences are mobilised in terms of the dispositions taken by individuals within the focus groups. In this final section, we want to ask whether there is a relationship between these personal dispositions and more macro-contexts. For instance, a key distinction among our groups was their access to cultural capital (such as further education) which served as the main determinant in mobilising the dispositions of outright refusal, processes of distancing and above all the ability to be analytical. The most obvious example in this respect was the group of upper-middle-class media professionals who lived in the Stoke Newington area of London. Throughout the discussion this group employed 'expert' frames of reference in talking about the magazines such as the following reference to 'classless laddism':

Kate: Is there a class element in *Loaded*'s appeal?
Monty: Classless laddism . . . an awful lot of culture has become tied into football, football's become very acceptable for all classes . . . you've got David Baddiel with his double first from Oxford, sat down with Frank Skinner and it's, that's hey, we're all guys together loving football and big-breasted women.

Most of the discussion within the group was about the culture of the magazines as a social phenomenon that can be analysed in terms of cultural trends and sociological shifts. Similarly the Counsellors were able to utilise an analytical discourse on masculinity and feminism not available to many of the other groups:

Nick: What is the New Man?
Chris: Emotional and caring (or at least pretends to be), a mythical creation, completely unrealistic and artificial, an attempt to redefine the masculine model if you wish . . . the final product of the women's movement.

The paradox here is that the notion of 'classless laddism' is employed to demonstrate commercial culture's ability to blur class boundaries, and yet such distinctions are reaffirmed in the way that they are spoken about. These groups who have access to more critical and analytical modes of discourse can both be seen in Giddens' (1994) description of 'clever people' and also in respect of Bourdieu's (1984) descriptions of the circuits of cultural capital. The expansion of a mediated culture within modernity has meant that within certain circles changes within public discourses and image repertoires are debated more intensely than ever before. While participation within further education is perhaps the 'gateway' to discourses of expertise generally, the specific forms they take are determined by access to more specific media and professional discourses.[11] To have an opinion about the magazines is to be 'included' within a rich cosmopolitan culture of consumption where group membership is determined culturally through the capacity to talk in an open and informed way. In this respect, we were often struck by the fact that many of the groups had picked up on the surrounding media debate and were able to offer an 'informed' discussion on the links between masculinity and consumer culture without being regular readers of the magazines.

This is not to argue that other groups did not have access to an analytic mode of talk but that it was mobilised quite differently. The most materially and socially excluded group (the unemployed men) are 'analytical' in the sense that they are surrounded by a culture that is difficult for them to participate fully within:

Martin: You see the magazines they're sort of like the upper classes and the middle class but the working class I don't see them as enjoying them you know. Because I think basically, I mean you're not talking, you're talking above. In the magazine you're talking above the poorer class you know. You know, you are talking above them and either way that can be derogatory.
Nick: And when you say derogatory?'
Martin: Looking down at them.

Martin's comment describes what it feels like to be excluded from a commercial culture of consumption. This is not so much a space of reflexivity or certitude but

11. Compare Mort's (1996) analysis of the various forms of discursive knowledge and complex professional alliances that facilitated the emergence of specific commercial cultures during the 1980s, associated with changing forms of masculinity.

a zone of marginalisation that is beyond the confines of contemporary commercial culture. Most pressing in this space is not the 'semiotic' ability to interpret contemporary lifestyle changes but the ability to raise questions about the link between culture and justice. Hence questions of masculine identity and ambiguity which are brought into play by most of the other groups hardly enter the frame.

Elsewhere, the young, unemployed working-class men from Sheffield also recognise certain exclusions but the culture of the magazines in not so much viewed analytically as in terms of certain pleasures of being male:

Kate: So if you had to say then what would be your ideal type of article, or whatever, what would be your kind of, what would you turn to first?

Mike: . . . for example, on that *FHM* with that Jenny McCarthy people probably go straight to that article straight away, you know, see it on the front and go, she looks quite nice [laughter] and they start looking at the pictures. Ooh!

The capacity of the group to offer a 'critical' account of the magazines is circumvented by two tropes: the first is connected to questions of masculinity, and the second the ability to give an opinion. This group mainly saw the magazines as 'reflecting' the lifestyle which they most aspired to in terms of the forms of masculinity represented in the magazines and the consumptive concern with clothes, style and gadgets. The sense of common identification (or sharing a similar sensibility to the magazines) had the effect of rendering the magazines relatively uncontroversial. As Bourdieu (1993: 157) argues, however: " there are dispositions, which by definition, are not opinion if one means by that . . . something that can be formulated in discourse with some claim to coherence". For Bourdieu, the ability to formulate an 'opinion' means the subject has access to certain symbolic codes and an 'educated' disposition towards culture. To have an opinion, the disposition we hold towards cultural forms has to be one of scrutiny rather than participation, enjoyment and pleasure. However there were spaces where this typology breaks down (the ability to formulate an opinion depends upon access to cultural capital) where access to more evaluative discourses had been arrived at by other means such as political involvement. The example, the Sheffield-based disabled group, while having little access to formal education, were used to offering 'opinions' as they did on the politics of disability.

Kate: What kind of person reads the magazines?

Dave: Somebody that to me is false. That to me is somebody having to go with their flow, you know. I'm not too sure who they really are, so they've picked up on this image and pay £500 just to have this particular jacket, that probably looks stupid, because the magazine said: This is in . . . You look fantastic ! And I'll pay for it just because of the label.

What mostly clearly differentiated the groups in terms of their dispositions towards the cultural domain was the ability to be analytical. As we have seen this mostly operated along the lines of social class (again confirming Bourdieu). However we also found that the kind of analysis offered depended upon access to certain professional codes of expertise, and that, following Bourdieu's critics, other forms of disposition were available dependent upon experiences (in this case political) not determined by class relationships. This points to a complex relationship between reflexivity and certitude, and the ability to hold a more analytic disposition that is mainly determined by class.

These features can be complicated further by arguing that the dispositions necessary to participate fully in contemporary culture are not only connected to the reproduction of distinctive consumptive relations but can also be derived from changes in production as well. As Scott Lash (1994) has pointed out, the demise of organised capitalism and its replacement with informational capitalism has meant that about a third of the British population is excluded at the point of production as well as consumption. The result of being excluded from the labour market is not reflexive individuation but alienation. According to a range of commentators including Campbell (1994), Lash (1994) and Segal (1990), it is precisely within these zones that 'lad culture' is most likely to make its mark with gang bonding replacing the disciplines of work. Such a picture not only suggests that there are structural limits to the ambivalences of masculinity in terms of the magazines themselves but also in terms of their cultural spheres of influence.

Conclusion: Ambivalent Spaces?

Don Slater (1997) has suggested that men's leisure pursuits (particularly their hobbies) are identified with times and spaces that are anomalous with respect to both home and work, occupying a space of 'ambivalent pleasure' for men who have no proper place either at work or at home.[12] Our understanding of men's 'lifestyle' magazines would certainly be consistent with such a view, often read literally in transit from home to work (on a train or bus) or in some other semi-public space such as at the hairdresser's. 'Private' consumption at home was consistently down-played in our focus groups with only a few participants describing the magazines as bedside reading:

> I tend not to bother. Unless I'm like at a railway station . . . I sometimes read them like round at other people's houses (18 year olds).

12. Compare Radway's comment about reading romantic fiction as connoting "a free space where [women] feel liberated from the need to perform [domestic] duties that they otherwise accept as their own" (1984: 92).

I guess I must have picked them up and browsed through other people's . . . *Loaded* was something that was passed around . . . I thought it was very funny (Journalists).

I used to read it [*Loaded*] just before I go to bed, that's the only time I read it . . . I can go back and read old ones, the articles are that good . . . I've got all my old ones (Bristol students).

[*Loaded*]'s on the settee by the side of our bed and if there's now't happening, I'll read it (Footballers).

The location of the magazines within the 'public' sphere was also significant in terms of their relationship with pornography (both 'gay' and 'straight'). For example, one man described the magazines as "the acceptable face of porn" (Unemployed men), while another referred to them as "a kind of softened pornography" (Musicians). In another group, one man said he would be embarrassed to take a copy of *Loaded* home and wouldn't read it in public, while another said he wouldn't feel embarrassed reading one on a busy train "because they are . . . acceptable" (Manchester lecturers). Another member of the same group said he had felt embarrassed reading *Men's Health* on a bus going through Manchester's gay village because "I thought people would just assume I'm gay", while a gay man said he wouldn't be embarrassed reading magazines like *Attitude* on a train because, unlike most gay magazines "they're not, like, explicit".

Through their emphasis on 'lifestyle', men's magazines signal a kind of paradoxical and ambivalent domesticity reflecting the contradictions of contemporary masculinity. Men read the magazines for advice on improving their appearance, looking good and keeping fit, yet they distance themselves from taking such advice 'too seriously'. Like the hobbyist who takes his obsession too far (satirised as an 'anorak' or 'nerd'), focus group participants were constantly asserting the 'correct' way to read the magazines ('for a laugh', not taking things 'too seriously'). The alternative, to be avoided at all costs, was the risk of appearing 'sad' or a 'loser': "it's just sad because it's about sex and the reason you're buying a magazine about sex is because you're not having sex" (Manchester lecturers).

The parallels between hobbies and magazine-reading can, of course, be overstated, with the almost fanatical devotion of the hobbyist in stark contrast to most readers' disavowal of the magazines' significance (picked up, flicked through and nonchalantly discarded as soon as anything more pressing occurs). But if hobbies once served to 'domesticate' potentially dangerous masculinities, structuring men's leisure time, assimilating them to the world of consumer goods and maintaining their distance from useful participation in domestic labour, there are some clear analogies with contemporary magazine reading. The rise of *Playboy* magazine in the US during the 1950s is often taken as a key moment of 'opposition' within this process, encouraging its readers to express a sense of 'freedom' from their imagined subordination to a (feminised) suburban domestic ideal (cf. Ehrenreich 1983). In a world where leisure interests of all kinds are increasingly commodified, 'hobbies' (such as magazine reading) can no longer be represented as a simple 'escape' from the worlds of paid work and domestic reproduction. Significantly, however, neither work nor home are treated seriously in the magazines. Work is represented as a semi-comical competitive struggle ("It's a jungle in there: as in football, office teams have eleven positions to fill. But it's every man for himself" *Maxim*, March 1997). The home is depicted as a potentially dangerous world of female entrapment ("Are you better off single? Meet the eternal bachelor, footloose and fancy-free for the foreseeable. Not for him the relentless grind of domestic life or the style-cramping mire of monogamy. No way, mate" *XL*, July 1997). While potentially enslaving, 'consumerism' is also represented as an escape route for men with sufficient resources, a convenient way of avoiding emotional commitment or domestic responsibility. As one participant declared:

> men have more freedom now than ever before, much much more. They're earning more, they can have as much sex as they want. They can go out and do what ever they want. You don't need to have a little wifey at home to darn the socks. You just throw the socks away and buy a new pair. That's really it. There's not the same kind of social pressure on men to have a family, to have a wife . . . you can do what you want . . . You don't need that support structure any more because you can pay your cleaner and pay someone to iron your shirt. (Journalists)

When we refer to the 'ambivalent spaces' of contemporary masculinity, therefore, we are referring to both metaphorical and literal spaces. Men's magazines provide a way of traversing the ambiguous (metaphorical) spaces of contemporary masculinity and consumer culture. As the editor of *Stuff for Men* put it: "small planet, loads of ideas, frequently churned out – what does it all mean? A planet chocka with stuff. And that's why *Stuff* is here: to help you navigate through a maelstrom of new things, sifting through the quantity to highlight the quality" (February 1997). But the magazines can also be thought of as occupying a more material space in terms of the semi-public places in which men's magazines are read and the newly 'public' discourses (about men's health, sexuality and bodily appearance) to which they refer.[13]

13. This combination of the material and the metaphorical is nicely caught in Frank Mort's reminder that: "Urban geographers have been telling us for a long time that space is not just a backdrop to real cultural relations. Space is material . . . it carries social meanings which shape identities and the sense we have of ourselves. For young men (and young women) it is the spaces and places of the urban landscape which are throwing up new cultural personas – on the high street, in the clubs, bars, brasseries, even on the terraces. It seems as if young men are now living out quite fractured identities, representing themselves differently, feeling different, in different spatial situations" (1988: 218–19).

The use of an ambivalent mode of address also suggests a parallel between the men's magazines and earlier interpretations of the contradictory appeal of women's magazines:

> perhaps the women's magazine does a better job of speaking for women, of empowering their voices, than does the feminist scholar who has set this as her task. I am not suggesting that we see women's magazines as some emancipatory institution, as the site of authentic resistance to the patriarchal norm [but that] . . . as feminists we might learn from the women's magazine as a pedagogical model, one that meanders yet remains contained, that offers information within a heteroglossia of narratives rather than from a univocal position, that accumulates rather than replaces, that permits contradiction and frag-mentation, that offers choice rather than conversion as its message. (Radner 1995: 135)

There may be few signs of 'authentic resistance' to the 'patriarchal norm' in the men's magazines we have studied or in the transcripts of our focus groups. But our analysis of the 'heteroglossia of narratives' reveals a number of contradictions (referred to here as ambivalences). And as the authors of *Women's Worlds* recognised in their analysis of ideology and femininity in women's magazines:

> The identification of 'contradiction' . . . fails to embarrass either editors, writers or readers. Indeed . . . the success of the women's magazine is no doubt connected with its ability to encompass glaring contradiction coherently in its pages. (Ballaster et al. 1991: 7)

The use of men's time in magazine reading and other leisure pursuits is, as Slater (1997) suggests, located at a weak point within masculinity, associated with significant pressures on men's changing roles within the privatised domestic context of the home and in the (increasingly uncertain) public world of work. Located at this intersection, the magazines address their readers' anxieties and aspirations. In turn, as the evidence of our focus groups suggests, readers negotiate these ambivalent spaces in contradictory fashion, searching for advice and reassurance while celebrating a return to a more 'natural' form of laddish masculinity. Reading men's magazines therefore has all of the ambiguity that Radway identified for women reading romantic fiction, including its 'incipiently oppositional character'. To paraphrase Radway (1987: 113): reading men's magazines, though often portrayed in more individualistic terms, also represents a collectively elaborated male ritual through which men explore the consequences of their common social condition.

Finally, we are also aware that men's lifestyle magazines open out certain political questions, which we have discussed at greater length elsewhere (Stevenson et al. 2000). We suggest that the political space opened up by the magazines is as ambivalent as the ways that they are talked about and the ideological contradictions that are evident in their content. Politically, then, we are able to open up the problem of ambivalence in a third sense, resisting the idea that there is anything to be done about the magazines, or hoping that they may eventually be replaced by forms of culture that might more directly meet with our approval. In one sense, the magazines can undoubtedly be linked to the defensive persistence of certain heterosexual norms, but in another they embody a number of fantasies about masculine behaviour and performance that continue to have a deep cultural purchase. Hence the magazines provide a zone of communication through which many men are able to explore the contradictoriness of modern masculinities, while simultaneously repressing certain key questions regarding their current construction. Viewed in terms of civil society we might suggest that the magazines have opened up questions of masculinity for wider political debate than would have been likely had it been left to more 'official' channels of political communication. Following Bauman (1991), however, we are left with the uncomfortable conclusion that the ambivalence and disorder of the magazines is such that their political significance cannot easily be categorised.

References

Ballaster, R., Beetham, M., Frazer, E. and Hebron, S. (1991), *Women's Worlds: Ideology, Femininity and the Woman's Magazine,* London: Macmillan.

Bauman, Z. (1991), *Modernity and Ambivalence,* Cambridge: Polity Press.

Beck, U. (1997), *The Reinvention of Politics: Rethinking Modernity in the Global Social Order,* Cambridge: Polity Press.

Bourdieu, P. (1984), *Distinction,* London: Routledge.

—— (1990), *In Other Words: Essays Towards a Reflexive Sociology*, Cambridge: Polity Press.

—— (1993), *Sociology in Question,* London: Sage.

Campbell, B. (1994), *Goliath: Britain's Dangerous Places,* London: Penguin.

de Certeau, M. (1984), *The Practice of Everyday Life,* Berkeley: University of California Press.

Chaney, D. (1996), *Lifestyles,* London: Routledge.

Connell, R.W. (1995), *Masculinities,* Cambridge: Polity Press.

Edwards, T. (1997), *Men in the Mirror,* London: Cassell.

Ehrenreich, B. (1983), *The Hearts of Men: American Dreams and the Flight from Commitment,* London: Pluto Press.

Fish, S. (1980), *Is There a Text in this Class?* Cambridge, MA: Harvard University Press.

Frazer, E. (1992), 'Teenage girls reading *Jackie*', in P. Scannell, P. Schlesinger and C. Sparks (eds), *Culture and Power,* London: Sage, 182–200; originally published in *Media, Culture and Society,* 9 (1987): 407–25.

Giddens, A. (1984), *The Constitution of Society: Outline of a Theory of Structuration,* Cambridge: Polity Press.

—— (1991), *Modernity and Self-Identity,* Cambridge: Polity Press.

—— (1994), *Beyond Left and Right: the Future of Radical Politics,* Cambridge: Polity Press.

Hall, S. (1980), 'Encoding/Decoding', in S. Hall, D. Hobson, A. Lowe and P. Willis (eds), *Culture, Media, Language,* London: Hutchinson, pp. 128–38.

Hall, S. and Jefferson, T. (eds) (1976), *Resistance through Rituals: Youth Subcultures in Post-War Britain,* London: Hutchinson.

Hermes, J. (1995), *Reading Women's Magazines,* Cambridge: Polity Press.

Hutcheon, L. (1994), *Irony's Edge: the Theory and Politics of Irony,* London: Routledge.

Jackson, P., Stevenson, N. and Brooks, K. (1999), 'Making sense of men's lifestyle magazines', *Environment and Planning D: Society and Space,* 17: 353–68.

Lash, S. (1994), 'Reflexivity and its doubles: structure, aesthetics and community', in U. Beck, A. Giddens and S. Lash (eds), *Reflexive Modernization: Politics, Tradition and Aesthetics in the Modern Social Order,* Cambridge: Polity Press, pp. 110–73.

Lash, S. and Friedman, J. (eds) (1992), *Modernity and Identity,* Oxford: Blackwell.

Levine, D. (1985), *The Flight from Ambiguity: Essays in Social and Cultural Theory,* Chicago: Chicago University Press.

McRobbie, A. (1978), 'Working class girls and the culture of femininity', in Centre for Contemporary Cultural Studies Women's Group, *Women Take Issue,* London: Hutchinson, pp. 96–108.

—— (1991), *Feminism and Youth Culture: from Jackie to Just Seventeen,* London: Macmillan.

Mort, F. (1988), 'Boy's own? Masculinity, style and popular culture', in R. Chapman and J. Rutherford (eds), *Male Order: Unwrapping Masculinity,* London: Lawrence & Wishart, pp. 193–224.

Mort, F. (1996), *Cultures of Consumption: Masculinities and Social Space in Late Twentieth Century Britain,* London: Routledge.

Nixon, S. (1996), *Hard Looks: Masculinities, Spectatorship and Contemporary Consumption,* London: UCL Press.

Nixon, S. (1997), 'Exhibiting masculinity', in S. Hall (ed.), *Representation: Cultural Representations and Signifying Practices,* London: Sage, pp. 291–336.

Parker, R. (1995), *Torn in Two: the Experience of Maternal Ambivalence,* London: Virago.

Pearce, L. (1997), *Feminism and the Politics of Reading,* London: Arnold.

Radner, H. (1995), *Shopping Around: Feminine Culture and the Pursuit of Pleasure,* London: Routledge.

Radway, J.A. (1987), *Reading the Romance,* London: Verso.

Segal, L. (1990), *Slow Motion: Changing Masculinities, Changing Men,* London: Virago.

Slater, D. (1997), 'Integrating consumption and leisure: "hobbies" and the structures of everyday life'. Paper presented at the European Sociological Association subgroup on the Sociology of Consumption, Essex, 27–31 August.

Southwell, T. (1998), *Getting Away With It: the Inside Story of Loaded,* London: Ebury Press.

Stevenson, N., Jackson, P. and Brooks, K. (2000), 'The sexual politics of men's lifestyle magazines', *European Journal of Cultural Studies,* in press).

Weger, K. (1992), 'The sociological significance of ambivalence: an example from adoption research', *Qualitative Sociology,* 15: 87–103.

Winship, J. (1978), 'A woman's world: *Woman* – an ideology of femininity', Centre for Contemporary Cultural Studies, Women's Group, *Women Take Issue,* London: Hutchinson, pp. 133–45.

—— (1987), *Inside Women's Magazines*, London: Pandora Press.

Part IV

Introduction:
Uncle Sam Invades?

Michelle Lowe

The announcement, in June 1999, of the imminent arrival of Wal-Mart – the United States' leading discount retailer – on British shores was greeted with both anticipation and horror by media, business and financial circles. Asda, one of the UK's big four food retailers, it was reported, had entered into a 'transatlantic romance' (*Observer,* 20 June 1999) with Wal-Mart and had seduced and sub-sequently persuaded the US retailer to bid £6.72bn for its company, the result of which merger, it was suggested, could 'revolutionize the way Britain shops' (*Guardian,* 15 June 1999). But whilst the possibility of lower food prices and fierce competition were universally viewed – particularly in the light of the ongoing Competition Commission Inquiry into UK food retail prices – as attractive facets of the Wal-Mart-Asda deal, other aspects of the operations of this American 'can do' company were seen as rather less welcome. Wal-Mart's accolades include being the first company to utilise 'people greeters' who stand at the front of the stores and beam at customers as they come in (*The Times,* 15 June 1999) and such characteristics were interpreted as signals to the further imposition on the UK of all that is bad about American retail capital. Hence, headline reports variously read 'How America shoplifted Asda' (*Observer,* 20 June 1999), 'Wal-Mart casts dark shadow over retailers' (*The Times,* 15 June 1999) and 'Uncle Sam invades' (*Guardian,* 15 June 1999) (see also Winship, this volume).

In reality, of course, America's retail giant does not at present aim to transport wholesale its US mode of operation into the UK. In the short term at least, Asda will retain its fascia and British planning regulation (let alone the UK's rather different urban geography, higher land and transport costs as compared to the US) means that it is extremely unlikely that Wal-Mart's supercentres of 200,000 square feet (into which you could fit seven British superstores) will ever arrive on British soil. Moreover, no one from the US is to be parachuted into Asda's head office in Leeds to run the UK operation. Rather, Asda's UK management are trusted by the US company as already being 'more Wal-Mart than Wal-Mart' (*The Times,* 15 June 1999). So whilst the rhetoric behind the Wal-Mart announcement specifically focussed on the clash of cultures between US and UK retail capital (Uncle Sam invades . . .), the reality of the merger deal with Asda is significantly more complex. Indeed, it is arguable that Wal-Mart explicitly targeted Asda for its first foray into the UK specifically because Asda had already taken on board many of Wal-Mart's retailing tools – 'Everyday low pricing', 'people greeters', staff equality measures such as the universal use of first names, etc. – and as such, Wal-Mart, in purchasing Asda, is effectively buying a British retail company in its own image, whilst simultaneously aiding its own struggle to internationalise. What Wal-Mart will allow Asda, however, is the sheer raw economic power necessary to make the retail culture which Asda has attempted to nurture work. As the world's largest retailer, Wal-Mart will bring vast economies of purchasing scale to the new Asda enabling it to carry through and sustain its price promises. (Wal-Mart, for example, buys and sells no less than 20 per cent of the world's 'Pampers' nappies through its US stores). Far from imposing its alien American culture on a raw British firm, then, the transformation Wal-Mart is accused of potentially bringing to Asda is already well underway (although to be fair Wal-Mart via its vast scale and phenomenal buying power will undoubtedly enable Asda to see their vision through in a way the company had failed to do in the past). Conversely, and contrary to the view popularly presented, Wal-Mart itself has consistently suffered opposition in its home environment where its enemies have dubbed the company 'sprawl-mart' and where, by the early 1990s 'Stop the Wal' clubs had formed in hundreds of towns (*Guardian,* 15 June 1999). The American retail giant is in no way universally popular even in the US.

Here then is a tale of the complexity of the relationship between the cultural and the economic and a clear example of the interconnections between the two. Like the earlier sections in this volume the three papers presented here all show the importance of transcending the simple dualism often erected between commerce and culture but also, and importantly, additionally highlight issues of *geographical difference*. In the recent past there has been a great deal of discussion in human geography concerning the various ways in which 'culture – in a variety of substantive and conceptual guises – is increasingly key to economic geography's research agendas' (Crang 1997: 4). The three papers in this part of our volume, like the Wal-Mart-Asda story recounted above, all provide within them 'culturally sensitive economic geographies . . . that recognise the social and cultural complexities of industrial organisation and economic change' (Hughes 1999: 364). Neil Wrigley, Michelle Lowe and Christopher Moore are all concerned with a similar theme, specifically the variation in commercial culture between the United States (often seen as the rampant home of consumerism run wild) and the UK (where historically, at least, consumer culture from the small shopkeeper onwards has been viewed as more 'gentlemanly' (sic) and sedate) (see also Winship, this volume).

Neil Wrigley's chapter draws on work carried out as part and parcel of a Leverhulme Trust funded research project on the reconfiguration of the US food retail industry during the 1990s and specifically focuses on 'some ingrained preconceptions which are held about US food retailing in particular and food retail and consumption more generally'. These preconceptions are organised as a series of 'myths' all of which demonstrate the various ways in which economic and cultural transformations take place hand in hand.

Myth 1 concerns a popular misconception that because the supermarket is an American invention the food retail industry more generally must reflect a US model. Here Wrigley demonstrates how the peculiarities of the US regulatory environment from the 1930s to the early 1980s mediated against the development of big retail capital and its associated market dominance. Rather, and in sharp contrast to the position in the UK and continental Europe, where food retailing had rapidly consolidated, 'by the late 1980s the share of the US food retail market accounted for by the top ten firms had barely changed in over 40 years'. Moreover, and again contra the image of the US as an innovator on the retail scene, the 1980s have been described as the 'dark ages' of supply chain management and systems development in US food retailing, whilst in the UK the rapid development of information technology (IT), electronic data interchange (EDI) etc., saw the food retailers responsible for what many see as key retail innovations e.g. own label produce, chilled ready meals and so on. In reality, then, it is clear that the situation in the US in the 1980s and early 1990s lagged considerably behind that of the UK, although more recent shifts in the economics and culture of US food retailing lead Wrigley to conclude that the US industry is rapidly being recast in a north-west European image.

Wrigley's second 'myth' concerns the perceived need for a regionally-structured food retail industry in the US due to the sheer scale and geographical variation of the country. Here Wrigley concludes that from 1995/6 a wave of consolidation involving the acquisition of many regional chains has led to the market share of the top four US food retailers increasing by 80 per cent in just three years. Myth 3 rests on what Wrigley terms the 'Wal-Martization' of America legend which has been in common circulation in the 1980s and 1990s as the world's largest retailer has grown explosively and transformed communities across the USA, and concerns the perceived threat posed by Wal-Mart's move into food retailing. Here Wrigley traces Wal-Mart's position viz-à-viz other US food retailers and demonstrates that the Wal-Mart 'myth' has not yet been substantiated by events as the leading firms in the industry have fought to defend their position. Moreover, and paralleling the argument presented above, even in the United States, Wal-Mart's supercentres have faced and continue to face considerable local opposition. Myth 4 is what Wrigley calls the 'mange tout' myth, that is to say that leading UK food retailers are masters of the food universe or at least highly significant global players. Here Wrigley interrogates this view in the context of the rapid reconfiguration of the US food retail industry during the 1990s, and concludes that UK food retailers are struggling to compete as part of an emerging global food retail elite.

Wrigley's four myths then all contradict aspects of a widely held belief in alternative commercial cultures between the US and the UK and demonstrate how a simplistic view of retail 'culture' is in reality far more complex. Rather the interconnections between commerce and culture have to be viewed through a more subtle lens.

The mythology of rampant American retail capitalism is also tackled in the second chapter in this section by Michelle Lowe. Lowe compares and contrasts the history and development of large out-of-town shopping centres in the US and UK and demonstrates that despite the fact that a political rhetoric emerged from the 1960s onwards in the UK in opposition to what were very much viewed as American concepts, the situation in the UK from the outset was fundamentally different. Once again, and like the Wal-Mart-Asda story recounted above, it is shown that whilst 'out-of-town' shopping in the UK is based rather loosely on an American model (from Brent Cross to Bluewater) and whilst American mall architecture has been universally imported, the UK's regional shopping centres are actually quite different from their American counterparts. More specifically, the regional shopping centres in the UK are essentially 'urban' in form and have arguably filled strategic gaps of underprovision in the UK's shopping geography. As such then, these regional centres have far more in common with the template propagated by Victor Gruen, the acknowledged founding father of US shopping malls, than their American cousins. Gruen envisaged that regional centres would provide scope for community activities and would be developed alongside offices, theatres, housing and so on, effectively forming new urban spaces focussed around the mall. In the US this vision has failed to transpire, but in the UK of the 1990s centres like Merry Hill near Dudley in the West Midlands are rapidly developing as new strategic centres within the urban fabric.

The final chapter in this section, by Christopher Moore, also engages with the critical interface between commerce and culture. Moore compares British and American fashion designer/retail capital and demonstrates how the differential economics of that capital have a distinct geographical effect in the fashionable shopping areas of London and New York. Moore charts the emergence in the 1980s and 1990s of the publicly owned American fashion design houses and provides a focussed explanation of the conditions which have enabled these American (and not British) fashion houses to develop the best recognised and most successful fashion brands in the world. Ralph Lauren, for example, had in 1998 worldwide sale in excess of $8 billion (more than that of Italy's three top design houses – Armani, Versace and Gucci – combined). For Moore, four interrelated dimensions serve to explain the international market success and dominance of American fashion designer/retail capital. First, stock market listing has enabled US companies to expand at an unprecedented rate. Second, a clever strategy of brand diffusion and a distinctive branding portfolio have allowed the American fashion houses to target the extremely lucrative 'middle market' whilst at the same time maintaining an aura of exclusivity. Third, an extensive network of licensing agreements mean that designers such as Ralph Lauren can take full advantage of a network of partners to manufacture, distribute and advertise their ranges. Fourthly and finally, the use of flagship stores located within the most fashionable districts of capital cities – e.g. London's Bond Street and New York's Madison Avenue – have proved a potent means of communicating brand image. Moore concludes by suggesting that it is the complex economics of American fashion designer/retail capital which lie behind the cultural facade of the high fashion districts of central London and New York. However, to reduce Moore's chapter to one which simply 'reads off' culture from a base of economic change would be far too simplistic. Rather Moore's paper, like those of Wrigley and Lowe, seeks to develop a culturally embedded economic geography. In this sense all three chapters in this section may be regarded as to some extent path breaking.

References

Crang, P. (1997), 'Cultural turns and the (re)construction of economic geography', in R. Lee and J. Wills (eds), *Geographies of Economies*, London: Arnold, pp. 3–15.

Hughes, A.L. (1999), 'Constructing competitive spaces: the corporate practice of British retailer-supplier relationships', *Environment and Planning*, A 31, pp. 819–39.

10

Four Myths in Search of Foundation: The Restructuring of US Food Retailing and its Implications for Commercial Cultures

Neil Wrigley

Introduction

The roots of this paper lie in a Leverhulme Trust funded research project on the reconfiguration of the US food retail industry during the 1990s. That project seeks to understand the transformations which, quite dramatically, and literally on a month-by-month basis, are profoundly reshaping the industry and remaking the map of US food retailing. My analysis in that project is essentially an economic one which positions an understanding of the current wave of consolidation and corporate reconfiguration in US food retailing (Wrigley 1999a) within a context of events ten years earlier – specifically the intense period of leveraged buyouts and recapitalisations which swept through corporate America between 1985 and 1988, restructuring and rebuilding firms and industries (Yago 1991; Cotterill 1993; Wrigley 1998a, 1999b). Nevertheless, although primarily economic in orientation, that project is centred upon intensive interview-based research involving the Chief Executives and Financial Officers (CEOs and CFOs) of the leading firms in the industry and, in particular, on a rather unusual and privileged level of access which I have succeeded in negotiating with Wall Street securities houses and their leading analysts. By participating, as the sole academic, in numerous meetings and site visits organised by these Wall Street institutions over a three-year period I have, as a result, been caught up – in a very real and intense sense – in the 'restructuring of commercial cultures', as an industry worth a massive $450 billion per annum has transformed itself before my eyes.

What I hope to provide in this paper are some broader reflections on that restructuring and transformation. In turn, I hope that these reflections will serve to unsettle some ingrained preconceptions which I often find are held about US food retailing in particular, and food retail and consumption more generally. My approach, like that of Daniel Miller in *Acknowledging Consumption* (1995) will be to pose and question a series of myths which seem to inform many of those preconceptions. Because of space constraints I will restrict my attention to just four of these myths. I offer them in no particularly profound order – simply to generate debate.

Myth 1: The supermarket is unequivocally American – it follows that food retail industries reflect the US model

In her essay 'Supermarket Futures', Rachel Bowlby (1997) has recently reminded a cultural studies and wider social science audience of the enormous significance attributed at the time to the emergence of the early supermarkets in the USA during the late 1920s and early 1930s. The intensely innovatory nature of large-format, self-service, food retailing – the spirit of which Bowlby captures very successfully in her essay – provided, as Michelle Lowe and I show in Chapter 4 of our forthcoming *Reading Retail: A Geographical Perspective on Retailing and Consumption Spaces* (2000) book, considerable profits of innovation for its early adopters and huge challenges to the incumbent leading food store chains of the period (e.g. A&P) who were initially slow to respond. But the arrival of self-service food retailing signalled not only an economic revolution – 'the supermarket could profitably sell goods at prices which would be ruinous to a conventional store' (Adelman 1959: 61) – but also a cultural one. As Bowlby (1997: 98–9) notes, self-service was associated 'with the unprecedented idea of the food store as potentially an attractive and comfortable place for the consumer to enjoy' – 'the looking and touching encouraged by the open displays suggested and permitted a taking that was not (yet) a commitment . . . in this interim provisional space, between the entrance and the checkout, [the consumer] really could have anything . . . this was the dream-like face of self-service, [where] all was possible, possessable, until the moment of reckoning'. Moreover, it was an economic and cultural revolution that would be repeated time and time again, as this 'unequivocally American invention . . . [and] the other features of twentieth-century consumer culture' which went with it (Bowlby 1997: 97) was exported, after the Second World War, to Europe and elsewhere.

It is that export, and the way it became ingrained in our image of the nature of societal change in the post-war period in Britain and continental Europe which, above all else, lies at the heart of the common preconception that food retail industries are cast in an American mould. My first task in this paper is to dispel that myth. Indeed, I will argue that by the late 1980s/early 1990s the US food retail industry had come to occupy a position which, in many important respects, was the polar opposite of that found in the countries of north-west Europe.

For almost fifty years in the USA – for the 1930s to the early 1980s – a regulatory environment had existed which was hostile to the development of 'big' retail capital and to market share being concentrated into the hands of a small number of major chains operating multiregionally and enjoying considerable purchasing leverage (Wrigley 1992). The effect had been to privilege the dominant position of the food manufacturer. Via price discrimination legislation (*Robinson-Patman Act,* 1936) aimed at protecting the smaller trader, via criminal and civil indictment of the leading US food retailers of the time (most famously the criminal prosecution of A&P in the 1940s), and via long periods of stringent anti-market-extension-merger regulation (*Celler-Kefauver Act,* 1950), a food retail industry had developed by the early 1980s which was far less consolidated than might have been expected. Moreover, despite the emergence of conditions during the 1980s which, on the face to it, were highly conducive to consolidation in the industry – notably the non-enforcement of US antitrust regulation under the Reagan administrations (Mueller and Paterson 1986) which allowed mergers and acquisitions to be contemplated 'which in the past would have been challenged and probably stopped on antitrust grounds' (Magowan, 1989) – curiously the consolidation of US food retailing still failed to occur.

The main reason (see Wrigley 1999b) for this lack of consolidation during the 1980s was a wave of financial re-engineering which accompanied the relaxation of US investment regulation. That relaxation fuelled the rapid growth of new financial instruments and markets – specifically the high-yield ('junk') bond market. In turn, it triggered, during the mid-1980s, the financial re-engineering of firms and industries across a wide swath of corporate America, creating immensely strong *deconglomeration* and *deconcentration* tendencies. The US industries most susceptible to restructuring in this way were those with stable demand and strong cash flows but urgently needing to increase efficiency and productivity. The food retail industry was quintessentially of this type and the consequence was that, between 1985 and 1988, nineteen of the fifty largest food retail firms undertook leveraged buyouts (LBOs) or leveraged recapitalisations, corporate debt levels in the industry rose sharply, and the leading firms rather than acquiring and consolidating were instead forced to divest thousands of stores and entire divisions of their operations to service those debt burdens (Cotterill 1993; Denis 1994; Chevalier 1995; Wrigley 1998a, 1999b).

The result was that, by the late 1980s, the share of the US food retail market accounted for by the top ten firms (at around 27 per cent) had barely changed for over forty years – indeed the market share of the top five firms had actually fallen during that period. This lack of consolidation was not only highly unusual in the context of the other US food system industries (Connor and Schiek 1997: 312), but stood in marked contrast to the position in Britain and its continental European neighbours where food retailing had very rapidly consolidated. In north-west

223

Europe the market shares controlled by the top ten and top five food retailers were typically at least double, and sometimes triple, the level found in the USA.

Within this significantly less consolidated US food retail industry, the shift in bargaining power from food manufacturers to retailers which had been such an important feature of the 1980s in Britain and its continental-European neighbours, as retailers in those countries 'increasingly assumed control over a range of functions traditionally performed by manufacturers, including physical distribution, advertising, packaging, product design and product development' (Grant 1987: 43), was far less advanced. Unlike their north-west European counterparts, US food retailers had not developed the same ability to control supply relations. As a result, fundamental differences had emerged in important operational areas – notably, supply chain management, distribution/logistics and systems, and own-label/retailer-brand development. Whilst essentially this reflected the inability of the leading US food retailers to match their European counterparts in terms of wresting control of the supply chain from the manufacturers, it also reflected the debt-encumbered, 'liquidity constrained' position which many of the US food retailers found themselves in at the end of the intense wave of leveraged restructuring which characterised the late 1980s. Faced with servicing huge debt burdens assumed during their LBOs and leveraged recapitalisations, many of the leading US food retailers were forced not only to divest assets (stores, distribution facilities, manufacturing plants) but also to reduce very severely their capital expenditures. In turn, this damaged their ability to invest in store renovation, supply chain management, distribution/logistics and systems innovations. The cuts in capital expenditure were often very substantial – 46 per cent in the four years following its leveraged recapitalisation in the case of the leading chain Kroger (Denis 1994) – and the contrast with the levels of capital expenditure of the major UK food retailers during the same period was dramatic (Wrigley 1998a, Table 5). Not surprisingly, and in marked contrast to our image of innovatory US food retailing ingrained from the birth-of-the-supermarket era, the 1980s was a period therefore which even sympathetic US analysts (Comeau 1995) have described as the 'dark ages' of supply chain management and systems development in US food retailing, in which the major firms struggled with fragmented divisional-based operating structures and in which manufacturers' promotions and forward-buying opportunities essentially drove their procurement practices.

Quite simply, by the late 1980s/early 1990s, the food retail industries of Britain and its continental-European neighbours did not reflect a US model. Rather, the 1980s had witnessed the increasing ability of ever larger retail corporations in north-west Europe to reshape supply relations in their favour. In the UK, for example, a revolution in physical distribution, logistics and IT systems had swept through the food retail industry (for further discussion see Wrigley 1998b) as the major retailers 'progressed from simply being the innocent recipients of manufacturer's transport and storage whims, to controlling and organizing the supply chain almost in its entirety' (Sparks 1994: 331). 'Quick response' distribution systems (Fernie 1992, 1994) had been widely adopted, retailer inventory holdings had progressively been reduced (see Figure 10.1 also Smith and Sparks 1993) – in the process passing those costs back to the manufacturer – and the retailers' sophisticated IT systems architecture had increasingly been linked back via EDI (electronic data interchange) into the manufacturers' systems. By the early 1990s, the EDI links of the major food retailers frequently covered more than 80 per cent of merchandise and lay at the heart of a logistically-refined 'demand pull' system of supply chain management. In addition, the own-label products of the major food retailers – a vital component of their increasing market dominance and supply chain control – had been repositioned during the decade, away from the inferior quality, cheap, generic or sub-brand image which had been common in the 1960s and 1970s, and towards that of high-quality, innovatory, 'retailer brands' (Sparks 1997; Hughes 1996).

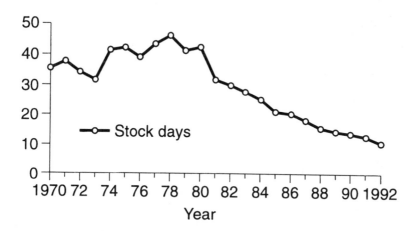

Source: redrawn from Smith and Sparks 1993

Figure 10.1   Reductions in inventory holdings in the 1980s – the case of Tesco

The growth of dynamically interactive 'retailer brand' supply chains based around the imperatives of continuous new product development during the 1980s – for example, those required to supply chilled ready meals, the first major food market segment in the UK to be totally dominated by own-label (Doel 1996, 1998; Hughes 1999) – was not only 'of immense symbolic significance . . . visibly epitomising the changing dynamics and shifting power balance within the food industry' (Doel 1996: 55), but also stood in marked contrast to the position in the USA. By the early 1990s, retailer own-label sales in the US industry represented only one-third of the equivalent UK levels, and the vital repositioning of own-label into 'retailer brand' with all that implied in terms of consumer perception of own-label quality was only just beginning to occur (Hughes 1996). In addition, own-label supply relations were often mediated by third-party brokerages – a type of supply chain organisation not conducive to the long-term growth of innovative own-label strategies (Marion 1995).

The importance of the reconfiguration of US food retailing which has taken place since the early 1990s as the industry has unwound from the highly leveraged position reached in the late 1980s (Table 10.1), and which has provided the focus

Table 10.1 Deleveraging of the US food retail industry, 1990–96[1]

	1990	1991	1992	1993	1994	1995	1996
Debt as % of total capitalisation	66.4	64.2	62.8	61.3	56.4	52.3	48.1
Interest expense as % of sales	1.65	1.47	1.24	1.13	1.02	0.93	0.87
Cash flow coverage ratio[2]	3.21	3.52	4.09	4.71	5.54	6.42	7.13
Capital expenditure as % of sales	2.14	2.32	2.48	2.60	2.64	3.40	3.42

1. Figures derived from a sample of 11 major chains – Albertson's, American Stores, Food Lion, Giant Food Inc, A&P, Hannaford Bros, Kroger, Safeway, Stop & Shop, Vons, Winn-Dixie.
2. Defined as EBITDA (earnings before interest, taxes, depreciation & amortisation) divided by interest expense.

of my Leverhulme Trust project, has not simply been that a wave of consolidation has at last begun to create food retail firms of equivalent relative size in the US economy to the giants of European food retailing. Rather, it is that as competitive advantage has shifted increasingly rapidly to the larger firms possessing critical mass and capital, and as those firms have been able to reverse the diseconomies of scale which dogged their fragmented divisional-based operating structures of the 1980s, so the balance of power in the US food system which traditionally favoured the manufacturer over the retailer (Wrigley 1992; Cotterill 1997) has begun to shift decisively in favour of the larger retailers. In the process, many of the contrasts which existed in the late 1980s/early 1990s between food retailing in north-west Europe and the USA have begun to break down. A profound shift has been underway in the 'commercial culture' of US food retailing as the increasingly deleveraged major firms have progressively been able to drive up their capital expenditure programmes (Figure 10.2), remove inefficiencies from their supply chains, and exploit potential synergies in administration, the buying process, and distribution/logistics by developing similar forms of centralised systems to those which the European retail giants had developed and refined a decade earlier. Rather than the food retail industries of north-west Europe reflecting the US model, a

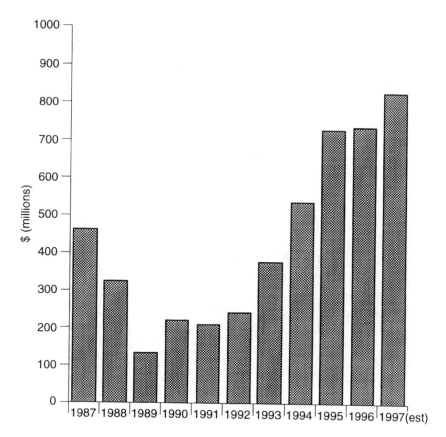

Figure 10.2   Kroger – annual capital expenditure levels, 1987–97

more reasonable interpretation is that having begun the 1990s at something of a polar extreme, the transformations currently reshaping the US industry and remaking both its economic geography and its prevailing commercial culture, are rapidly recasting the US industry in a north-west European image.

Myth 2: The US is so huge it demands a regionally structured food retail industry

In attempting to account for the relatively low level of market concentration in US food retailing in the 1980s and early 1990s, it was often argued that such a huge country in which major markets are separated by considerable distances does not lend itself to the development of national food retail chains. Instead it was suggested that regional chains possess certain intrinsic competitive advantages. The very notion that a centralized buyer in somewhere like Boise, Idaho could be sufficiently sensitive to the different product mixes required by consumers in cities ranging from New Orleans, Louisiana through El Paso, Texas and Portland, Oregon to Boston, Massachusetts, to exercise competitive advantage over local buyers within the regional chains operating in each of these areas, was a notion treated by some commentators as patently absurd.

In addition, a more considered academic version of this argument was also frequently advanced. That version, as exemplified by Cotterill (1997: 128), suggested that, although the national level of concentration in US food retailing – as measured by the market shares held by the top ten or top five firms – was considerably lower in the 1980s and early 1990s than the levels found in the countries of north-west Europe, 'the geographical size disparity between markets vitiates any comparison of concentration numbers'. Instead, Cotterill and others argued that the true comparison should be between the market concentration levels found in individual regions or states of the US and individual European countries. For example, California with a population of 29.8 million in the early 1990s or Florida with a population of 12.9 million are, it is argued, larger in population terms than several of the north-west European countries and are examples of states with significant food retail market concentration – with the top five food retailers in these states controlling 55.5 per cent and 82.8 per cent respectively of the market in 1993. As a result it is argued that, 'when one takes geography into account, retailing [in the early 1990s was] no less concentrated in the US' (Cotterill 1997: 128). However, for two interrelated reasons – beyond the obvious point that distance of itself is not an important issue given the relatively small proportion of a retailer's costs which relate to transportation – I suggest that these arguments are significantly flawed.

First, what mattered during the 1980s and early 1990s in terms of many of the critical US-European differences outlined above, was the *relative* power of food retailers compared to food manufacturers and suppliers within the individual national economies. In the UK, for example, the major food retailers rose rapidly to prominence in the economy during the 1980s, and began to exceed 'the sizes of their suppliers in terms of sales, assets and stock market capitalisation' (Grant 1987: 45). Sainsbury, for example, rose from a position as the 51st largest UK company in terms of turnover in the late 1970s to the 14th largest by 1988/89 with a turnover of £5.9 bill (approximately $9.5 bill). In the process, it eclipsed many of the largest manufacturing firms in the UK economy. In the USA, in contrast, the major food retailers occupied a far less prominent position in the national economy. Indeed, the leading food retailer in 1988/89, Kroger, had a turnover of just $17.5 bill – that is to say considerably less than double the Sainsbury turnover in a country which was almost *five* times larger in population terms than the UK. To have approached parity with its European counterparts, Kroger's turnover and market share should have been at least twice as large as that actually achieved.

Moreover, during the late 1980s and early 1990s, the position of the major US food retailers, if anything, weakened in the US economy relative to the leading firms in other food system industries and other retail sectors. For example by 1995, the US had five food manufacturing/processing firms (see Connor and Schiek 1997: 98) with US food sales exceeding $15 bill per annum (Phillip Morris, ConAgra, Cargill, PepsiCo and Coca-Cola) but only one food retail firm (Kroger). It also had twenty-one food manufacturing firms with sales exceeding $5 billion per annum (the five above plus firms such as Archer-Daniels-Midland, Sara Lee, HJ Heinz, RJR Nabisco, Campbell Soup Co., Kellogg, Ralston Purina, and General Mills), but only nine food retailers (see Table 2). In the UK, in contrast, this relative position of the food retailers and manufacturers in the economy was reversed with, in 1995/96, four major food retailers (Tesco, Sainsbury, Safeway, Asda) in the top thirty companies by turnover (Sainsbury and Tesco in 6th and 7th positions) compared to just two major food manufacturers (Unilever and Associated British Foods). Similarly, in comparison to the leading firms in other US retail sectors, the position of the major US food retailers had also weakened during the late 1980s and early 1990s. For example, in comparison to the spectacular growth achieved during the period by the discount general merchandiser, Wal-Mart – which increased its sales more than 700 per cent to over $100 bill per annum by the mid-1990s – the leading food retailer, Kroger, could only achieve a 25 per cent increase in sales to $25 bill per annum.

Second, the fact that no true national food chains emerged in the US during the 1980s, should not be taken to imply that competitive advantage lies for some intrinsic but rather ill-defined reason of 'geography' with the regional chains in the US, or that national chains with European levels of market share in the industry could not emerge. Indeed, as noted above, a consistent feature of the 1990s has been the attempts by the major US food retailers to reverse the diseconomies of scale which dogged their fragmented divisional-based operating structures of the 1990s. Heavy investment in the IT systems necessary to allow centralised administration and control of both logistics and the buying process, has been matched by major 'self-consolidation' programmes. The most ambitious of these has been American Stores' 'Delta' programme initiated in 1994, and which, by 1997, was achieving benefits which significantly exceeded implementation costs. But there are many other examples, including Ahold's 'Project Compete', which focused on the integration of the regional chains in the Dutch retailer's rapidly expanding US business – beginning with financial, logistic and supply-chain management functions and the merger of the individual chains' own-label programmes. Rather than basing most decisions about buying, pricing, advertising and investment at the regional/divisional level, as was the norm in the 1980s, even the most devolved of the major US food retailers have been heavily involved during the 1990s in co-ordination of technology, consolidation of administrative functions, centralised own-label development programmes, co-ordinated corporate buying, integrated logistics management, and 'best practice' dissemination. Indeed, during this process, it is the major multi-regional firms who have learned to appear 'local' to the consumer whilst at the same time exercising significant scale economies in their upstream activities that have grown differentially rapidly.

Furthermore, the notion that US food retailing cannot support European levels of market share controlled by the major food retailers, or potential national chains, is easily exposed. A glance at the history of US food retailing shows that in the early part of the twentieth century, when the fledgling US food chains began to expand, the retailer A&P grew from less than 400 stores in 1910 to 15,100 stores in 1930 – in the process capturing a remarkable 12.1 per cent of total US food store sales by 1933 (Adelman 1959, Appendix Tables 10.2 and 10.5), compared to just 5 per cent held by the leading chain in the late 1980s. The fact that A&P did not build on this share of the market and evolve into a national chain, was a function not only of corporate strategy failings within A&P but vitally, as noted above, of the harsh regulatory environment which constrained the emergence of 'big' retail capital in US food retailing from the mid-1930s to the early 1980s, followed by the demands of an intense wave of financial re-engineering in the late 1980s.

The significance of the recent reconfiguration of US food retailing, which has provided the focus of my Leverhulme Trust project, is that it has destroyed this myth of an intrinsically regionally structured US food retail industry. Beginning in earnest in 1995/96, a wave of consolidation has swept through the industry as the newly deleveraged major food retailers have turned to merger and acquisition as the best means of growth available to them in a low inflation environment in which the potential of 'organic' (new-store-development driven) growth has become limited. A succession of acquisitions of the regional chains including: Stop & Shop and Giant Food Inc. by Ahold; Vons, Carr Gottstein, Dominick's and Randall's by Safeway; Kash n' Karry and Hannaford by Food Lion; Buttrey and Sessells by Albertson's; Smith's/Smitty's, Ralphs/Food-4-Less, Quality Food Centers/Hughes by Fred Meyer, has been topped by two mega deals – the $11 bill Albertson's acquisition of American Stores announced in August 1998 and the $13 bill Kroger acquisition of Fred Meyer announced in October 1998. In the process, as Table 2 shows, the market share of the top ten US food retailers has risen over 40 per cent in three years from 27.7 per cent in 1995 to 39 per cent (on a pro forma basis) in 1998. The market share of the top five has risen even more dramatically – over 60 per cent in three years to reach almost 30 per cent of the US market. As a result, the US suddenly has three food retailers – Kroger, Albertson's and Safeway –

with individual market shares of over 5 per cent of total US food store sales, plus a fourth firm, Ahold, which is likely to soon reach this level. In addition, it has a leading food retailer, Kroger which, with sales (on a pro forma basis) of $43 bill in 1998 and a market share of almost 10 per cent, holds a position not substantially dissimilar to the leading firms in north-west European markets.

Table 10.2 Rapidly increasing concentration in US food retailing 1995–98 – market shares of top 10 food retail chains*

	1995		1997		1998 (Pro forma)		
Rank	Firm	Share	Firm	Share	Firm	Share[1]	Share[2]
1	Kroger	5.7	Kroger	6.1	Albertson's	6.7	
2	American	3.2	Safeway	4.4	Kroger	6.5	9.9
3	Safeway	3.1	Albertson's	3.4	Safeway	4.8	5.4
4	Albertson's	3.1	Ahold	3.3	Ahold	4.3	5.2
5	Winn-Dixie	3.1	American	3.1	Fred Meyer	3.4	mrgd
6	Publix	2.3	Winn-Dixie	3.1	Winn-Dixie	3.1	
7	A&P	2.0	Publix	2.6	Publix	2.7	
8	Ahold	2.0	Food Lion	2.4	Food Lion	2.4	
9	Food Lion	2.0	A&P	1.9	A&P	1.9	
10	Vons	1.2	Fred Meyer	1.3	H.E. Butt	1.3	
Top 10 market share (%)		27.7		31.6		37.1	40.0
US food store sales ($ bill)		409.6		432.1		440.7	

* Market share figures exclude drug store division sales of American Stores and Canadian food sales of Safeway and A&P. For further details of definitions and sources see Wrigley (1999a)
1. Pro forma market share following August 1998 announcement of Albertson's acquisition of American Stores
2. Pro forma market share following October 1998 announcement of Kroger acquisition of Fred Meyer and Safeway acquisition of Dominick's, and March 1999 announcement of Ahold's acquisition of Pathmark. (Pathmark acquisition subsequently blocked by FTC.)

As Figure 10.3 shows, Kroger, following its acquisition of Fred Meyer, will operate in every state of the US except those in the North-East, Minnesota, Wisconsin and Hawaii. In addition, both Albertson's and Safeway now operate coast to coast – with Safeway also in Alaska and Hawaii. The myth of the US not being able to support national food retail chains is well on the way to being laid to rest.

Neil Wrigley

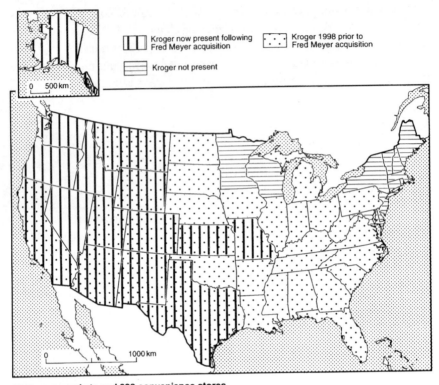

2200 supermarkets and 820 convenience stores

Major trading names :
Kroger
Dillon Food Stores
Fry's
King Soopers

Fred Meyer
Smiths/Smitty's
Ralphs/Food-4-Less
Quality Food Centers/Hughes

Figure 10.3   Kroger following acquisition of Fred Meyer

Myth 3: The rise of Wal-Mart as a food retailer will seriously harm the major US food retailers

This view, at its heart, rests on the 'Wal-Martization of America' legend which has been in common circulation in the 1980s and 1990s as the world's largest retailer has grown explosively and transformed communities across the USA. By the late 1980s, facing a future of increasingly saturated markets for the continued expansion of its traditional discount general merchandise/department stores, Wal-Mart began to experiment with a new format – the so-called 'supercentre'. Pioneered earlier in the 1980s by the food retailers Meijer in Michigan and Fred Meyer in the Pacific Northwest, 'supercentres' are huge stores, typically around

232

190,000 sq. ft., in which one quarter of the floor space is devoted to food. In turn, this space generates about 40 per cent of the store's sales. Essentially they are a much larger version, with a higher proportion of non-food sales, of the 100,000 sq. ft. French 'hypermarkets' of Carrefour, Auchan and Promodès.

The economic logic of the supercentre format for Wal-Mart rested on the potential cross-over of shoppers from food to non-food. Although food is sold at lower profit margins than the other merchandise in the supercentre it serves to generate a considerably increased frequency of consumer visits (relative to the traditional Wal-Mart discount store), and the cross-shopping from food to non-food which occurs on those visits increases sales of the non-food merchandise compared to the traditional discount store. The result is that, even if the supercentres only manage to break even on the food proportion of their business, they can still generate better returns than the traditional Wal-Mart discount stores – a situation reminiscent of the economic advantages which the prototype US supermarkets of the 1920s and 1930s held over the conventional food stores of that period. Yet a firm such as Wal-Mart, which led the US retail industry in the 1980s in terms of its adoption of centralized buying, logistics and IT systems, had the technological efficiency to ensure that its supercentre food sales were in fact significantly profitable in their own right. This merely strengthened the already considerable economic advantages of the format to Wal-Mart, given its position as a highly dominant firm facing market maturity in its original retail sector and seeking a new growth vehicle.

As Table 10.3 shows, from a position of having just ten supercentres in 1991, Wal-Mart had opened over 550 with sales of over $32 bill by late 1998. Best estimates currently suggest that there will be around 1,600 supercentres in the US by the year 2001 with combined sales of approximately $92 bill per annum, with Wal-Mart accounting for almost two-thirds of those totals (Merrill Lynch 1998). Not surprisingly, faced during the early 1990s with early indications of the scale of this growth, considerable debate and concern was generated in the US, not least within the food retail industry itself, about the threat which supercentres posed to the industry. A view gained currency that the fragmented and unconsolidated US food retail industry would be relatively easy prey, and that a huge firm like Wal-Mart with serious capital and commitment might rapidly, and perhaps as early as the turn of the century, become *de facto* the largest food retailer in the US.

The significance of the events that have provided the focus of my Leverhulme Trust project are that they are in the process, at the very least, of tempering this new version of the 'Wal-Martization of America' legend. As Figure 10.4 demonstrates, because of the rapid consolidation which had taken place between 1996 and mid-1998 (see Table 10. 2) – that is to say, before the announcement of Kroger's $13 bill merger with Fred Meyer – the best estimate available suggested that Wal-Mart would by the year 2002 rank as only the third largest US food retailer with

Table 10.3 Growth of the US supercentre format, 1991–2001

	1991	1992	1993	Actual 1994	1995	1996	1997	1998E	Estimated 1999E	2000E	2001E
Total US supercentres	249	297	344	495	656	780	855	1006	1181	1381	1616
of which: Wal-Mart	10	34	72	147	239	344	441	564	694	834	984
Sales of US supercentres ($bill)	9.3	11.0	14.3	19.8	27.9	35.5	43.3	52.8	64.1	77.3	92.2
of which: Wal-Mart*	0.2	1.0	2.7	6.1	11.2	17.7	24.5	32.3	41.2	51.2	61.8

* Wal-Mart's food-related supercentre sales approximately 45 per cent of these totals.
Source: adapted from Merrill Lynch (1998)

food-related sales of approximately $42 bill and a market share of around 7.5 per cent (Wrigley 1999a). Following the Kroger/Fred Meyer merger, it now appears likely that Wal-Mart will rank at best as the fourth largest US food retailer in 2002 – significantly behind Kroger (which is likely to have an 11.5 per cent market share), Albertson's and Safeway – and perhaps even fifth largest if Ahold continues its rapid pace of acquisition in the USA.

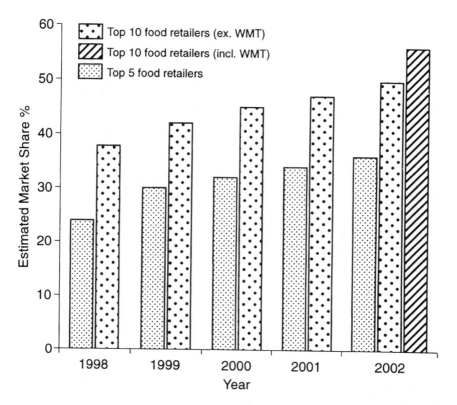

Source: Wrigley (1999a)

Figure 10.4   Forecast market share of leading US food retailers 1998–2002

In addition, it is vital not to over-extrapolate the growth of the US supercentres. Stores of 190,000 sq.ft. requiring 15-20 acre development sites and extensive trade areas face considerable difficulties in their attempts to expand into the urban and inner suburban areas of the major US metropolitan markets where suitable real estate is both scarce and expensive. In addition, in several regions of the US – notably New England – supercentres face increasingly vocal and effective community resistance, and significant difficulties in obtaining zoning approval.

As a result, Wal-Mart has already been forced to develop a smaller, more flexible, supercentre format of 109,000 sq. ft. and, most significantly, has recently announced major plans to experiment with 40,000 sq.ft. 'small marts' or 'neighbourhood markets'. However, it is possible that lack of real estate availability for the development of any of these formats might force Wal-Mart to join the accelerating acquisition wave in the US food retail industry and to acquire regional chains in order to reach critical mass more rapidly. In that case the transformations discussed above will simply be ratcheted up to a more extreme level.

Myth 4: British food retailers have risen to a position of unprecedented prominence, they shape global supply chains, it follows that they are part of an emerging food retail global elite

Finally, it is useful to reverse our perspective and examine British food retail in the context of the transformation of the US industry. That is to say we will consider what might be termed the *Mange Tout* myth following the well-known BBC television documentary of that title. Because British food retailers have risen to a position of unprecedented prominence in the UK economy (see Marsden et al. 1998), and because they shape global networks of commodity production in the way that documentary so vividly portrayed and as Cook (1993, 1994), Arce and Marsden (1993) and Crang and Jackson (in press) have traced and debated to different levels of abstraction in the geographical literature, there has emerged a widely held, but rarely probed, belief that the leading UK retailers are 'masters of the food universe' or, at least, highly significant global players. But how does this view stand up in the context of the reconfiguration of US food retailing outlined above?

During the mid to late 1980s, the leading UK food retailers perceived the emergence of considerable opportunities for expansion into what they saw as a highly fragmented, and fortuitously (from their perspective) debt-encumbered, US food retail industry. As Sainsbury Executive Director, Ian Coull, acknowledged in interviews which I conducted in 1996:

> The US was more attractive than Europe to us because it was a very regionalized and fragmented market and the main players were (in our view at the time) nowhere near as sophisticated as most of the European players. But then having made that decision (to enter the US), purely by chance in the mid 1980s, we had all these LBOs, and that was a wonderful boost to us because all these companies became cash limited and they were unable to expand.

On the basis of these, and related views, on the attractions of the US market (Wrigley 1989), both Sainsbury and Marks & Spencer entered US food retailing

– Sainsbury acquiring the New England chain, Shaw's, and Marks & Spencer the small New Jersey chain, Kings. By 1996/97 heavy capital investment by Sainsbury in its US subsidiary had successfully transformed Shaw's from a minor to a major regional chain (see Wrigley 1997a for details), more than double the size of that originally acquired, operating in all six New England states, and competing strongly for regional market leadership. In addition, Sainsbury had made a second major US acquisition – 50 per cent of the voting stock (20 per cent of the total equity) of Giant Food Inc, the market leader in the Washington DC/Baltimore area (see Wrigley 1997b for details). Poised to purchase full control of Giant, and promoting a major expansion of the firm northwards into the greater Philadelphia market, Sainsbury appeared to be on the verge of becoming a significant force in the north-east US market controlling over 300 stores with an annual turnover of $7 bill. Statements by its incoming Deputy CEO, to the effect that a minimum scale of $10 bill p.a. turnover would be required to compete effectively, made it clear that the firm was also sensitive to the consequences of the impending consolidation wave in the US industry. It appeared that like Ahold, the leading Dutch retailer which through a series of US east coast acquisitions from Bi-Lo in South Carolina to Stop & Shop in New England had propelled itself into a top five position in the US industry (Wrigley 1998c), Sainsbury was also poised to become one of the elite food retailers in the US. In so doing it would have put into place an international diversification strategy with the potential to generate 30 per cent of the firm's annual sales from outside the UK.

However, during the intense wave of consolidation and reconfiguration in the US food retail industry which has taken place over the past two years, none of this has materialised. Having experienced severe and unanticipated difficulties with both of its US operations in 1997 (see Wrigley 1997c, 2000a) whilst attempting to nurse to fruition a fragile recovery of strength in its core UK food business, Sainsbury found itself in a position where the UK capital markets were extremely hostile to any further US expansion. As a result, Sainsbury was unwilling to pay the price of joining the rush to consolidate which began to dominate US food retailing and which drove up the so-called 'acquisition multiples' strategic buyers were required to pay for their target firms to historically high levels (Wrigley 1999b). Having positioned itself, therefore, over a three-year period to acquire full control of what Merrill Lynch (1997: 15) described as 'cash rich Giant . . . one of the few great regional supermarket franchises that is both independent and financially unleveraged', and despite being reminded consistently by the Wall Street investment banks that 'if Sainsbury concludes that it is unwilling or unequipped to complete this purchase, we believe that others would be prepared to step in' (Merrill Lynch 1997: 15), Sainsbury was summarily ejected from its position in Giant in May 1998, and forced to selling its 50 per cent voting share, as Ahold acquired the firm for $2.7 bill. In the process, and with its subsequent proposed acquisition of Pathmark, Ahold increased the turnover of its US operations to $20 bill p.a., reinforced its position within the top five firms in the US industry, and emerged as the dominant east coast US food retailer (Figure 10.5).

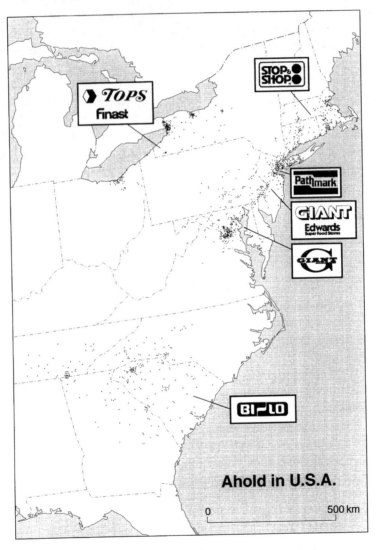

Note: Ahold withdrew from acquisition of Pathmark, December 1999, following opposition to acquisition from Federal Trade Commission
Source: author based on store listings supplied by Ahold

Figure 10.5   The US operations of Royal Ahold in 1999 – the creation by acquisition of a chain of over 1000 stores with a turnover of $20 bill p.a.

Ahold's acquisition of Giant clearly left the international diversification of the UK's second largest food retailer in disarray. Although Sainsbury's subsequently acquired the Boston-based chain, Star Markets, to add to Shaw's (Wrigley 2000a) it was left essentially with just a medium-sized ($4 bill p.a. turnover) regional chain, marginalised from the pace of US food retail consolidation and just one-fifth the size of Ahold's US business. As analysts at Credit Suisse First Boston (1998: 24) reflected at the time of Sainsbury's exit from Giant:

Sainsbury's determination to avoid overpaying and to achieve respectable returns on further investment in the US makes it difficult to see how it would be able to compete with those retailers that either already have:

- a more substantial presence in the US than Sainsbury and thus a more substantial sunk cost base against which to extract synergy; and/or
- a management/shareholder base which is willing to accept materially lower returns from acquisitions than Sainsbury's

However, this is a problem which is not unique to Sainsbury. Despite the 'mange tout' myth, successful internationalisation remains the Achilles Heel of the British food retail industry within the wider context of a rapidly emerging global food retail elite (Wrigley 2000b). Even though Tesco, the leading UK food retailer, has spent £1.4 bill building up an international presence in central Europe (Poland, Hungary, Czech Republic, Slovakia), the Irish Republic and, most recently, Thailand and South Korea, important questions still surround Tesco's ability to develop, *independently*, a substantial profitable business outside the UK. In contrast to other leading European retailers – particularly Carrefour and Ahold – with long-standing international operations, and what often appears to be a startling appetite for highly-geared somewhat risky expansion, the UK food retailers have struggled to compete as part of an emerging global food retail elite (Wrigley 2000b). Figure 10.6, in contrast, shows the extent of Ahold's global empire in 1998, by which point its sales outside its core market in the Netherlands accounted for no less than 75 per cent of its turnover.

The significance of the events that have provided the focus of my Leverhulme Trust project are that they are in the process of exposing, within the context of the giant US food retail market, how false in important senses is the image of globally powerful UK food retailing that we receive via the 'mange tout' myth. The rapid reconfiguration of US food retailing currently underway and transmitted via its impacts on leading European retailers, has, I would suggest, much wider implic-ations for our understanding of the restructuring of commercial cultures in the global food system. It is clearly time to reappraise some of the myths through which our views of that global system are filtered.

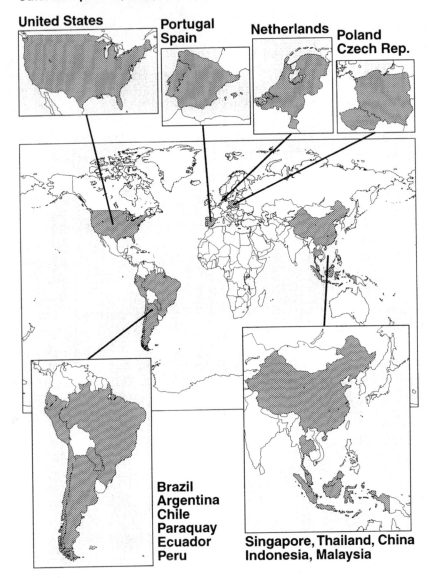

Ahold - Global Operations 1998
Turnover : $29.5 bill (2000 est : $42..2 bill)
Domestic market share of sales : 25%
USA : 55%, Latin America, 11%
Other Europe : 7%, Asia, 2%

United States

Portugal
Spain

Netherlands

Poland
Czech Rep.

Brazil
Argentina
Chile
Paraguay
Ecuador
Peru

Singapore, Thailand, China
Indonesia, Malaysia

Figure 10.6   Royal Ahold: global operations 1998 – 75% of sales outside its core
market in the Netherlands

Conclusion

As Richard Longstreth (1999) so vividly illustrates in *The Drive-In, the Super-market, and the Transformation of Commercial Space in Los Angeles*, the invention of two radically new forms of commercial space – the supermarket and the drive-in shopping centre – in the US during the 1920s had a profound effect on the twentieth-century American city. As those unequivocally American inventions, and the revolution in consumer culture which accompanied them, were exported to Europe after the Second World War, so they became ingrained in the image of the nature of post-war societal change. The common preconception that the food retail industries of Britain and continental Europe and their commercial cultures must inevitably be cast in an American mould has its roots in that image. Yet, as this chapter suggests, the reality is far more complex and contradictory. By the late 1980s/early 1990s hugely important differences had emerged between the US and European industries. In that sense, the dramatic transformations that have swept through the US food retail industry since the mid-1990s, and which I have reflected upon above, have in a very real sense served to reshape the prevailing commercial culture of the US industry, recasting it in certain important respects in a European image. But, in turn, many of the leading firms in that European industry have since the mid-1990s shifted their focus to the challenge of globalisation (Wrigley 2000b), drawing lessons from the synergist benefits which the rapid consolidation of the US industry has demonstrated can flow from mergers and acquisitions in a low price-inflation environment, and from the mechanisms and cultures of within-firm 'best practice' knowledge transfer adopted during those US mergers and acquisitions. In turn, both industries, American and European, face the common challenge of the rise of e-commerce as a potentially destabilising force, and the transformation of their commercial culture which might result from e-commerce's ability to short-circuit existing product and service chains.

Acknowledgements

This chapter forms part of wider research on 'The Post-LBO Reconfiguration of US Food Retailing' supported by The Leverhulme Trust under a 1997 Individual Research Award. The author is grateful to Gary Vineberg and Andrew Wolf of Merrill Lynch, New York; Ed Comeau and Christina Boni of Donaldson, Lufkin and Jenrette, New York; and to Ron Cotterill of the University of Connecticut for on-going discussions on the nature of the US food retail industry. Thanks also go to Ian Coull, Executive Director, J Sainsbury plc; Stuart Brown, Royal Ahold; James Martin, Credit Suisse First Boston; Mark Wasileswki, ABN-AMRO and Tony MacNeary, Bankers Trust Alex Brown for discussions on European food retailers in the USA.

References

Adelman, M.A. (1959), *A&P: A Study in Price-Cost Behaviour and Public Policy,* Cambridge, MA: Harvard University Press.

Arce, A., and Marsden, T.K. (1993), 'The social construction of international food: a new research agenda', *Economic Geography,* 69: 293–311.

Bowlby, R. (1997), 'Supermarket futures', in P. Falk and C. Campbell (eds), *The Shopping Experience,* London: Sage.

Chevalier, J.A. (1995), 'Capital structure and product-market competition: empirical evidence from the supermarket industry', *American Economic Review,* 85: 415–35.

Comeau, E. (1995), *Food and Drug Retailers Industry Viewpoint,* Donaldson, Lufkin and Jenrette Securities Corporation, New York, 9 October.

Connor, J.M. and Schiek, W.A. (1997), *Food Processing: An Industrial Powerhouse in Transition,* 2nd Edition, New York: John Wiley.

Cook, I.J. (1993), 'Constructing the exotic: the case of tropical fruit'. Paper presented at Institute of British Geographers Annual Conference, Royal Holloway and Bedford New College, University of London, 5–8 January.

—— (1994), 'New fruits and vanity: symbolic production in the global food economy', in A. Bonanno, L. Busch, W.H. Friedland, L. Gouveig and E. Mingiovie (eds), *From Columbus to ConAgra: The Globalisation of Agriculture and Food,* Lawrence, Kansas: University Press of Kansas, pp. 232–48.

Cotterill, R.W. (1993), 'Food retailing: mergers, leveraged buyouts and performance', in Duetsch, L. (ed.), *Industry Studies,* Englewood Cliffs: Prentice Hall, pp. 157–81.

—— (1997), 'The food distribution system of the future: convergence towards the US or UK model', *Agribusiness,* 13: 121–35.

Crang, P. and Jackson, P. 'Consuming geographies: localizing the global and globalizing the local', in K. Robins and D. Morley (eds), *British Cultural Studies,* Oxford: Oxford University Press, in press.

Credit Suisse First Boston (1998), *Food Retail Sector: Corporate Activity, Diversification and the Pursuit of Growth,* Credit Suisse First Boston, London, 28 July.

Denis, D.J. (1994), 'Organizational form and the consequences of highly leveraged transactions: Kroger's recapitalization and Safeway's LBO', *Journal of Financial Economics,* 36: 193–224.

Doel, C. (1996), 'Market development and organizational change: the case of the food industry', in N. Wrigley and M.S. Lowe (eds), *Retailing, Consumption and Capital: Towards the New Retail Geography,* Harlow: Addison Wesley Longman, pp. 48–67.

—— (1998), 'Towards a supply chain community? Insights from governance processes in the food industry', *Environment and Planning A,* 31: 69–85.

Fernie, J. (1992), 'Distribution strategies of European retailers', *European Journal of Marketing*, 26 (8/9): 35–47.

—— (1994), 'Quick response: an international perspective', *International Journal of Physical Distribution and Logistics Management*, 24(6): 38–46.

Grant, R.M. (1987), 'Manufacturer-retailer relations: the shifting balance of power', in Johnson, G. (ed.), *Business Strategy and Retailing*, London: Wiley, pp. 43–58.

Hughes, A.L. (1996), 'Retail restructuring and the strategic significance of food retailers' own-labels: a UK-USA comparison', *Environment and Planning A*, 28: 2201–26.

—— (1999), 'Constructing competitive spaces: the corporate practice of British retailer-supplier relationships', *Environment and Planning A*, 31: 819–39.

Longstreth, R. (1999), *The Drive-In, the Supermarket, and the Transformation of Commercial Space in Los Angeles, 1914–41*, Cambridge, Mass.: MIT Press.

Magowan, P.A. (1989), 'The case for LBOs: the Safeway experience', *California Management Review*, 32: 9–11.

Marion, B.W. (1995), 'Changing power relationships in the US food industry: brokerage arrangements for private label products.' Paper presented at conference on 'Food Retailer-Manufacturer Competitive Relationships in the EU and USA', Univ. of Reading, July.

Marsden, T.K., Harrison, M. and Flynn, A. (1998), 'Creating competitive space: exploring the social and political maintenance of retail power', *Environment and Planning A*, 30: 481–98.

Merrill Lynch (1997), *US Food and Drug Merchandising: Investment Snapshots*, Merrill Lynch & Co, New York, 15 April.

—— (1998), *Supercenter Forecaster*, Merrill Lynch & Co, New York, 4 May.

Miller, D. (ed.) (1995), *Acknowledging Consumption: A Review of New Studies*, London: Routledge.

Mueller, W.F. and Paterson, T.W. (1986), 'Policies to promote competition' in B.W. Marion (ed.), *The Organization and Performance of the US Food Industry*, Lexington, Mass., Lexington Books, pp. 371–412.

Smith, D.L.G. and Sparks, L. (1993), 'The transformation of physical distribution in retailing: the example of Tesco plc', *International Review of Retail, Distribution and Consumer Research*, 3: 35–64.

Sparks, L. (1994), 'Delivering quality: the role of logistics in the post-war transformation of British food retailing', in G. Jones and N.J. Morgan (eds), *Adding Value: Brands and arketing in Food and Drink*, London: Routledge, pp. 31–5.

—— (1997), 'From coca-colonization to copy-cotting: the Cott Corporation and retailer brand soft drinks in the UK and US', *Agribusiness*, 13: 153–67.

Wrigley, N. (1989), 'The lure of the USA: further reflections on the internationalisation of British grocery retailing capital', *Environment and Planning A*, 21: 283–8.

—— (1992), 'Antitrust regulation and the restructuring of grocery retailing in Britain and the USA', *Environment and Planning A*, 24: 727–49.

—— (1997a), 'British food retail capital in the USA. Part 1: Sainsbury and the Shaw's experience', *International Journal of Retail and Distribution Management*, 25: 7–21 (Reprinted in British Food Journal, 99, 412–26).

—— (1997b), 'British food retail capital in the USA. Part 2: Giant prospects?', *International Journal of Retail and Distribution Management* 25: 48–58 (Reprinted in *British Food Journal*, 99: 427–37).

—— (1997c), 'British food retail capital in the USA. Preface and update', *British Food Journal*, 99: 409–11.

—— (1998a), 'Corporate finance, leveraged restructuring and the economic landscape: the LBO wave in US food retailing' in R.L. Martin (ed.), *Money and the Space Economy,* John Wiley: Chichester, pp. 185–205.

—— (1998b), 'How British retailers have shaped food choice', in A. Murcott (ed.), *The Nation's Diet: The Social Science of Food Choice,* Harlow: Addison Wesley Longman, pp. 112–28.

—— (1998c), 'European retail giants and the post-LBO reconfiguration of US food retailing', *International Review of Retail, Distribution and Consumer Research,* 8: 127–46.

—— (1999a), 'The consolidation wave in US food retailing: characteristics, causes and consequences', *Agribusiness,* 15.

—— (1999b), 'Market rules and spatial outcomes: insights from the corporate restructuring of US food retailing', *Geographical Analysis,* 31: 288–309.

—— (2000a), 'Strategic market behaviour in the internationalization of food retailing: interpreting the third wave of Sainsbury's US diversification', *European Journal of Marketing,* 34: 891–918.

—— (2000b), 'The globalization of retail capital', in G.L. Clark, M.S. Gertler and M. Feldman (eds), *The Oxford Handbook of Economic Geography,* Oxford: Oxford University Press, pp. 292–313.

—— and Lowe, M.S. (2000), *Reading Retail: A Geographical Perspective on Retailing and Consumption Spaces,* London: Edward Arnold.

Yago, G. (1991), *Junk Bonds: How High Yield Securities Restructured Corporate America,* New York: Oxford University Press.

II

From Victor Gruen to Merry Hill: Reflections on Regional Shopping Centres and Urban Development in the US and UK

Michelle Lowe

Introduction

Victor Gruen, pioneering architect of the shopping mall in 1950s North America, envisaged that his enclosed shopping centres would parallel the ancient agora, the medieval market place and the town square – that they would provide space and scope for community activities and would be developed alongside apartments, office buildings, theatres and so on. Tragically, Gruen was to become disillusioned by the way his ideas were diluted by other developers who built their malls with minimal regard for public activities. In his final years, he practically disowned the mall industry, returning to his native Vienna where he died in 1980. But the idea of the shopping centre as the focal point for public life which Gruen and his associates propagated was never totally lost. Indeed, in his 1980s tour of American malls, William Kowinski suggests that such malls 'have more than financial significance; they are becoming a way of life . . . these meticulously planned and brightly enclosed structures . . . have taken the concept of one-stop shopping, as old as the ancient public markets, and turned it into a virtual one-stop culture, providing a cornucopia of products nestled in an ecology of community, entertainment and societal identity' (Kowinski 1985: 21–2). Ironically, though, it was not until nearly half a century later, and on the other side of the Atlantic, that Gruen's ideas began to bear fruit. Many of Britain's regional shopping centres, themselves modelled on North American megamalls, are arguably in the process of transforming themselves into centres of community life, and reinventing many of Gruen's design principles. This chapter traces that transformation, focussing specifically on a case study of the Merry Hill regional shopping centre in the West Midlands. At Merry Hill it has recently been argued that the centre and its immediate environs have already de facto evolved into a 'high level town centre' (Hall 1996: 14) and as such that Merry Hill increasingly combines shopping into an 'ecology of community, entertainment and societal identity' in the way Kowinski and Gruen suggested. But other UK regional shopping centres are also in the process of becoming far more than commercial centres and attention is also given to several of these other cases.

This chapter begins by comparing and contrasting the history and development of large out-of-town shopping centres in the US and the UK. It is suggested that despite a political rhetoric in opposition to the import of what were very much viewed as American concepts, the situation in the UK was from the outset fundamentally different. The example of Brent Cross, Britain's first 'out-of-town' shopping mall (Miller et al. 1998) serves to illustrate this important point. At Brent Cross the American concept of 'out of town' shopping and American mall architecture were imported wholesale into north-west London, but this is where the simplicity of the comparison between US and UK centres ends. The chapter then considers how Brent Cross has more in common with the regional shopping centres of the 1980s and 1990s than is commonly suggested. Like Brent Cross before them these centres – Metrocentre in Gateshead; Meadowhall in Sheffield; Merry Hill near Dudley in the West Midlands; Thurrock Lakeside by the M25 to the east of London; Bluewater in Kent; The Trafford Centre in Manchester; Cribbs Causeway, Bristol; White Rose, Leeds; and Braehead near Glasgow – are becoming enmeshed into Britain's urban fabric, as by definition, will be the most recent of these regional scale centres – White City in West London. To varying degrees all of these centres are in the process of becoming central components in Britain's evolving urban structure and are likely to be important urban forms in the twenty-first century. The paper concludes by suggesting that the common knee-jerk reaction against Britain's regional shopping centres is somewhat misplaced. These new centres can be viewed as merely the latest in a long line of twentieth-century urban (re)developments and as such (and whether we like it or not) deserve to be taken seriously.

The Malling of the American Landscape

As many US commentators noted in the 1980s, 'in a rather short time span the planned shopping centre has become a dominant component of the American retail landscape' (Lord 1985: 209). Between 1950 and 1980 the number of shopping centres in the USA grew from approximately 100 to more than 22,000, and this expansion was accompanied by the now well-documented decline in retailing in city and town centres (see for example Guy and Lord 1993). The majority of the new centres were established, as Victor Gruen had recommended, as focal points of the rapidly growing American suburbs. Shopping centre developers essentially followed the flight to the suburbs of the mainly white, affluent, population. Increasing levels of car ownership combined with growing consumer demand to feed the evolution of the new suburban centres and set the seeds of decline for many of America's inner cities, where poor, mainly black, populations remained in the urban core (Guy and Lord 1993).

The strong racial and class divisiveness of America's suburban shopping malls has resulted in fierce opposition to such retail developments. Highly critical readings of these consumption spaces, specifically concerning malls as private as opposed to public spaces and the clear geographies of exclusion evidenced in such centres are provided by John Goss, Jeffrey Hopkins and Rob Shields in particular. These authors cite the various ways in which mall owners filter the public, excluding certain individuals from their spaces (Hopkins 1990), and contrast the idealised semi private interiors of the malls with the more egalitarian geographies of the street (Shields 1989). In the UK opponents of out-of-town retail developments reference the American example and experience in order to support their arguments. From Brent Cross to Bluewater, opposition has often focused around the fact that these centres are North American in origin, concept and architecture. It is to the situation in the UK that this chapter now turns.

High Streets 'Out-of-Town'

In the light of the current evidence presented in this chapter, it is fascinating to reflect on the history of opposition to 'out-of-town' retailing in the UK. 'The first genuine out-of-town centre had been proposed as early as the 1960s at Haydock Park near Liverpool and it was the perception of the effects such centres had upon US downtowns as much as anything else which united planning authorities against this and subsequent proposals in the 1960s and 1970s' (BDP Planning/OXIRM 1992). Parallels were drawn between what was thought to have happened to city centre retailing in the US and what could happen in the UK if large-scale regional shopping centres were built (Distributive Trades EDC 1988). But, in addition, from the outset, and somewhat prophetically perhaps, fears about the impact of such centres appeared to:

stem not only from the competitive effects of such developments on the traditional hierarchy of shopping centres but also from the prospect that such centres might become new nuclei for ectopic urban planning growth attracting a wider range of functions and breaking the British planning conventions of urban containment. (Lee Donaldson Associates 1986)

However, as Hall and Breheny noted over a decade ago, 'as part of the debate in the UK about the impact of regional shopping centres we must be conscious not only of *similarities* with the experience in the US but also *differences* that may be crucial to our understanding of what may happen' (1987: 255). They point to a number of important differences between out-of-centre retail developments in the US and UK, not least the *scale* of development (the US has much higher levels of out-of-centre provision than is ever likely to occur in the UK), and the continued confidence in established centres in the UK despite strong moves to 'out-of-town'. Over ten years on, and with the benefit of hindsight, it is possible to further probe the essential points of distinction between out-of-centre retailing in the US and UK. Further detailed information on the history of Britain's regional shopping centre phenomenon enables advancement of this argument.

Following the refusal of the Haydock Park proposal in 1964 by the Ministry of Housing and Local Government, there was a considerable lull in the pressure for regional centres in the UK. Indeed, the only such centre built in the 1970s was Brent Cross in suburban North-West London. Brent Cross has been, and continues to be, viewed as a distinctly different entity from the later 1980s and 1990s generations of regional shopping centres. But further consideration of the Brent Cross example, a case often lost in the history of Britain's regional centres, serves, it is suggested, to illustrate the fundamental difference between the situation in the US and that in the UK. It is to the detail of the Brent Cross development and its parallels with later generations of the UK regional shopping centres that this chapter now turns.

Brent Cross: North America comes to North-West London?

The first major comparison-shopping complex to be established outside existing town and city centres in the UK – was opened at Brent Cross in North-West London in 1976. Brent Cross was designed to be a centre of 'North American style for people who wish to use their cars for shopping' and to fill a gap identified in London's shopping structure (Greater London Development Plan, 1969). The centre was unusual at the time in that it was the only purpose-built shopping centre in the UK which was outside the established shopping hierarchy and was not part of a new town development (Miller et al. 1998: 32). The application for a shopping centre at Brent Cross was first made in January 1966 but was withdrawn in April 1967. A new application for a large scheme was submitted in the following year. This application was called in and a Public Inquiry held in December 1968. Ultimately, approval for the centre was granted on the grounds of 'need' for such a centre in that area of London as identified in the GLC's plan, together with the fact that the application by the developers Hammersons was supported by Barnet, the local authority. The centre is often viewed as distinct from later UK regional shopping centres, because it is 'within an urban area' (BDP Planning/OXIRM 1992: 25) and 'not truly outlying' (Howard 1989), since it was built on land that previously comprised allotments and wasteland including a disused greyhound stadium. In reality, of course, it is possible to argue that the vast majority, if not all, of the UK's subsequent regional shopping centres are equally 'within an urban area' and are certainly 'not truly outlying'. The example of Brent Cross helps then to illustrate a fundamental and *persisting* difference between out-of-centre shopping development in the US and the UK. Whilst many of the 1980s and 1990s generation of regional centres have been established in what Howard (1989) terms 'non traditional locations' and may possibly be 'edge-of-centre', many are not truly – in common with Brent Cross – 'out-of-town' in the American sense (see Guy 1994a). Rather, and almost by definition, given their origins in enterprise zones and on brownfield sites, the majority, if not all of the UK's 1980s and 1990s regional shopping centres, are clustered in and around major cities and like Brent Cross before them, fill 'strategic' gaps of underprovision. As such, they are very much part and parcel of the UK's evolving urban form. Moreover, moves to combine their shopping functions with broader cultural and community activities, together with often strong local support for these emerging centres once again distance them from some of their US counterparts. Unlike North American megamalls, many of the UK's regional shopping centres are indeed emerging as far more than commercial centres and are in the process of transforming themselves into centres of community life in the way that Gruen envisaged. It is to this process that this chapter now turns.

Britain's Regional Shopping Centres – New Towns?

In recounting the history of the regional shopping centre in the UK this chapter has thus far failed to mention an important and often overlooked era. Indeed, few commentators on the UK regional shopping centre phenomenon include in their remit the major 'out-of-town' centres that were built in the context of the government-sponsored 1960s and 1970s new and expanded towns. That is to say, the shopping centres built in connection with the development and/or expansion of towns such as Harlow, Basildon, Stevenage, Bracknell, Crawley, Runcorn, Telford and Milton Keynes. Indeed, Guy (1994a) is almost unique in drawing attention to several regional-sized shopping centres which were built in government-financed new towns during the 1970s. In Guy's view 'the centres in Runcorn, Telford and Washington were built well away from existing town centres, and thus could be regarded as the first free-standing regional centres to be built in Britain' whilst 'the first free-standing super regional centre to be built in Britain was central Milton Keynes opened in 1979'. In the UK, then, there is an often neglected history of large new shopping developments being planned as part and parcel of new and expanded towns, and it is important to bear this in mind when thinking through the recent history and development of the UK's 1980s and 1990s regional shopping centres.

Indeed, there have recently been a number of attempts to represent the latest generation of regional shopping centres in the UK as effectively being the cores of proto new towns and such proposals have frequently found strong support at local level. At Metrocentre, for example, John Bryson, the General Manager, in attempting to convince the Government that the project he has nurtured on the edge of Gateshead has evolved into something much bigger than an out-of-town shopping centre – effectively a town in its own right (Hetherington 1997) – has been supported by Gateshead MB, the local authority (Guy 1998: 26). Capital Shopping Centres (CSC) the current owners of Metro argue that the centre is a town centre because 'it has most of the infrastructure you would expect in a town centre. It has a railway station, a bus station, a church, a medical centre, banks, post office, etc., etc. . . . It also has a hotel and residential development around it . . . it has a leisure content as well with cinemas and Metroland so to a large extent it is quite complete' (Abel, personal communication, 1999). CSC also own Thurrock Lakeside and the soon-to-be-opened Braehead in Glasgow. In both cases these centres are seen by the company as far more than retail developments. Lakeside, with the adjacent Chafford Hundred residential development, has, they suggest, effectively become a town centre and is proving to be an important catalyst for further development in the region whilst negotiations are currently taking place with the Scottish local authorities of Glasgow and Renfrew in the hope that Braehead will be recognised as a second-tier Scottish town. Elsewhere, Bluewater, which opened in March 1999 on an abandoned cement works near Dartford in north-west Kent is viewed by Land Lease (its Australian developers) as the retail hub of a new city which is to include business and housing – effectively a private sector city of the future – plans which have been substantially aided by Bluewater's proximity to Ebbsfleet station on the planned Channel Tunnel highspeed rail link (Chaplin 1998). Meanwhile, the White Rose Centre, four miles south-west of the city centre of Leeds, has been nominated for inclusion as a 'town centre' in the Leeds UDP Inspector's report, since the Inspector was satisfied that White Rose 'does make provision for and is used by the local community and that it acts as a focus for public transport' (Leeds City Council 1999). Needless to say, and in the context of tightened land of use planning regulation (PPG6) which now restricts further 'out-of-town' retail development in the UK (DoE 1993, 1996a; Guy 1998c; Wrigley 1998) the outcome of the White Rose decision is eagerly awaited by the property and planning communities.

But, thus far, it is the Merry Hill Centre in the West Midlands which has seen this argument taken furthest. Indeed, as Peter Hall (1996: 14) argued in evidence at a recent Public Inquiry, Merry Hill and its immediate environs have already de facto evolved into a high-level town centre. To what extent then can centres like Merry Hill be viewed as new towns of the twenty-first century? And are we effectively seeing a new generation of private sector British 'new towns' constructed around a retail core in the same way that the 1970s new towns – for example Telford or Milton Keynes – were themselves centred around new shopping and other facilities? The 1996 Inquiry regarding plans to expand Merry Hill brought into sharp focus a number of facets of these questions and it is to an examination of the Merry Hill case that this chapter now turns.

The Merry Hill Case

A detailed and contextualised account of the 1996 Merry Hill Inquiry has been published elsewhere (Lowe 1998). Suffice it to say here that a proposal by owner–developers Chelsfield to expand the centre was ultimately rejected by the Secretary of State for the Environment on the grounds that 'Merry Hill is a regional shopping centre in an out-of-centre location' . . . 'not a town centre', and thus constitutes a form of retail development discouraged under tightened land-use planning regulations relating to retail development – PPG6 (DOE 1993, 1996a). Critically, though, it was conceded in the 1996 Inquiry report that the case was not 'absolutely clear cut' (DOE 1996b: 86). Here a number of issues arising from the 1996 Inquiry are examined and a case made that Merry Hill – when viewed in its local context – is in the process of emerging as a new town of the twenty-first century.

In Chelsfield's final submission to the Inquiry the company argued that 'The Merry Hill Centre, when placed . . . in its locality, becomes part of an urban node, where the retail uses, the high-prestige offices, the industry, the leisure uses and the complex services – banks, building societies and others, unite in an effective mixture of uses serving the public similar to a town centre' (Merry Hill Centre Public Inquiry 1996, Applicants Final Evidence, 6). The key to the owner-developers' arguments here, is a view of 'Merry Hill' that comprises far more than the regional shopping centre which was the definition of 'Merry Hill' for the purposes of the Inquiry. Indeed, 'Merry Hill' as a new town centre comprises Chelsfield's shopping centre, leisure and office uses at the adjacent Waterfront, together with Brierley Hill district centre (see Figure 11.1). These three components of a 'new town' have been dubbed the Brierley Hill/Merry Hill/Waterfront triangle by Dudley MBC and are viewed as having developed 'complementary roles' (Dudley MBC 1997). An examination of the three components of the 'triangle' helps to develop the argument.

Figure 11.1   Merry Hill shopping centre in its local context.

The regional shopping centre

The Merry Hill Centre has developed incrementally over the past decade. Originally the brainchild of local entrepreneurs, Don and Roy Richardson, and in the first instance comprising retail warehousing (Lowe 1991, 1993), by the mid-1990s Merry Hill retail at 1,515,000 square feet was very similar in size and type to the other regional shopping centres constructed during the 1980s – Metrocentre, Meadowhall and Lakeside (Guy 1994a). As well as its retail functions, the centre provided a ten-screen cinema, banks and building societies, post office, tourist information centre and a range of community facilities such as bridge and chess club, careers service, Age Concern, Citizens Advice Bureau, chiropodist, disability helpline etc.

The waterfront

Part and parcel of the Richardsons' original Merry Hill scheme, the Waterfront, adjacent to the shopping centre, has evolved into an important employment location in the West Midlands region. The Waterfront comprises over 700,000 square feet of office, leisure and retail uses and has attracted central government offices (Child Support Agency and Inland Revenue), local business organizations (Dudley TEC and Dudley Chamber of Commerce and Industry), plus service industries and electronics firms. Large employers at the Waterfront (in addition to CSA and IR) include Barclays, Prudential and Cable Midlands. The development employs over 3,000 people (mainly (60 per cent +) women) in clerical (65 per cent) and other occupations. The Waterfront also has a thriving night-time economy centred around its bars and restaurants which have provided a new social focus in Dudley borough. The vast majority of its evening visitors are aged 20–39 in socio-economic groups C1/C2 (skilled manual and clerical). The Waterfront is also home to a 4-star (Copthorne) hotel (Dudley MBC 1997).

The district centre

Brierley Hill and its high street, immediately to the south of the shopping centre, is a locally important centre with a range of community facilities including a public library, council offices, police station, civic hall, churches, health and leisure centres. Brierley Hill remains the main focus for local shopping, administrative, community and recreational activity in the area. Despite original concerns that the district centre would be massively negatively impacted by the opening of the adjacent regional shopping centre, fears apparently confirmed by the relocation of MFI in 1986, and a subsequent loss of 13,000 square feet of comparison shopping floorspace after the opening of Phase Five of Merry Hill in 1989, the overall loss of Brierley Hill's retail space by 1992 amounted to only 3 per cent of its 1986 total (Roger Tym and Partners 1993). The centre has subsequently stabilised and indeed may have experienced certain positive washover effects from trade drawn into the area. Brierley Hill – with its distinctive retail and service flavour – has arguably developed a complementary and symbiotic relationship with the Merry Hill Centre.

A New Urban Geography

By the mid-1990s, Dudley MBC had acknowledged that 'in terms of retail floorspace, in terms of business activity, in terms of employment, the urban structure of Dudley has refocused itself at Merry Hill' (Merry Hill Centre Public Inquiry 1996, Applicants Final Evidence: 15). But what evidence was there for such a statement? In particular, how was the new urban geography of the area actively being created by residents of Dudley? Sean Nethercott, from Dudley MBC's Planning Department explains:

> People on the ground have started to use the three elements together and perceive the area as a town centre . . . because that's how it operates . . . People go shopping at Merry

Hill, they go out for the evening and they work there. They'll go to the Waterfront in the evening, or work there and then go out . . . it's the major leisure destination in the Borough. You've got Brierley Hill, a district centre, the library, the leisure centre . . . People are using it as such without it being called a town centre. (Nethercott, personal communication, 1997)

In this context, surveys undertaken in the mid-1990s suggested a relatively tight catchment area for the centre – with 68 per cent of visitors living within fifteen minutes drive time. Notably, and contra to popular opinion on modes of transport to regional shopping centres, over 13,000 visits to the centre per week were in fact taking place on foot – reflecting the centre's embedded urban location with 25,000 people living within one mile – with a further 36,000 visitors (11 per cent) reaching the centre by bus (Merry Hill Centre Public Inquiry 1996, Applicants Final Evidence 59–60). Although complementary figures on the use of the Waterfront's leisure facilities are not available, Perkins' (1996) survey of households in Dudley suggests that amongst the under 40s, over 50 per cent were visiting Merry Hill more than once a week.

It is in relation to this and much similar evidence obtained by the local authority in the mid-1990s, that Dudley MBC proposed the reclassification of the three components of 'Merry Hill' as a new town centre under the Borough's Unitary Development Plan (UDP). In this respect Dudley was, it felt, merely reflecting the reality of usage by ordinary citizens who had by this point come to regard Merry Hill as their town centre. Indeed, Dudley billed revisions to the UDP as 'perhaps the most exciting change in the urban geography of the Borough since the Industrial Revolution' (Dudley MBC 1998). Notwithstanding the clear evidence of use at a local level, combined with Dudley MBC's commitment to a new urban centre at the heart of the Borough, however, the transformation of Merry Hill from a 'regional shopping centre' to a 'new town centre' was unlikely to be a smooth or uncontested process.

At the 1996 Inquiry strong opposition was mounted by a Consortium of local authorities in the immediate region and beyond, anchored by Birmingham City Council. The Consortium argued that expansion proposals at Merry Hill were:

Conflicting with all the efforts that most of the authorities and private sector partners were making to enhance existing centres in various ways. It would undermine efforts that had been made and would potentially undermine upgrading or further development in centres. (Carter, personal communication, 1997)

But in practice, this amounted to an attempt to preserve the existing urban hierarchy at the expense of the newcomer – Merry Hill. In contrast, Dudley MBC were of the view that Merry Hill should be given the same opportunity to expand as 'traditional' centres in the region like Wolverhampton or Birmingham (*Stourbridge Chronicle* 1998) and that the opposition of the Consortium was merely an attempt to preserve the status quo. Dudley clearly faces a considerable task under current planning regulations if it is to counter this strong 'preservationist' argument.

During the Inquiry much emphasis was placed by owner-developers, Chelsfield, on comparisons of Merry Hill, not with 'traditional' town centres, but with new towns such as Telford or Milton Keynes. The owner-developers argued that objections concerning public transport usage (and comparisons of that usage) with established town centres were unreasonable in the context of a centre developed during the 1980s. Rather, they suggested, Merry Hill should be more fairly compared with new towns where the modal split car/public transport is much more similar. Indeed, Chelsfield suggested that when Telford and Merry Hill are examined closely they are remarkably similar – 'When both are looked at in context, both are locations for diverse uses serving the community beyond mere shopping need' (Merry Hill Centre Public Inquiry 1996, Applicants Final Evidence 16). As such, and as in the case of Telford or Milton Keynes, Merry Hill serves as both a 'regional shopping centre' *and* as a 'new town centre' for its immediate hinterland. In this respect it is interesting to reflect on Guy's (1994b) view (above) that any listing of 'regional shopping centres' should include those constructed as part and parcel of Britain's new towns. But again, this comparison of Merry Hill to 'new towns' argument was overruled during the course of the Inquiry. The Secretary of State maintained that there were sufficient grounds to reject Chelsfield's case despite the 'new town' thesis.

The Merry Hill Inquiry pointed to the potential of Merry Hill as a new town centre – an emerging new town even of the twenty-first century. But what are the implications of that evidence for UK planning policy and what does it suggest, more widely, about the place of the regional shopping centres of the 1980s and 1990s within Britain's evolving urban form? It is to these broader discursive issues that this chapter now turns.

Beyond the Merry Hill Case: Regional Shopping Centres and Evolving Urban Form

It has clearly always been the case that the UK's built environment and urban hierarchy have been dynamic entities. Indeed, as Peter Hall (1996: 8) argued in his evidence at the Merry Hill Inquiry:

New Centres have constantly arisen in the history of urban development; examples are new suburban centres such as Ealing Broadway and Muswell Hill in the late nineteenth-century tramway era, Slough in the interwar era, and the relocation of the prime town centre shopping in Southampton and Portsmouth in the post-World War II period; other examples are provided by the new towns, including Hemel Hempstead, Stevenage and Runcorn, where new centres were built at some distance from the old ones.

Hall's commentary concerning the historic emergence of new town centres (see also Hall and Ward 1998), via both the operation of market forces and by conscious public action, is a convincing one and one which deserves considerable consideration. Whilst the Merry Hill case, as the evidence outlined above attests, may lie at one end of a spectrum in respect of this process, it is arguable that many of Britain's other regional shopping centres, as noted above in the case of Metrocentre, Lakeside, Braehead, Bluewater and White Rose, are some way towards, or have the potential for transforming themselves into new town centres – new towns even of the twenty-first century. In part, of course, this process reflects, as highlighted above, the largely urban nature of many of the regional shopping centres. Whilst Merry Hill with its proximity to areas of high population, its divorce from motorways and its high degree of local connectivity is an obvious example – indeed it is interesting to reflect on the fact that the Secretary of State in rejecting expansion plans at the Inquiry stopped short of declaring the site an 'out-of-town' centre – it is equally the case that several of the other regional shopping centres are similarly not 'out-of-town'. Moreover, even in instances where the argument for 'out of town' status could potentially be made – for example at Thurrock Lakeside – the building of new residential developments will eventually embed the centre more fully into the urban fabric. In the case of Metrocentre and Meadowhall, constructed as they were on abandoned industrial sites, it is hard to imagine how the label 'out of town' could ever realistically be applied. Indeed, the very nature and raison d'être of regional shopping centres explicitly demands access to large catchment populations and thereby de facto assumes considerable urban linkage.

In the context of the above discussion, it is pertinent here to consider the place of planning policy – specifically the tightened regulation of PPG6 – in relation to the existing regional shopping centres. At Merry Hill, plans to expand the centre clearly fell foul of the basic principles and philosophy underlying PPG6 (Lowe 1998), specifically its concern with reinvestment in *existing* town centres in order to ensure their 'vitality and viability' (DOE/URBED 1994; Guy 1998a, 1998b; Wrigley 1998). But surely many regional shopping centres developed in the 1980s, could by the mid-1990s also be labelled as 'existing centres'? Indeed, Peter Langley (Government Office for the West Midlands) suggests that:

> [Regional shopping centres] do not fit comfortably within a policy framework whose main purpose is to protect historic or traditional town centres and address the problems of out of town superstores and warehouse parks. (Langley, personal communication, 1997)

In this respect it is important to remember the fact that notwithstanding the emphasis placed on 'protecting' existing centres from the might of regional shopping centres, in practice, a larger threat is posed by the retail parks which have developed apace on the edges of many of Britain's towns and cities (indeed total floorspace in retail parks is currently estimated at ten times that of the regional shopping centres of the 1980s (Guy 1998b)). Moreover, intensification of retail usage in existing regional shopping centres can often permit significant expansions in retail sales without any growth in overall centre size. At Merry Hill, for example, the acquisition of a 40,000 square feet Littlewoods store by Marks and Spencer (the latter trading at approximately £400 per square foot above the former at Merry Hill), has significantly expanded the centre's overall trade without any recourse to planning policy. In the light of the above issues, the knee-jerk reaction to developments which further transform regional shopping centres into town centres, would seem to be somewhat misplaced. But despite this fact, and despite a mounting groundswell of opinion which supports moves such as those of Dudley MBC to incrementally transform Merry Hill and its environs into the 'new Dudley' (*Guardian* 1996; *The Times* 1997; *Sunday Times* 1998), there remains considerable opposition to this and similar proposals, in particular from the local authorities covering the established centres.

Writing as long ago as 1987, Hall and Breheny argued that Britain's regional shopping centres 'constitute the final confirmation that the urban structure of Britain has been undergoing a sea change with the growth of new major economic nodes and the inevitable decline of established urban centres'. Evidence presented in this paper confirms this view. Britain's regional centres are in the process of creating new urban forms. At Merry Hill, for example, following the 1996 Inquiry, owner-developers Chelsfield are putting together a comprehensive area development framework. This will include new street layouts in the Merry Hill/Brierley Hill/Waterfront area which will aid physical connectivity, improved public transport access to the site and the further diversification of uses to include public buildings, open spaces and so on. Merry Hill 'town centre' is here to stay. But whilst the initial concept of 'out of town' shopping developments and much of the architecture of Britain's regional shopping centres may be American in origin, this is where the simplicity of the comparison between US and UK centres ends. Ironically, perhaps, Victor Gruen's vision may be in the process of becoming more of a reality in the UK of the 1990s than in the mid-west American heartland and in which it was first developed. In the UK large shopping malls have the potential perhaps, as Gruen envisaged, to become: 'antidotes to suburban sprawl . . . centralizing influences, organizing principles as well as adaptable mechanisms for creating community centres where there were none'. Like Brent Cross and Milton Keynes before them Britain's new generation of regional shopping centres are rapidly becoming enmeshed into the urban fabric. The popularity of these new centres alone is clearly a signal to their success and as a result it is surely time that we took these new urban spaces seriously?

References

BDP Planning/OXIRM (1992), *The Effects of Major Out of Town Retail Development,* London: HMSO.

Chaplin, S. (1998), Bluewater: out of town, out of mind? *Architectural Design Profile,* No. 131, 67.

Department of the Environment, (1993), *Planning Policy Guidance 6: Town Centres and Retail Developments,* London: HMSO.

—— (1996a), *Planning Policy Guidance 6: Town Centres and Retail Developments,* London: HMSO.

—— (1996b), *Merry Hill Shopping Centre – Proposed Expansion 1996 Inquiry Report.,* London: Department of the Environment.

DOE/URBED (1994), V*ital and Viable Town Centres: Meeting the Challenge,* London: HMSO.

Distributive Trades EDC (1988), *The Future of the High Street,* London: HMSO.

Dudley MBC (1997), *The Waterfront Impact Study,* Dudley: Dudley MBC.

—— (1998), *The New Town Centre at Brierley Hill,* Dudley: Dudley MBC.

Goss, J. (1993), 'The "magic of the mall": an analysis of form, function and meaning in the retail built environment', *Annals of the Association of American Geographers,* 83, 18–47.

Greater London Council (1969), *Greater London Development Plan,* London: GLC.

The *Guardian* (1996), 'The future is here and now: lots of happy smiling people tripping to the shopping mall. But does it work?' 8 October, 2.

Guy, C. M. (1994a), *The Retail Development Process,* London: Routledge.

—— (1994b), 'Whatever happened to regional shopping centres?' *Geography,* 79, 293–312.

—— (1998a), 'Off-centre retailing in the UK: prospects for the future and the implications for town centres', *Built Environment,* 24, 16–30.

—— (1998b), 'Alternative use valuation, open A1 planning consent, and the development of retail parks', *Environment and Planning A,* 30, 37–47.

Guy, C. M. and Lord, J.D. (1993), 'Transformation and the city centre', in R.D.F. Bromley and C.J. Thomas (eds), *Retail Change: Contemporary Issues,* London: UCL Press, pp. 88–108.

Hall, P. and Breheny, M. (1987), 'Urban decentralization and retail development: Anglo-American comparison', *Built Environment* 13, 244–61.

Hall, P. (1996), *The Merry Hill Centre: Proof of Evidence at Public Inquiry,* Department of the Environment, Ref WMR/P/5106/223/9A.

—— and Ward, C. (1998), *Sociable Cities: the Legacy of Ebenezer Howard,* Chichester: Wiley.

Hetherington, P. (1997), 'Mega malls become a battlefield', *Guardian,* 5 November, 23.

Hopkins, J. (1990), 'West Edmonton Mall: landscapes of myths and elsewhereness'. *Canadian Geographer,* 34, 2–17.

Howard, E. B. (1989), *Prospects for Out-of-Town Retailing: the Metro Experience*, London, Longman.

Kowinski, W. S. (1985), *The Malling of America: an Inside Look at the Great Consumer Paradise*, New York: Morrow.

Lee Donaldson Associates (1986), Shopping centre appeals review Research Study 2, London: Lee Donaldson Associates.

Leeds City Council (1999), *Leeds Unitary Development Plan Inspectors Report*, Leeds City Council.

Lord, J. D. (1985), 'The malling of the American landscape', in J. A. Dawson and J. D. Lord (eds), S*hopping Centre Development: Policies and Prospects*, London: Croom Helm, 209–25.

Lowe, M. S. (1991), 'Trading places: retailing and local economic development at Merry Hill, West Midlands', *East Midland Geographer*, 14, 31–48.

—— (1993), 'Local hero: An examination of the role of the regional entrepreneur in the regeneration of Britain's regions', in G. Kearns and C. Philo (eds), *Selling Places: the City as Cultural Capital, Past and Present*, Oxford: Pergamon Press, 211–30.

—— (1998), 'The Merry Hill regional shopping centre controversy: PPG6 and new urban geographies', *Built Environment*, 24, 57–69.

Merry Hill Centre Public Inquiry (1996), *Applicants Final Evidence*, Department of the Environment, Ref WWR/P/5160/223/9A.

Miller, D., Jackson, P., Thrift, N. J., Holbrook, B., and Rowlands, M. (1998), *Shopping, Place and Identity,* London: Routledge.

Perkins, S. (1996), 'The social effects of retail decentralisation: a multi method impact assessment', *Unpublished PhD thesis*, University of Swansea.

Roger Tym and Partners (1993), *Merry Hill Impact Study*, London: HMSO.

Shields, R. (1989), 'Socio spatialization and the built environment: the West Edmonton Mall', *Environment and Planning D: Society and Space*, 7, 147–64.

Stourbridge Chronicle (1998), 'Merry Hill goes to town', 26 June, 1.

Sunday Times (1998), 'Changes in store', 15 February, 3/2.

Times (1997),'Landmark decision for out of towners', 10 October, 27.

Wrigley, N. (1998), 'Understanding store development programmes in post-property-crisis UK food retailing', *Environment and Planning A*, 30, 15–35.

Streets of Style: Fashion Designer Retailing within London and New York

Christopher M. Moore

The opening of the new six-floor Ralph Lauren store, the new Tommy Hilfiger and Calvin Klein stores, cumulatively represent a total investment of over £20 million in Bond Street for these three companies alone. In the past five years, the international fashion designers have invested over £120 million in property in a street no longer than a mile long. *Menswear*, March 1999

The landscape of fashion designer retailing, particularly within Western Europe and the USA, has changed fundamentally in the past twenty years or so. Previously, the fashion design market was dominated by family-owned, typically French, sometimes Italian (and to a lesser extent, English), fashion houses, which normally offered a limited number of products (invariably evening gowns), to a limited clientele (usually the very rich), within a limited number of locations (normally the world centres, such as London, New York and Paris). However, by the mid-1990s, the balance of power within this market had changed and was principally manifest in the emergence of publicly-owned, American fashion design houses. Through their effective marketing communications management, the extension of the product lines to include branded clothing, cosmetics and home furnishing lines, and the opening of "lifestyle-superstore" flagship outlets, the American fashion houses have expertly re-engineered the nature and characteristics of fashion designer retailing to include the lucrative middle retailing market, and in so doing have established a wider constituency of active consumers and as a result, a multi-billion dollar market.

Based upon the findings of a longitudinal study of fashion designer retailing in general, and of fashion designer flagship stores in London and New York in particular (and which included extended interviews with senior representatives from more than twenty international fashion design houses), this chapter will seek to identify the conditions which have enabled the American (and not the British) fashion houses to develop the best recognised and most successful fashion brands in the world. For reasons of respondent confidentiality, the identities of the fashion companies involved in this study cannot be disclosed.

Identifying the International Fashion Designers

An obvious, but critical starting point for this research was the need to provide a definition of what actually constitutes an 'international fashion design retailer'. After consultation with the British Fashion Council, the Editors of the International Fashion Magazines and Journals, as well as with various other fashion journalists, experts and commentators, a clear agreement was reached as to the defining characteristics of the international fashion design retailers. This consensus identified that such firms:

- have an international profile in the fashion industry as evidenced in their having a bi-annual fashion show in one of the international fashion capitals (i.e. Paris, Milan, London or New York);
- have been established in the fashion design business for at least two years;
- retail merchandise either through outlets bearing the designer's name (or an associated name), and/or within other outlets within two or more countries,
- market their own label merchandise.

It should be noted that those fashion designers who distribute their ranges internationally via wholesale arrangements to third party retailers, and who do not have any direct involvement in foreign markets (by operating stand-alone stores, franchised outlets, rented in-store concessions etc.), were excluded from the above definition.

From the above criteria, a database of international fashion design retailers was established using such sources as international fashion brand directories, international retailing intelligence reports, internet sites, and pre-established databases comprising details of international fashion shows held in 1997/98, and new store openings by fashion design houses worldwide (which were provided by a British fashion publishing house). From this database, a total of 114 international fashion design houses were identified. Of these, over 80 per cent were found to originate from four countries, notably Italy, France, the USA and the UK (see Table 12.1).

By way of explaining this concentration, industry experts suggested that the large size of these national markets, each with sizeable proportions of wealthy consumers prepared to pay the premium prices typical of fashion design houses, meant that it was inevitable that these countries should produce and sustain a disproportionately high number of fashion design houses in the first place. The fact that these fashion design houses were also the most likely to trade internationally was partly explained by the fact that each of these countries (with the possible exception of the USA) have long enjoyed a global reputation for excellence in fashion design, manufacturing and retailing.

Table 12.1 Country of Origin of International Fashion Designers

Country of Origin	Number of International Fashion Designers
France	30
Italy	26
UK	27
USA	12
Others	19
Total	114

That only twelve of the 114 international fashion design houses were found to originate from the USA underplays the market domination of the American designers. America's most successful international fashion designer, Ralph Lauren, had, in 1998, world-wide sales in excess of $8 billion (Anon 1998a), a sales level that was greater than Italy's three top design houses (Giorgio Armani, Versace and Gucci) combined (Anon 1998b). Perhaps what is more remarkable is the fact that sales of Ralph Lauren worldwide were more than the total sales of the twenty-seven British fashion design houses in 1998. The success enjoyed by the Ralph Lauren Corp. are not atypical of the American fashion design sector. America's second most successful designer, Calvin Klein had sales of over $3 billion in 1998, while the third and fourth contenders, Tommy Hilfiger and Donna Karan, each had sales of over $1 billion in that year. While no official figures exist to confirm the total sales of America's twelve international fashion design houses, a conservative estimate based upon figures released by the varies companies would suggest total sales of $15 billion in 1998. In contrast, an estimate for the total sales of the UK twenty-seven international designer's would be unlikely to exceed $3 billion.

In the light of the above estimates, the inevitable question that arises is – *What is it that makes American fashion designers so successful and British fashion designers markedly less so?* According to representatives from the American and British fashion design houses, representatives from the European design houses, as well as other industry commentators, there are four, interrelated dimensions which serve to explain the international market success and dominance of the American designers.

The remainder of the chapter will consider each of these dimensions in turn, and will then reflect upon the micro level impact of these factors upon the premier fashion design shopping districts of Central London and New York.

From Private to Public Ownership

> Stock-market listing is really a key to understanding our growth and success. To achieve a listing, we had to commit to a strategy of international growth so as to show we were a strong viable company. Post-listing gave us the financial muscle to continue the push for international growth. (Vice-President, Corporate Affairs)

An analysis of the ownership characteristics of American fashion design companies highlights the transformation of the most successful companies from being private (invariably family-owned) firms, to stock market listed concerns. The Tommy Hilfiger Corp. was among the first to achieve a listing in 1992, followed by Donna Karan in 1995. The move to public ownership by Ralph Lauren was incremental. In 1994 the company raised £80 million by selling a 28.5 per cent stake to the investment house, Goldman Sachs. In late 1997 the company was floated on the New York Stock Exchange, with Lauren himself retaining a 44 per cent share of the company. Calvin Klein, while still wholly owned by the designer and his business partner, have indicated that it is their intention to float the company in 2001/2002. In contrast, none of the major British fashion design houses have achieved stock market listing, and none have declared an interest to do so in the foreseeable future.

There are a number of reasons as to why the American design houses have become public companies, among the more important being their desire to raise revenue so as to fund the continued development of their businesses, as well as to secure a significant financial reward from a stock market flotation for the original owners (invariably the designers themselves). The Vice-President responsible for International Sales and Marketing of one company provided a very succinct explanation as to why his company had moved to public ownership:

> We had a fine brand and we knew it would work in Europe. But, to take it there, we needed finance. Most fashion design houses, us included, are small in scale, in terms of available finance and expertise. By going public, we were able to obtain the finance required in order to develop the business. And we then could buy in the expertise to take us fully into international markets.

The change in ownership status has provided a clear impetus for business growth for some of the designers. In the case of the Tommy Hilfiger Corp., share issue revenue has provided the finance for the company to significantly extend the number of domestic outlets and engage in international expansion through the creation of a network of flagship stores and shop-in-shops in department stores. New revenue and net income increases of 93 per cent and 53 per cent respectively for the period March 1998/March 1999 serve to highlight the continued growth enjoyed by the company (Anon 1998c).

Public-ownership status has not always proved to be a "bed of roses" for all designers. One company that has experienced the pressures of stock market participation and with it the hazards of a belligerent press railing against disappointing performance is Donna Karan International Inc. Floated on the New York Stock Exchange in 1995 at $24 a share, the highest level the company were able to achieve in 1998 was $17, and throughout the first half of 1999 the company's shares were valued at $6. Industry commentators claim that analysts' scathing appraisals of the company's management and trading strategy cost Donna Karan, the company's namesake, chairman and chief designer, her position as CEO in 1997. Her replacement as CEO, John Idol, who was recruited from the more successful Ralph Lauren Corp., sought immediately to placate investors by cutting costs and signing brand licensing deals as a remedy for poor company cash flow. Idol's inability to achieve an immediate improvement in company performance has meant that he too has faced significant hostility from market commentators. Indeed, criticism of the Donna Karan Corp. among city analysts reached such an extent that *Fortune* magazine suggested that the "market has treated one of the most glamorous names in a fashion like a tacky mall rat" (Goldstein 1999).

Given the potential for hostile trading, and compounded by the volatile and unpredictable nature of the fashion market, it is perhaps not surprising that British fashion design houses should fastidiously avoid stock market listing. But there are a number of other reasons which account for their avoidance. Perhaps the most significant is the apparent lack of faith among market analysts in the investment potential of British designers. Those that were surveyed as part of this research maintained that (with a very few exceptions) British fashion designers lacked the drive, the management competency, and the marketing aplomb to create and maintain a strong brand, with an international appeal, that could rival those of the American and Italian companies. To paraphrase the words of one analyst, British designer fashion is an investment "no-go area".

Within the context of such hostility from the financial community, it is perhaps no surprise that British designers appear to have little appetite for stock market involvement. Alongside their recognition of the market's lukewarm regard for fashion companies, many British fashion designers themselves recognise that a stock market flotation would not be feasible because of the limited earnings potential of their businesses, as is evident from the remarks of a director of one of the British companies :

Yes, we are successful, but in a small scale. British designer fashion is by its nature small scale. Going public requires a big brand, a big identity. No British designer, other than perhaps Paul Smith, has that international profile. And none of us could compete internationally with the likes of Lauren or Armani. Our earnings potential is terminally limited.

Arguably, it is that limited earnings potential which lies as the central difference between American and British fashion design houses. British designers, with a few exceptions such as Paul Smith and Jasper Conran, have generally held to the traditional model of the fashion designer as courtier, serving a rich market segment, located within Central London, and with a narrow product range. As such, British fashion design has largely remained exclusive, and as a result, is intentionally limited in its appeal since according to one such designer, "real and actual, as opposed to perceived exclusivity" is central to British designer's positioning and appeal.

In contrast, the most successful American fashion designers, such as Ralph Lauren and Calvin Klein, have "traded-up" from being ostensibly mass-market jeans and casualwear manufacturers with limited international recognition, to reposition themselves as up-market fashion design houses that provide couture for the rich but at the same time dress the considerably less well-off around the world. The apparently insatiable demand for their products would appear to suggest that the American designers have convinced their customers that brand exclusivity is reconcilable with wide availability. As to how they have achieved this is largely explained by the other three defining dimensions identified by this study, notably those of product line extension and brand diffusion, product manufacturing under licence, as well as international expansion through flagship store openings. The following sections will consider each of these dimensions in particular detail.

Brand Diffusion – Brand Democracy

Traditionally, the international fashion design houses, such as Chanel and Hermes, have targeted only the very rich with a relatively limited range of formal wear garments. And as has been previously suggested, this also has largely been the strategy adopted by the majority of British designers. In contrast, and by virtue of their more mass-market origins, American designers have evolved to provide more extensive product ranges, and have tended to concentrate, in particular, upon casualwear rather than couture clothing. The companies themselves explained that their focus upon casualwear was a response to American customer demand and mirrored the more casual approach to dressing which was, and remains, an important feature of the American fashion market. With the advent of more casual dressing worldwide, increased consumer leisure time and affluence, and a greater interest among consumers in conspicuous fashion consumption, particularly in the form of designer branded clothing, companies such as Ralph Lauren and Calvin Klein (and unlike the British fashion designers), have been well placed to respond to the clothing needs of diverse customer segments, worldwide.

Evidence of this diversity in approach is evident in the way in which American designers have been adept in the development of a portfolio of brands, each of which is promoted using a distinct brand name (while still retaining some connection with the designer's name) has a distinct visual brand identity and is managed and distributed using quite separate channels to quite distinct customer groups. Figure 12.1 illustrates the brand segmentation strategy of three American designers. Of the three brand categories, diffusion ranges have proved to be the most financially rewarding for the American fashion houses, and this success can, in the main, be attributed to the fact that these diffusion brands are targeted towards the large and lucrative "middle retail market". The TMS Partnership, an international fashion research agency, define the middle retail market to include social groups B to C2, and identified that within both Europe and the USA, these consumers spend three times more on clothing than those within social group A, the fashion designer's typical target customer (Anon 1998d).

The development of these diffusion brands has been a key element of the American fashion designers' growth strategies, and has had a fundamental impact upon the merchandising and distribution strategies of these companies. Where previously a fashion designer's store typically offered between two and three hundred product lines per season, the introduction of a diffusion brand at Ralph Lauren has swelled that company's product range to more than 6,000 lines per season. And where previously the fashion designer's ranges were distributed through a small number of company-owned stores in the fashion capitals of Paris, London, Milan and New York, as well as select department stores worldwide, the desire to attract the middle retail market has required that they adopt less narrow distribution methods. A more extensive market coverage has been achieved largely through the development of wholesale distribution to third party stockists. Through the extensive use of wholesaling, the Polo Ralph Lauren brand is now sold in over 1,600 department and speciality stores, as well as through 200 Polo Ralph Lauren shops and outlet stores worldwide, the majority of which are operated under franchise agreements with local partners in over twenty countries. Distributing their diffusion brands through wholesaling and franchising has proved to be a low-risk, high-return strategy, and on average, this study found that while diffusion ranges accounted for between 50–60 per cent of companies' sales turnover, their contribution to gross profit was often as high 90 per cent.

Brand Category	Description	Examples
Couture	• Collections featured in fashion shows and the media; • Garments are hand-made and made to measure; • Collection consists of no more than 100 pieces; • Targeted towards the world's richest women; • Evening gowns can cost upwards of £8,000; • Designer responsible for design; • Rarely profitable.	Donna Karan Couture Calvin Klein Couture Ralph Lauren Couture
Ready-to-Wear (RTW)	• Garments featured in fashion shows and the media; • Designer shares design responsibility with design team; • Garments sold off-the-peg; • Premium prices; • Net margins typically between 25–50%; • Targeted towards men & women in wealthy social groups; • Marketed under a distinct brand name.	Donna Karan CK Collections Ralph Lauren
Diffusion	• Aimed at the middle retail market (e.g. B – C2); • Designer has minimal, often no involvement in design; • Mid-high prices; • Marketed under a distinct brand name; • Net margins are high.	DKNY CK Jeans Polo Ralph Lauren / Chaps

Figure 12.1   The Brand Segmentation Strategy of American Designers.

A defining characteristic of diffusion brands is the extensive use of branding trademarks, such as in the form of brand logos, which are normally prominently placed on the product to be as visible and recognisable as possible. These brand trademarks do not only have a denotative function, but also have a connotative meaning. Through the adoption of seemingly complex, and certainly expensive communication strategies, the American designers have proved highly expert in the process of developing a lifestyle association for their brands. Through memorable, often controversial advertising campaigns, the Calvin Klein Company have developed an image for their CK jeanswear line which is urban, modern and confident. Through the purchase of CK jeanswear, consumers, it would seem, seek to associate themselves with these specific values. Likewise, the Ralph Lauren Corporation has sought to associate their Polo brand with a quintessentially English, aristocratic lifestyle. The brand name, itself, the logo of a horseman playing polo, as well as the stores, with props that include cricket bats, sculling oars and croquet trophies all blend to connote a clear brand positioning. Here the brand is truly aspirational: buying a part of the brand is like buying into this lifestyle.

The diffusion brands have now become lifestyle brands, and the diffusion stores which have been opened separately from the designers' up-market stores, couture and ready-to- wear stores (partly so as to avoid confusion between their different brand positioning, but mostly to avoid alienating rich customers who do not want to shop with, what one marketing executive described as, "those of the lower social orders), carry ranges which go beyond clothing and include jewellery, perfume, eyewear (spectacles), luggage, furniture, paint, fabrics, sheets, towels and bedding.

The primary aim of this product line extension is to allow a greater number of customers access to the brand, be it through a $5 candle, a $3 bottle of (branded) mineral water, or a $500 suit.

The extensive range of products now sold by the American designers has meant that stores have expanded significantly in size, and to such an extent that companies, such as Ralph Lauren, now identify their flagship stores as department stores, trading on as many as six floors, with ten or more departments, and as many as one hundred people employed in each store.

The extension of their diffusion brands into a wide and varied assortment of product areas, while often conceptually developed by the American design houses themselves, has been made possible through the skills and co-operation of license partners. It is the licensees' skills and expertise that has enabled the designers to diversify into diverse product markets swiftly and so successfully.

Licensees – the Drive behind the Brand

Marks and Spencer were once described as a manufacturer without factories (Tse 1985) and in many ways this description could also be readily applied to Ralph Lauren, Tommy Hilfiger, Calvin Klein and the other leading American designers. The fashion designers' virtual production capacity is made possible through an extensive network of licensing agreements. These licensing agreements function on the basis of an exchange between the designer, who provides the product design, (whether that be for a garment or for a range of bedding), and most importantly of all, permission to use their brand name, and the licensee, who pays to make, distribute and advertise the branded product on the designer's behalf. As their reward from the deal, the designers obtain a proportion of sales (in the case of the Ralph Lauren Corporation that cut is 6%) (Caminiti 1998) as well as guaranteed minimum payments each season, while the licensee obtains the exclusive right to manufacture and distribute for a brand that has an established reputation and appeal among consumers.

Clearly, it is the combination of the strength of the designers' brands, and the manufacturing and distribution expertise of licensing partners, that has enabled the American fashion design houses to so successfully expand and diversify their range of branded products. Again, using the example of Ralph Lauren, more than thirty companies are licensed to manufacture, distribute and advertise his ranges which include jeanswear, underwear, jewellery, cutlery (flatware), and furniture in over one hundred countries. Many of Lauren's licensees are well respected brands in their own right, and include Rockport/Reebok, who manufacture the Ralph Lauren footwear ranges, WestPoint Stevens who make Ralph Lauren sheets, towels and bedding, while Clairol, the international cosmetics conglomerate, hold the licensee for the production and distribution of Ralph Lauren perfumes world-wide. The partnership with Clairol has been especially lucrative for the Ralph Lauren Corp., and in 1997 earned the company in excess of $20 million in brand loyalty payments alone (Caminiti 1998).

As has been identified, a clearly positioned and successful brand is a crucial element of the partnership with licensees, serving as it does to both attract and retain them. Given the importance of the brand to the success of both licenser and licensee, it is incumbent on both sides to ensure that the brand maintains its profile, allure and clear market positioning. Retaining the existing fashion customer and attracting the new, depends upon considerable, and regular advertising support in order that the values, images and lifestyle association of the brand can be communicated and reinforced. Having taken responsibility for the creation and initial development of their successful brand, the responsibility for funding the continuing advertising support of the brand usually does not remain with the designer's company, but instead is normally transferred to license partners. This transference of financial responsibility was explained by a senior executive responsible for licensee relations in his organisation:

> The licensees are initially attracted to the company because we have a strong brand. They commit to production, and distribution and they start to realise that the success they enjoy through us depends upon the continued success of the brand. So we take advantage of that dependence and shift the responsibility of maintaining and supporting the brand, by that I mean in the form of advertising costs, to them.

As an example of this shift in responsibility, the advertising budget of $20 million for the Polo jeans brand was paid for entirely by Sun Apparel, the licensee responsible for the manufacture, distribution and promotion of the jeans brand, worldwide (Caminiti 1998). Sun Apparel's financial support of the Polo brand is by no means unique within the sector. Indeed, one company that participated in the survey indicated that all of their brand advertising and promotional costs were met by their licensee partners.

And while the American designers are happy to delegate the responsibility for manufacturing and distributing diffusion brands to their licensee partners, they nevertheless retain full control over all aspects of designing, manufacturing and distributing their couture and ready-to-wear ranges. These collections, while not as financially significant, are arguably the more important in terms of the development of the designers overall brand image and allure, since these are the garments that are featured in their twice-yearly fashion shows, receive the extensive media coverage and which diffusion brand customers ultimately aspire to wear. Therefore, given the importance of these ranges and so as to avoid the threat of design espionage (American designers are particularly sensitive to the threat of other companies plagiarising their work before the launch of a collection), the designers prefer to manage the couture and ready-to-wear lines themselves. Added to this is the fact that the sales volumes attached to these more up-market lines are considerably less, and as such, obtaining access to the large volume production capacity and distribution capability of the typical licensee partner is not a requirement or priority.

The Flagship Store – the ultimate in Brand Communications

A fashion designer's flagship store has a number of defining features. Typically, they are located within capital cities, and more precisely, within the most fashionable districts of these cities. Their purpose is to act as a conduit, linking the designer and his or her premium-priced clothing ranges with the designer's target market, the wealthy, urban, cosmopolitan types. For many designers, these flagship stores are their only method of distribution and for that reason, are regarded as critically important and are worthy of substantial resource investment.

For both British and American designers, their couture, and in some cases, the ready-to-wear lines, are distributed solely through flagship stores. But in terms of the number of flagship stores, in 1998 American's twelve international fashion designers operated, on average, seventeen couture and ready-to-wear flagships worldwide, while British designers averaged no more than four. This difference is partly due to American designers' willingness to operate some of their flagships on a franchise basis, and so avoid the high start-up and operating costs associated with flagship stores, but is also due to the fact that stock market listing provides capital to finance the opening of company-owned flagships stores.

Over 90 per cent of American designers' diffusion ranges are distributed through wholesale agreements with speciality fashion retailers and department stores. Given the ready availability of these brands, it would be reasonable to assume that the role of flagship stores in the marketing of diffusion ranges would be redundant. However, flagship stores devoted to the promotion and distribution of diffusion brands are an important feature of the American designers' businesses. On average, in 1998, the designers operated thirty seven flagships devoted to diffusion ranges (the Tommy Hilfiger Corporation have fifty-five, while Ralph Lauren operate over 140), and these were typically four to five times the size of the typical couture/ready-to-wear flagship stores.

These diffusion flagships are normally located in close proximity to the couture/ready-to-wear flagship, but remain separate and distinct through differences in store design, the range of customer services offered and the target customer profile. Generally, the target customer for the diffusion flagship is younger and less affluent than the couture customer. A further distinction is that these diffusion stores are also located within other major and secondary cities within the home and foreign markets, and are not confined necessarily to capital cities in the same way as couture flagship stores.

Given the size and up-market location of most diffusion stores, the associated set-up and operating costs are usually very high. As an example, it has been estimated that Ralph Lauren's Polo flagship in London's Bond Street cost £10 million to develop and requires weekly sales of £250,000 to break-even (Fernie et al. 1997). Similarly, it has been suggested that Lauren's New York flagship loses £1 million each month (Caminiti 1998). Given the high costs associated with these flagships, and the fact that the stores duplicate the product offering of nearby wholesale stockists, it is difficult to find an obvious justification for their existence. However, from the companies' perspective, the primary purpose of the diffusion flagship store is to serve as a promotional device to showcase the brand in a coherent and closely managed setting, and encourage brand awareness and interest, and so stimulate sales either in the store itself, or in the stores of wholesale stockists. Their purpose was explained by one executive as follows:

> The flagship is the nerve centre of the brand in a local market. Wholesale stockists may not have the space to take a whole collection, and the flagship does and is able to show the brand in its entirety. The flagship raises the profile and the image. The store is a metaphor for the brand. It helps to create the feeling of exclusivity and aspiration.

Categorising the diffusion flagship as an integral part of their corporate communications strategy is a view commonly shared by the American designers as is evidenced by the incorporation of flagship store opening and operating costs into their advertising budgets. In effect, the costs are written-off as part of effective brand communications. And among wholesale stockists, the existence of a flagship store is not viewed as an unfair form of competition, but is recognised as a powerful means of reinforcing the prestige of the brand through its up-market location and expensive shopfit.

The purpose of these diffusion flagships is perhaps best summarised by the director responsible for the management of one such store in London:

> The flagship store does not operate under the traditional rules of profit and loss. If we get some good sales from the store, that is a bonus. No, the purpose of the flagship is to show-off, to show the power of the brand, to show that this brand is as good as Chanel and Hermes, who are just along the road. It is about image, and where image is concerned the rules of accounting have to go out the window.

So far, this chapter has delineated the metamorphosis of the American designers from being family-owned, US-focused businesses to stock market quoted concerns that have diversified into many and varied product areas, through the support of licensees, and which now operate directly, in the form of flagship stores, and indirectly through wholesaling, in as many as one hundred foreign markets. While, in contrast, the British fashion designers, with only a few exceptions, have remained small scale, are privately owned and have engaged in international expansion and market development in a very limited way.

At the beginning of this chapter it was claimed that the American fashion designers had prompted the reconfiguration of the international landscape of designer retailing. In order to illustrate that influence in a more specific way, the final section of this chapter will consider the micro level impact of the strategies of US designers upon the premier fashion design shopping districts of London and New York.

How an Address Sells the Dress, and the Paint, and the Candle . . .

The migration and concentration of international fashion designers to economically and culturally important cities, such as London and New York, and specifically to particular streets within both, is neither a new nor accidental occurrence. Since the Industrial Revolution dressmakers have located in affluent areas of important cities primarily to be near to their wealthy clients. But as well as for these practical reasons, fashion designers have also recognised for a long time the important role that store location has in the development of a prestigious brand image. Hollander

(Hollander 1970) termed this the "New York, London, Paris syndrome", and suggested that their choice of prestigious addresses in important world centres was as much motivated by the fashion houses' desire to create a cosmopolitan image and international allure for their companies, as it was for reasons of customer accessibility.

More than a century after the first couturiers first opened stores in Central London and New York, the major fashion companies continue to locate in the most fashionable districts for reasons of both access and prestige. Of the 114 international fashion designers identified, 84 had stores in Central London and 53 in New York, in December 1998. Within both cities, these stores are clustered around two distinct shopping districts; in London these are Bond Street in Mayfair, and Sloane Street, in the Knightsbridge area, while in New York, Madison Avenue and Fifth Avenue are the important streets.

In the past ten years the total number of flagship stores operated by British designers in London has remained relatively unchanged at between twenty-eight and thirty, while in New York, British designer representation has remained small, with only two stores. The majority of these are flagship couture and ready-to-wear stores and only two are diffusion stores, and both are located in London. In contrast, the number of American flagships in London has risen markedly from only two in 1992 to twelve in 1998, with three more under construction and due to be opened in late 1999, while in New York, their flagship store numbers have increased five-fold in the same period. And of the six new flagship stores opened by the American designers in London since 1995, all but one of the six are dedicated to diffusion brands.

Since 1992, and paralleling the increased involvement of American designers within the fashionable shopping areas of London and New York, rental increases for Bond and Sloane Streets have been above the average for Central London (with an annual percentage increase of 12 per cent compared to a Central average of only 6.8 per cent) while in Madison Avenue, rental prices increased by 13 per cent to compared to an annual rate increase of 8 per cent for Central New York. As a result of these increases, the annual rent for the Polo Ralph Lauren in London's Bond Street in 1998 was estimated as £2.5 million, while the rental for Calvin Klein's diffusion store, CK, was £500,000 the same year (Anon 1998e). As a result of these rental increases, British fashion designers have been totally displaced from the prestige locations of London, mainly because they are unable to afford the high rents there. Instead, the leading British designers, such as Paul Smith, have opted for less expensive areas, such as Covent Garden, while the niche dressmakers, such as Amanda Wakeley, who designed for the late Princess of Wales, have located 'off-centre' into South Kensington. Similarly, in New York, the two flagship stores operated by British designers are located 'off-centre' in the Soho district, again because the rental costs of Fifth and Madison Avenues are prohibitively high.

As well as paying high rents for their flagship stores, the American designers have made considerable financial investment in store design, both in the opening of new stores, as well as the renovation and development of their existing stores. It is estimated that the development cost for Tommy Hilfiger's store in Bond Street was in excess of £2 million, while the new London flagship for Klein's diffusion range, CK, was estimated to be in the region of £2.5 million (Moore and Fernie 1998). None of the British designers were prepared to disclose the amount that they had spent on their flagship stores. However, one company stated that it was very considerably less than that spent by the American houses.

A further defining feature of the newly opened American diffusion flagship stores is their size. In order to provide the required selling space needed to accommodate the extended product ranges offered, the average size of these new stores has risen dramatically. In 1993, in Central London, the average size of a designer's flagship store was 4,700 sq ft over one selling floor. In comparison, the average size of the five new diffusion stores opened by American companies was 12,300 sq ft, over at least two selling floors. The flagship store opened by Ralph Lauren in 1999 at No 1 New Bond Street is 30,000 sq ft and operates over four floors. With the exception of Paul Smith's street of adjacent stores in Floral Street, Covent Garden, and despite their less costly locations, the average size of British designer's flagship stores in London is comparatively small and averages between 1,200–1,500 sq ft, and is normally confined to one sales floor. Likewise, in New York, the two British flagship stores are significantly smaller than the 14,000 sq ft average of their American counterparts.

With their opening of new, large and expensive flagship stores in London, the American designers have sought to develop not only a thriving business within the lucrative British market, but have also used the UK as a gateway into the rest of Europe. All of the major American designers opened their first European stores in London and did so for a variety of reasons. Of the more important, the Americans recognised that cultural affinity, a common language and similar business practices help to eliminate some of the difficulties normally associated with establishing a foreign subsidiary and that the British market could be used as a "market barometer" to measure the likelihood of commercial success within the rest of Europe. In addition, they typically regard the British market as highly influential in Europe, in that it is held in high regard by European retailers and that prospective wholesale stockists and franchise partners would be more interested in an American brand that had proven successful within the British market than in one that entered their market untested in Europe. The significance of the British market, and of London in particular, to entry into the rest of Europe was described by a senior market development executive:

We opened a store in London not just for the benefit of the British market. We used London as a European launch-pad. We recognised the importance of London in terms of media coverage – the British fashion media is the most influential in Europe. To get coverage in the British media, we had to have a London flagship store to focus media attention. Brands in this market suffocate without the air of the media. We also knew that most fashion retailers come to London to see which brands are best. We needed to be successful in London so as to encourage other stockists in Europe to take us. And we needed to be in London to learn about the latest fashion trends. London leads the world in fashion ideas, it does not come from the USA. A presence in the UK is as much about gathering market intelligence than anything else.

Concluding Remarks

Clearly, it is beyond the scope of this chapter to provide a definitive explanation as to why the American fashion design companies have become so much more successful than their British counterparts. It could be suggested that differences in corporate culture, variations in the availability of business acumen and support from financial institutions, may account for the contrasting performances. But perhaps the somewhat contentious but nevertheless very interesting explanation provided by the managing director of a leading French design house shed some light:

> The British are expert at design, but not good at selling. They do not have the skills of branding. At this time, it is the brand and not the product that matters. Expertise in design is not enough. The Americans' product is always predictable, and it is dull. But they have the great, memorable, advertised, well recognised brand. The Americans invented all the great brands of the Twentieth Century. MacDonalds, Coke, so why should we be surprised that should have the best fashion brands? The first and last reason for why they are successful is because Americans are masters of branding. And that is all that really matters in a post-modern world. Ralph Lauren and Calvin Klein, they are the MacDonalds of fashion.

Whether British fashion designers could, or would want to develop their businesses using the "MacDonald's model" remains to be seen. But it is unlikely that a double Paul Smith burger with Jasper Conran on the side will be on the menu in the Fashion Cafe in the foreseeable future . . .

References

Anon. (1998a), 'The Polo Ralph Lauren Corporation', *Hoover's Company Capsules,* Austin, Texas: Hoover's Inc.

Anon. (1998b), *Fashion Designers in Central London and New York*, London: Hillier Parker Retail Research.

Anon. (1998c), 'Tommy Hilfiger Corp', *Hoover's Company Capsules*, Austin, Texas: Hoover's Inc.

Anon. (1998d), 'Premium Potential', *TMS Partnership Research Publications*, London, UK.

Anon. (1998e), *Fashion Designers in Central London and New York*, London: Hillier Parker Retail Research.

Caminiti, Susan (1998), 'Ralph Lauren: the emperor has clothes', *Fortune*, 11 Nov, Vol. 137, No. 9, pp. 80–9.

Fernie, J., Moore, C. and Lawrie, A. (1998), 'A Tale of Two Cities : an examination of fashion designer retailing within London and New York', *Journal of Product and Brand Management*, 7, 5: 366–78.

Goldstein, Lauren (1999), 'Can Donna Karan get back into Black?' *Fortune*, April 12, Vol. 139, No. 7, p. 31.

Hollander, S. C. (1970), *Multinational Retailing* MI: Michigan State University.

Moore, C. and Fernie, J. (1998), 'How address Sells the Dress – An examination of Fashion Designer Retailing within London and New York', *The Journal of the Textile Institute*, 89: 81–95.

Tse, K. K. (1985), *Marks and Spencer: Anatomy of Britain's Most Efficiently Managed Company,* Oxford: Pergamon.

Index